Saul Bellow and the Critics

About Irving Malin

IRVING MALIN teaches at The City College of New York. He is the author of *William Faulkner: An Interpretation*, *New American Gothic*, and *Jews and Americans*; he is the editor of *Psychoanalysis and American Fiction* and *Breakthrough: A Treasury of Contemporary American-Jewish Literature* (with Irwin Stark).

Saul Bellow

AND THE CRITICS

Edited by Irving Malin

New York · NEW YORK UNIVERSITY PRESS
London · UNIVERSITY OF LONDON PRESS LIMITED
1967

ACKNOWLEDGMENTS

ACKNOWLEDGMENT is made to publishers, periodicals, and authors for permission to reprint the following:

"Saul Bellow," by Leslie A. Fiedler. Reprinted from *Prairie Schooner* 31 (Summer, 1957). Copyright © 1957 by the University of Nebraska Press.

"Saul Bellow: Novelist of the Intellectuals," by Maxwell Geismar. Reprinted from *American Moderns: From Rebellion to Conformity* by Maxwell Geismar. Copyright © 1958 by Maxwell Geismar. Reprinted by permission of Hill and Wang, Inc. and W. H. Allen and Co.

"The Adventures of Saul Bellow: The Progress of a Novelist," by Richard Chase. Reprinted from *Commentary* 27 (April, 1959). Copyright © 1959 by the American Jewish Committee.

"Bellow's Dangling Men," by J. C. Levenson. Reprinted from *Critique* 3 (Summer, 1960). Copyright © 1960 by *Critique*.

"Saul Bellow: The Illusion of Environment," by Ralph Freedman. Reprinted from *Wisconsin Studies in Contemporary Literature* 1 (Winter, 1960). Copyright © 1960 by Wisconsin Studies in Contemporary Literature.

"Reality and the Hero: *Lolita* and *Henderson the Rain King*," by Daniel Hughes. Reprinted from *Modern Fiction*

v

Studies 6 (Winter, 1960–1961). Copyright © 1960 by the Purdue Research Foundation.

"A Discipline of Nobility: Saul Bellow's Fiction," by Marcus Klein. Reprinted from *Kenyon Review* 24 (Spring, 1962). Copyright © 1962 by Kenyon College.

"Caliban on Prospero: A Psychoanalytic Study on the Novel, *Seize the Day*, by Saul Bellow," by Daniel Weiss. Reprinted from *The American Imago* 19 (Fall, 1962). Copyright © 1962 by *The American Imago*.

"Bellow in Occupancy," by Earl Rovit. Reprinted from *The American Scholar* 34 (Spring, 1965). Copyright © 1965 by the United Chapters of Phi Beta Kappa.

"*Herzog*: A Review," by Forrest Read. Reprinted from *Epoch* 14 (Fall, 1964). Copyright © 1964 by Cornell University.

"The Complacency of *Herzog*," by John W. Aldridge. Reprinted from *Time to Murder and Create* by John W. Aldridge. Copyright © 1966 by John W. Aldridge. (New York, 1966) Used by permission of David McKay Co. Inc.

"Where Do We Go From Here: The Future of Fiction," by Saul Bellow. Reprinted from *To The Young Writer: Hopwood Lectures, Second Series* ed. A. L. Bader by permission of the University of Michigan Press. Copyright © 1965 by the University of Michigan.

Illustrative passages of unusual length from the following works by Saul Bellow—*Henderson the Rain King*, copyright © 1958, 1959, by Saul Bellow; *Herzog*, copyright © 1961, 1963, 1964 by Saul Bellow; and *Seize the Day*, copyright © 1956 by Saul Bellow—are reprinted by permission of Saul Bellow, The Viking Press, Inc. and Weidenfeld and Nicolson, Ltd. Shorter passages are quoted from Saul Bellow's *The Adventures of Augie March* (The Viking Press, Inc. and Weidenfeld and Nicolson, Ltd.), *Dangling Man* and *The Victim* (The Vanguard Press, Inc. and Weidenfeld and Nicolson, Ltd.).

INTRODUCTION

THE TWELVE ESSAYS which I have collected vary in length, scope, and point of view, but they affirm that Bellow is an important, gifted novelist whose achievement must be explored in depth. They are not unusual in the latter respect. Tony Tanner has just published a short book on Bellow in the Writers and Critics series; Keith Opdahl is revising his dissertation for publication; Earl Rovit is working on a pamphlet for the University of Minnesota Press; and I am preparing a book for the Twayne series. Here I wish to outline some problems raised in the present collection—problems which must be studied by future critics.

I. THEME

The theme of alienation (and accommodation) is continually emphasized by the twelve critics. Leslie A. Fiedler views the "dangling man" as "essential man, man stripped of success and belongness, even'of failure." Richard Chase thinks that Bellow fails at times to clarify what "his heroes want to be free *from*." Marcus Klein views the novels as "dialogues between alienation and accommodation." John W. Aldridge argues that this dialogue may not even exist in *Herzog*; complacency and vagueness have triumphed.

We can move easily from this general theme to related ones. Many of the critics represented here discuss "reality" in Bellow. Ralph Freedman, for example, asserts that there is no simple reality from which any character is alienated; in the later novels the "typical relations between self and world" become even more problematical. The early novels—which also questioned the very notion of "social reality"—give way to "increasingly artificial illusion." Daniel Hughes is able to show us how this theme is at the heart of *Henderson the Rain King* and *Lolita*; both "novels about the quest for reality" insist, ironically, upon unreality or madness.

Not only is Bellow interested in profound philosophical problems—he also studies such "down-to-earth" ones as the American-Jewish experience. Leslie Fiedler regards "assimilation" as an important theme; he argues that the heroes—and Bellow himself—must be seen in terms of their attraction toward and repulsion from the bourgeois community. Maxwell Geismar claims that Jewishness is never clarified in the novels because the author refuses to commit himself to any real description of community life or social actualities. John W. Aldridge cannot understand how Herzog, "the Jewish intellectual," becomes a symbol of "contemporary Everyman."

The matter is complicated by the fact that Bellow also deals with the quality of "American" life. J. C. Levenson, Earl Rovit, and Richard Chase mention Emerson, Twain, and Whitman as possible ancestors, but they don't inform us in great detail how or why Bellow is an *American* writer. Does he offer us any substantial, new picture of our national experience? Are Henderson and Herzog "representative" or abstract?

These questions can, indeed, be raised about the few themes I have noted. Once we accept that Bellow is an intellectual novelist—whatever this means!—we are prone to congratulate him because he is such a "rare bird"—at least in our country. But Geismar, Aldridge, Rovit, *et al* are disturbed by such quick congratulation. They believe that at times Bellow slips into somewhat careless resolution of problems; ideas *per se* are not artistic.

II. CHARACTERIZATION

Many critics of Bellow shun individual psychology because they submit to his anti-Freudian bias. They talk about *types*: the dangling man, the "reality instructors," the American, the Jew, or the intellectual. Rarely do they explore psychological motivation which may underlie social or metaphysical abstractions. I have included several critics who do face the matter of quirky characterization. Leslie A. Fiedler may discuss "essential man" in Bellow, but he qualifies him as "man disowned by his father, unrecognized by his son, man without woman, man face to face with himself . . ." He is the first critic to stress the "emotional transactions of males" in the fiction, but he does not have the space in which to elaborate. Maxwell Geismar mentions the latent homosexuality of *The Victim* and *Seize the Day*. Daniel Weiss painstakingly delineates the father-son relationship in the latter work (using Kafka in his range of references). Richard Chase points out the dramatized figure which may incarnate Reality or Society. I would suggest that before we can talk about reality or society we must investigate the family. The "natural" father is often missing or weak in the novels; only in *Herzog* does he appear strong. Why? What meanings does he hold? Does he help to explain the odd behavior of victims? Obviously, these rhetorical questions imply that I think psychology, in effect, precedes philosophy.

I am troubled by the absence of any lengthy discussion of Bellow's women. Critics assert they are stylized or unreal. But these adjectives are not enough to explain the *complexity of recurring stereotyped roles*. Only after *Herzog* do critics describe "characteristics"; Ramona and Madeleine force them to do so. (See Forrest Read's essay for some brilliant remarks about the two heroines.) But it is time for someone to write an entire essay on all the women.

There are other critical problems in understanding characterization. Does Bellow "stack the cards" against certain minor figures as John W. Aldridge asserts? Does he tend to duplicate characters so much, say, in *The Adventures of Augie March*, that we care little about the differences among the spiritual guides encountered by the hero? Does he sacrifice personality to philosophical design? Can picaresque tale or romance give us the *depth of character* we desire? These questions—and there are, of course, many additional ones—appear in the twelve essays.

III. IMAGERY

I have included a rather long essay from 1962 in which I attempt to show that various images used by Bellow deserve

close attention. These images are, in part, alluded to by
other critics—Marcus Klein, Daniel Hughes, and Forrest Read
are especially good on *density* and *beastliness* in the novels—
but as far as I know, few critics have bothered with textual
analysis. Why? The answer is clear. They have accepted
Bellow's attack on "the deep reader. He falls wildly on any
particle of philosophy of religion and blows it up bigger than
the Graf Zeppelin." Or they have felt that a *literary* task can
disrupt *the flow of conversational thought* in his fiction. I don't
agree. I believe that, in the long run, it is relatively fruitless to
discuss conformity or freedom or suffering without seeing how
these concepts are imbedded in images.

It is especially helpful to survey one image—mirror, parasite, beast, prison, movement, or weight—so that we can see how
it moves not only in one novel but in the canon. Dangling is
mentioned often by critics; so is voyaging. Few connect the two
to discuss the quality of *movement* in the novels and, more, to
relate this movement to other principles of structure and
theme. Such surveys lead to many questions. Does Bellow use
natural or exotic images? When is his imagery effective? Can
his imagery be archetypal? Is it very literary? In my essay I
suggest that Bellow uses such "natural" images as deformity,
resemblance, and weight as facts *and* symbols of our destiny.
He does not usually strain for exotic ones because he realizes
that there are universal pressures—that for example, the pressures felt by Tommy Wilhelm or Asa Leventhal are burdens
or "crosses" like the one borne by Christ. If we read him carefully, we see that as modern as his heroes are, they enact mythic
trials. Am I right? I think so, but I would like to see a *deep
reading* of the novels which agrees or disagrees with my
admittedly "schematic" position.

IV. STYLE

Bellow is such a remarkable novelist that it is hard to
place him. He refuses to rest in one style; he asserts that there
is more than one way—realistic, fantastic, comic, etc.—of confronting life.

I have suggested that he is concerned with "eternal"
tensions—alienation *versus* accommodation; fathers *versus* sons;
Jew *versus* Gentile; prisons *versus* voyages. It is appropriate

that his various styles—although clearly one or two dominate any novel—oppose one another. They are "human," clamoring for attention, wanting to take the center of the stage. They make the confident reader uncomfortable, dramatizing for him the painful struggles of existence. That these styles are *organized* and *mastered* symbolizes an even deeper message: the novelist, like his readers, can govern himself. *In the shaping process lies sanity, freedom, and power.*

There are at least five important styles ("modes of perception") used by Bellow: realism, fantasy, comedy, pastoral, and prophecy. Although no critic included here discusses all of these, many do note stylistic tensions. Leslie Fiedler believes that the language is, at times, "centrifugal" and "centripetal"—in *Seize the Day* the two tendencies find a "sort of perilous rest." Marcus Klein mentions the city-country opposition (realism and pastoral). Richard Chase describes the debate between naturalism and transcendentalism; so does J. C. Levenson. He also makes much of the comic voice: "the interanimation of American and Jewish strains is a matter of gesture, language, and conception." Ralph Freedman and Daniel Hughes, as I have mentioned earlier, emphasize the struggle between realism and fantasy. Forrest Read attempts to put *Herzog* in a tradition, but he finds that it contains "elements of the historical, ideological, metaphysical, romantic, anti-romantic, erotic, and picaresque novels; of the novel of manners, the anti-novel, the romance, etc. But above all, it is a great comic novel." Earl Rovit captures the narrative tension in *Herzog*: "The device of multiple perspective tends to cancel out the actual lack of movement since awareness of self-awareness creates a dynamic psychic motion in itself, and it is this rhythm that dominates the structure of the novel."

But we cannot stop here. Are these critics correct? Or do *they* create the tension? Are John W. Aldridge and Maxwell Geismar more to the point when they claim that Bellow's style —his current "philosophy of life"—is fat, complacent, and safe?

v. SOURCES

I have not pursued "sources" because I do not think they are as important as the fiction itself. But future essays could easily be written on the relation of Bellow to Joyce (see Forrest

Read), Dostoyevsky (see J. C. Levenson), Emerson (see Earl Rovit and Richard Chase), and such Jewish contemporaries as Isaac Rosenfeld (see Leslie Fiedler). These comparative studies will help to disclose his tradition and originality.

I regret not including an essay on Bellow's short stories. Although such works as "The Mexican General," "Two Morning Monologues," and Dr. Pep's sermon have never been fully discussed—Marcus Klein, Tony Tanner in his short book on Bellow, and I have hinted at their importance—they deserve careful attention. So do the many critical essays and reviews by Bellow; such essays as the one I have included as an appendix help us to understand the theoretical problems he confronts in writing his novels.

Bellow demands that we read his fiction closely and imaginatively. I hope that this collection will help us to meet his challenge.

I. M.

Queens Village
March 18, 1966

for my son Mark
who doesn't dangle

CONTENTS

Saul Bellow and the Critics

1·SAUL BELLOW

WITH THE PUBLICATION of *Seize the Day*, Saul Bellow has become not merely a writer with whom it is possible to come to terms, but one with whom it is *necessary* to come to terms—perhaps of all our novelists the one we need most to understand, if we are to understand what the novel is doing at the present moment. Bellow has endured the almost ritual indignities of the beginning fictionist: his first novel a little over-admired and read by scarcely anyone; his second novel once more critically acclaimed, though without quite the thrill of discovery, and still almost ignored by the larger public; his third novel, thick, popular, reprinted in the paperbacks and somewhat resented by the first discoverers, who hate seeing what was exclusively theirs pass into the public domain; and now a fourth book: a collection of stories, most of which have appeared earlier, a play, and a new novella.

Suddenly, the novelist whom we have not ceased calling a "young writer" (it is a habit hard to break and the final indignity) is established and forty, a part of our lives and something for the really young to define themselves against. But it has become clear that he will continue to write, that he is not merely the author of a novel or two, but a *novelist*; and this in itself is a triumph, a rarity in recent American literary history and especially among the writers with whom we associate Bellow. We think of the whole line of Jewish-American novelists, so like him in origin and aspiration, of Daniel Fuchs and Henry Roth and Nathanael West, those poets and annalists of the thirties who did not survive their age, succumbing to death or Hollywood or a sheer exhaustion of spirit and subject. Or we think of Bellow's own contemporaries, the *Partisan Review* group, urban Jews growing up under the threat of failure and terror, the depression and Spain and the hopelessly foreseen coming of war. We remember, perhaps, Isaac Rosenfeld or H. J. Kaplan or Oscar Tarcov or Delmore Schwartz or even Lionel Trilling, who had also to be twice-born, committed first to Stalinism and then to disenchantment, but who were capable of using imaginatively only the disenchantment. And remembering these, we recall beginnings not quite fulfilled, achievements which somehow betrayed initial promises. Certain short stories remain in our minds (flanked by all those essays, those explanations and rejoinders and demonstrations of wit): Kaplan's "The Mohammedans," Rosenfeld's "The Pyramids," Schwartz's "In Dreams Begin Responsibilities," Trilling's "The Other Margaret"; but where except in *The Dangling Man* and *The Victim* and *Augie March* do the themes and motifs of the group find full novelistic expression?

We must begin to see Bellow, then, as the inheritor of a long tradition of false starts and abject retreats and gray inconclusions. There is a sense in which he fulfills the often frustrated attempt to possess the American imagination and to enter the American cultural scene of a line of Jewish fictionists which goes back beyond the postwar generation through Ben Hecht and Ludwig Lewisohn to Abe Cahan. A hundred, a thousand one-shot novelists, ephemeral successes and baffled eccentrics stand behind him, defining a subject: the need of the Jew in America to make clear his relationship to that country in terms of belonging or protest—and a language: a speech enriched by the dialectic and joyful intellectual play of Jewish conversation.

Bellow's own story is, then, like the archetypal Jewish dream a success story; since, like the standard characters in the tales of my grandfather (socialist though he was!), the novelist, too, has "worked himself up in America." Bellow's success must not be understood, however, as exclusively his own; for he emerges at the moment when the Jews for the first time move into the center of American culture, and he must be seen in the larger context. The background is familiar enough: the gradual breaking up of the Anglo-Saxon domination of our imagination: the relentless urbanization which makes rural myths and images no longer central to our experience; the exhaustion as vital themes of the Midwest and of the movement from the provinces to New York or Chicago or Paris; the turning again from West to East, from our own heartland back to Europe; and the discovery in the Jews of a people essentially urban, essentially Europe-oriented, a ready-made image for what the American longs to or fears he is being forced to become.

On all levels in the years since World War II, the Jewish-American writer feels imposed on him the role of being The American, of registering his experience for his compatriots and for the world as The American Experience. Not only his flirtation with Communism and his disengagement, but his very sense of exclusion, his most intimate awareness of loneliness and flight are demanded of him as public symbols. The Southerner and the Jew, the homosexual out of the miasma of Mississippi and the ex-radical out of the iron landscape of Chicago and New York—these seem the exclusive alternatives, contrasting yet somehow twinned symbols of America at mid-century. *Partisan Review* becomes for Europe and *Life* magazine the mouthpiece of intellectual America, not despite but because of its tiny readership and its specially determined contributors; and in Saul Bellow a writer emerges capable of transforming its obsessions into myths.

He must not, however, be seen only in this context. His appearance as the first Jewish-American novelist to stand at the center of American literature is flanked by a host of matching successes on other levels of culture and subculture. What Saul Bellow is for highbrow literature, Salinger is for upper middle-brow, Irwin Shaw for middle middlebrow and Herman Wouk for lower middlebrow. Even on the lowbrow levels, where there has been no such truce with antisemitism as prosperity has brought to the middle classes, two young Jews in contriving Superman have invented for the comicbooks a new version of the Hero, the first purely urban incarnation of the most ancient of mythic figures. The acceptance of Bellow as the leading novelist of his generation must be paired off with the appearance of Marjorie Morningstar on the front cover of *Time*. On all levels, the Jew is in the process of being mythicized into the representative American.

There is a temptation in all this to a kind of assimilation with the most insipid values of bourgeois life in the United States. It is to Bellow's credit that he has at once accepted the full challenge implicit in the identification of Jew with America, and yet has not succumbed to the temptation; that he has been willing to accept the burden of success without which he might have been cut off from the central subject of his time; and that he has accomplished this without essential compromise. In *Augie March*, which is the heart of his work (though technically not as successful as *The Victim* or *Seize the Day*), he has risked the final absurdity: the footloose Jewish boy, harried by urban machiavellians, the picaresque *schlimazl* out of Fuchs or Nathanael West, becomes Huck Finn; or, if you will, Huck is transformed into the footloose Jewish boy. It is hard to know which way of saying it gives a fuller sense of the absurdity and importance of the transaction. The point is, I think, that the identification saves both halves of the combination from sentimental falsification: Huck Finn, who has threatened for a long time to dissolve into the snubnosed little rascal, barefoot and overalled; and the Jewish *schlimazl*, who becomes only too easily the liberals' insufferable victim, say, Noah Ackerman in Irwin Shaw's *The Young Lions*.

The themes of Saul Bellow are not, after all, very different from those of the middlebrow Jewish novelists in step with whom he has "worked himself up"; but in treatment they become transformed. Like Wouk or Shaw, he, too, has written a War Novel: a book about the uncertainty of intellectual and Jew face to face with a commitment to regimentation and violence. But unlike Wouk and Shaw, Bellow has not merely taken the World War I novel of protest and adulterated it with popular front pieties. His intellectual is not shown up like Wouk's Keefer; his Jew does not prove himself as brave and brutal as his antisemitic buddies like Shaw's Ackerman or Wouk's Greenspan, whose presumable triumphs are in fact abject surrenders. The longing to relinquish the stereotyped protest of the twenties, no longer quite believed in, is present in Bellow's *Dangling Man*, but present as a *subject*: a temptation to be confronted, not a value to be celebrated.

Dangling Man is not an entirely successful book; it is a little mannered, a little incoherent, obviously a first novel. But it is fresh beyond all expectation, unlike any American war book before or since; for Bellow has realized that for his generation the war itself is an anticlimax (too foreknown from a score of older novels to be really lived), that their real experience is the waiting, the dangling, the indecision before the draft. His book therefore ends, as it should, with its protagonist about to leave for camp and writing in his journal: "Hurray for regular hours! And for the supervision of the spirit! Long live regimentation!" In the purest of ironies, the slogans of accommodation are neither accepted nor rejected, but suspended.

Similarly, in *The Victim* Bellow takes up what is, perhaps, the theme *par excellence* of the liberaloid novel of the forties: antisemitism. In proletarian novels, though many were written by Jews, this was a subject only peripherally treated; for the Jew in the Communist movement, Judaism was the enemy, Zionism and the Jewish religion the proper butt of satire and dissent. But Hitler had made a difference, releasing a flood of pious protests against discrimination; from Arthur Miller's *Focus* to John Hersey's *The Wall*, via *Gentlemen's Agreement*, *The Professor's Umbrella*, etc., Jew and Gentile alike took up the subject over and over. In a time when the Worker had been replaced by the Little Man as a focus for undiscriminating sympathy, the Little Jew took his place beside the Little Negro, the Little Chinese, the Little Paraplegic as a favorite victim. Even what passed for War Novels were often merely anti-antisemitic fictions in disguise, the war itself being treated only as an occasion for testing a Noble Young Jew under the pressure of ignorant hostility.

In the typical middlebrow novel, it was seldom a real Jew who was exposed to persecution; rather some innocent gentile who by putting on glasses mysteriously came to look Jewish or some high-minded reporter only pretending to be a Jew. In part what is involved is the commercial necessity for finding a gimmick to redeem an otherwise overworked subject; but in part what is at stake is surely a confusion in the liberal, middlebrow mind about what a Jew is anyhow: a sneaking suspicion that Jew-baiting is real but Jews are imaginary, just as, to the same mind, witch-hunting is real but witches only fictions.

In Bellow's book about antisemitism, *The Victim*, once

more the confusion becomes the subject. It is Asa Leventhal, not the author, who is uncertain of what it means to be a Jew, because he does not know yet what it is to be a man; and neither he nor his author will be content with the simple equation: the victim equals the Jew, the Jew the victim. In *The Victim*, Jew and antisemite are each other's prey as they are each other's beloved. At the moment when the Jew in general, when the author himself as well as his protagonist, have moved into situations of security, however tenuous, inflicting injury in their scramble to win that security, Bellow alone among our novelists has had the imagination and the sheer nerve to portray the Jew, the Little Jew, as victimizer as well as victim. Allbee may be mad, a pathological antisemite and a bum, but his charge that Leventhal's success was achieved somehow at his expense is not utter nonsense. It is the necessary antidote to the self-pity of the Jew, one part of a total ambiguous picture. In the slow, gray, low-keyed exposition of *The Victim*, Leventhal's violence and his patience, his desire to exculpate himself and his sense of guilt, his haunting by the antisemite he haunts, become for us truths, part of our awareness of our place as Jews in the American scene.

As *The Victim* is Bellow's most specifically Jewish book, *Augie March* (in this, as in all other respects, a reaction from the former) is his most generally American. Its milieu is Jewish American, its speech patterns somehow molded by Yiddish, but its theme is the native theme of *Huckleberry Finn*: the rejection of power and commitment and success, the pursuit of a primal innocence. It is a strangely non-Jewish book in being concerned not with a man's rise but with his evasion of rising; and yet even in that respect it reminds us of *David Levinsky*, of the criticism of David implicit in the text and entrusted to the Socialist characters. It is as if David had been granted a son, a grandson, to try again—to seek a more genuine Americanism of noncommittal. Certainly, Bellow's character is granted a symbolic series of sexual successes to balance off the sexual failures of Cahan's protagonist. But the socialism of Cahan does not move his descendant; it has become in the meanwhile Soviet Communism, an alternative image of material success, and has failed; so that there is left to Augie only the denial of the values of capitalism without a corresponding allegiance, a desire to flee success from scene to scene, from girl to girl, from father to father—in favor of what? The most bitter of Happy Endings as well as the most negative, the truly American Happy Ending: no reunion with the family, no ultimately happy marriage, no return to the native place—only a limitless disponibility guarded like a treasure. It is, of course, the ending of *Huckleberry Finn*, an ending which must be played out as comedy to be tolerable at all; but unlike Twain, Bellow, though he has found the proper tone for his episodes, cannot recapture it for his close. *Augie*, which begins with such rightness, such conviction, does not know how to end; shriller and shriller, wilder and wilder, it finally whirls apart in a frenzy of fake euphoria and exclamatory prose.

Seize the Day is a pendant and resolution to *Augie March*. Also a study of success and failure, this time it treats them in contemporary terms rather than classic ones, reworking directly a standard middlebrow theme. Call it "The Death of a Salesman" and think of Arthur Miller. It is the price of failure in a world dedicated to success that Bellow is dealing with now; or more precisely, the self-consciousness of failure in a world where it is not only shameful but rare; or most exactly of all, the bitterness of success and failure become pawns in the deadly game between father and son. Bellow is not very successful when he attempts to deal with the sentimental and erotic relations that are the staples of the great European novels; his women tend to be nympholeptic projections, fantasies based on girls one never had; and his husbands and wives seem convincing only at the moment of parting. But he comes into his own when he turns to the emotional transactions of males inside the family: brother and brother, son and father—or father-hating son and machiavellian surrogate father. It is the muted rage of such relationships that is the emotional stuff of his best work; and in *Seize the Day*, it is the dialogues of Tommy and his old man, Tommy and the sharper Tamkin that move us, prepare us for Tommy's bleakest encounter: with himself and the prescience of his own death.

But how, we are left asking, has Bellow made tragedy of a theme that remains in the hands of Arthur Miller sentimentality and "good theater"? It is just this magical transformation of the most travestied of middlebrow themes which is Bellow's greatest triumph. That transformation is in part the work of style, a function of language. Bellow is in no sense an experimental writer; the scraps of avant-garde technique which survive in *The Dangling Man* are purged away in *The Victim*; yet he has managed to resist the impulse to lifeless lucidity which elsewhere has taken over in a literature reacting to the linguistic experiments of the twenties. There is always the sense of a living voice in his prose, for his books are all dramatic; and though this sometimes means a deliberate muting of rhetoric for the sake of characterization, it just as often provides occasions for a release of full virtuosity. Muted or released, his language is never dull or merely expedient, but always moves under tension, toward or away from a kind of rich, crazy poetry, a juxtaposition of high and low style, elegance and slang, unlike anything else in English except *Moby Dick*, though at the same time not unrelated in range and variety to spoken Yiddish.

Since Bellow's style is based on a certain conversational ideal at once intellectual and informal, dialogue is for him necessarily a distillation of his strongest effects. Sometimes one feels his characters' speeches as the main events of the books in which they occur; certainly they have the impact of words exchanged among Jews, that is to say, the impact of actions, not merely overheard but *felt*, like kisses or blows. Implicit in the direction of his style is a desire to encompass a world larger, richer, more disorderly and untrammeled than that of any other writer of his generation; it is this which impels him toward the picaresque, the sprawling, episodic manner of *Augie March*. But there is a counter impulse in him toward the tight, rigidly organized, underplayed style of *The Victim*: and at his best, I think, as in *Seize the Day*, an ability to balance the two tendencies against each other: hysteria and catalepsy, the centrifugal and the centripetal in a sort of perilous rest.

But the triumphs of Bellow are not mere triumphs of style; sometimes indeed they must survive the collapse of that style into mannerism, mechanical self-parody. Beyond an ear, Bellow possesses a fortunate negative talent: a constitutional inability to dissolve his characters into their representative types, to compromise their individuality for the sake of a point. It is not merely that his protagonists refuse to blur into the generalized Little People, the Victims of sentimental liberalism; but that they are themselves portrayed as being conscious of their struggle against such debasement. That struggle is, indeed, the essence of their self-consciousness, their self-definition. Their invariable loneliness is felt by them and by us not only as a function of urban life and the atomization of culture, but as something *willed*: the condition and result of their search to know what they are.

More, perhaps, than any other recent novelist, Bellow is aware that the collapse of the proletarian novel, which marks the starting place of his own art, has meant more than the disappearance of a convention in the history of fiction. With the disappearance of the proletarian novel as a form there has taken place the gradual dissolution of the last widely shared definition of man: man as the product of society. If man seems at the moment extraordinarily lonely, it is not only because he finds it hard to communicate with his fellows, but because he has lost touch with any overarching definition of himself.

This Bellow realizes; as he realizes that it is precisely in such loneliness, once man learns not to endure but to *become* that loneliness, that man can rediscover his identity and his fellowship with others. We recognize the Bellow character because he is openly what we are in secret, because he is us without our customary defenses. Such a protagonist lives nowhere except in the City; he camps temporarily in boardinghouses or lonely hotels, sits by himself at the corner table of some seedy restaurant or climbs backbreaking stairways in search of another whose existence no one will admit. He is the man whose wife is off visiting her mother or has just left him; the man who returns to find his house in disorder or inhabited by a squalid derelict; the man who flees his room to follow the funeral of someone he never knew.

He is essential man, man stripped of success and belongness, even of failure; he is man disowned by his father, unrecognized by his son, man without woman, man face to face with himself, which means for Bellow face to face not with a fact but a question: "What am I?" To which the only answer is: "He who asks!" But such a man is at once the Jew in perpetual exile and Huck Finn in whom are blended with perfect irony the twin American beliefs that the answer to all questions is always over the next horizon and that there is no answer now or ever.

2 · SAUL BELLOW: Novelist of the Intellectuals

JUST AS J. D. Salinger, by the middle Fifties, was the literary spokesman of the college undergraduates, Saul Bellow was the favorite novelist of the American intellectuals. This is a heavy burden for a fiction-writer to bear, and Bellow's work is interesting to the degree that it conforms to the prevailing values and standards of his "class," and to the degree that it goes beyond them. This writer, as I have said elsewhere, is a novelist in spite of himself; part of our sympathy and concern with his career lies with his own struggle to break through a predominantly intellectual and moral approach to life.

His first book, *Dangling Man,* in 1944, was acclaimed by the critics of the Partisan-Kenyon Review orbit as an "unassailable moral effort" in its attempt to chart the uncertainty of modern man caught between the military and the civilian worlds. "One of the most honest pieces of testimony on the psychology of a whole generation," said Edmund Wilson. Beneath the contemporary surface of the novel, there were echoes and parallels from Dostoyevsky's *Notes from the Underground.*

Books—"these guarantors of an extended life"—are the primary life medium of the Dangling Man. But this early hero, in a state of demoralization, is waiting for his draft call in a war that he supports but refuses to profit from (a different stand from that in our World War I writing). He has become indifferent to his friends, his family; what point is there in getting or holding a job? In the solitude of his room, while his wife becomes the breadwinner, even his new-found "freedom" seems futile. He resigns himself to a "narcotic dullness," broken by fits of hysterical anger at those who do not understand his devotion to principle.

He is already a "moral casualty of the war," as he feels; he has assumed that "weariness of life" which Goethe described. If he finds urban life particularly hideous and joyless—and particularly the lower middle-class segment of society that he frequents—yet he still tries continually to find "clear signs of their common humanity." There must be a difference, he thinks, between things and persons and even between acts and persons. Otherwise the people who lived and died in these ugly modern American cities were actually a reflection of the conditions they lived among.

> I had always striven to avoid blaming them [he adds] because I was involved with them; because, whether I liked it or not, they were my generation, my society, my world. We were figures in the same plot, eternally fixed together. I was aware, also, that their existence, just as it was, made mine possible. And if, as was often said, this part of the century was approaching the nether curve in a cycle, then I, too, would remain on the bottom and there, extinct, merely add my body, my life, to the base of a coming time.

This was probably a condemned age, the hero reflects, in which, among the violent political factions, even simple human communication had become impossible. At the dreadful parties of rootless middle-class intellectuals and Bohemians, which he attends, he sees only a modern parody of the Eleusinian spirit where "the charge of feeling in the pent heart" was now released without grace or mystery. Nor is he better off with his rich brother Amos, the complacent and comfortable Dolly, and their spoiled daughter Etta, who wants Cugat, not Haydn, to be played on *her* phonograph.

Joseph finally spanks this brat in a rare act of aggression (after Etta claims he has attacked her sexually). For the Bellow protagonist has also rejected—along with the militant pacifism of our World War I literature, and the adolescent modes of social protest—the Hemingwayish code of dead-pan virility. "Do you have emotions? Strangle them," he thinks, ironically. But what is the fundamental cause of his moral despair and spiritual apathy? Is it really because, as we are told here, "God is dead," and we no longer operate in that medieval hierarchy where man's place was given, fixed and immutable in a ceaseless conflict between good and evil, or between Satan and the redeeming Church?

But, since, the stage has been reset and human beings only walk on it, and, under this revision, we have, instead, history to answer to. We were important enough then for our souls to be fought over. Now, each of us is responsible for his own salvation, which is in his greatness. And that, that greatness, is the rock our hearts are abraded on. Great minds, great beauties, great lovers and criminals surround us. From the great sadness and desperation of Werthers and Don Juans we went to the great ruling images of Napoleons; from those to murderers who had that right over victims because they were greater than the victims; to men who felt privileged to approach others with a whip; to schoolboys and clerks who roared like revolutionary lions; to those pimps and subway creatures, debaters in midnight cafeterias who believed they could be great in treachery and catch the throats of those they felt were sound and well in the lassos of their morbidity; to dreams of greatly beautiful shadows embracing on a flawless screen. Because of these things we hate immoderately and punish ourselves and one another immoderately. The fear of lagging pursues and maddens us. The fear lies in us like a cloud. It makes an inner climate of darkness.

Now this is beautifully said, with a certain truth—but it summarizes almost too neatly the prevalent post-Marxist, nostalgically semireligious American intellectual view of our modern dilemma. Aren't these eloquent words a little odd, after all, coming from a writer who bases his work firmly, as Bellow has, on the social-environmental nexus? And particularly from a writer (as we shall see in the subsequent novels) who has within him a deep and primary core of Jewish feeling and of Biblical righteousness? "If there is no God, anything is possible," said Dostoyevsky, after he had returned to his own particular complex of religious and nationalistic "authority." But what the devil are the descendants of Jehovah and Jefferson doing in this gallery? If indeed *Dangling Man* caught the notice of our intellectual and literary journals, it was because it represented their own inner world view so accurately and so smoothly. In this sense, the

early Saul Bellow was the Herman Wouk of the academic quar-
terlies; and there are other interesting comparisons in fact between these two assimilated (in their art) Jewish writers and
prophets, one speaking for the elite of the 1940's and '50's, and
the other for the masses.

In the purely literary aspects of the novel, too, it was a
youthful and ambiguous work, for all its expression of the time
spirit. "It's months and months since you took an interest in
me," says Joseph's despairing wife, and this indictment could
extend to all the other characters in the book whom this hero
regards with, so to speak, an enforced humanity. He is a narrow,
a self-enclosed auctorial spokesman who is so concerned "with
keeping intact and free from encumbrance a sense of his own
being" that his separation from his own society seems as much
personal as social. The integrity of the hero's moral principles
is matched by the shallow penetration of those sensual or material levels of human experience on which a novelist's work usually rests. But this typical hero of isolated sensibility appears
again in Bellow's subsequent books, and the constricted psychic
syndrome at the center of the moral vision becomes tormented
in his second novel.

Three years later, in 1947, *The Victim* marked a sharp
advance in Bellow's craft, even while it was an elaboration of
Dangling Man in certain aspects. (Like William Dean Howells,
this later fictionalist showed a certain caution, even timidity, in
the development of his career.) There was again the use of a
purely literary source for the new novel in Dostoyevsky's *The
Eternal Husband*; there were literal repetitions of certain "effects," while the energy of the novel was transferred from the
cuckold-lover to the Jew-anti-Semite theme. But who is really
the "victim" in this ironic fable of a lower middle-class world of
commercial journalism? The poor, pathetic, moralistic, and tormented "hero," Leventhal, is made to feel responsible for having
ruined another man's life.

The ostensible "victim," Allbee, has lost his job through one
of Leventhal's fits of anger; he has taken to drink and is at the
edge of that bottomless social abyss that Leventhal himself fears
and dreads. In revenge—or is it simple human need and ele-
mentary justice?—Allbee fastens himself upon Leventhal in a

parasitical relationship. He moves into the apartment while Leventhal's wife is away, takes over Leventhal's affairs, pries into the most intimate affairs, brings a prostitute into Leventhal's marital bed, and finally attempts a "mutual suicide pact" without, however, first consulting Leventhal's wishes about the matter. The worst of it all is that Allbee, a decadent New Englander, has a morbid curiosity about the Jews which he is at no pains to conceal; he taunts Leventhal, whom he is slowly destroying. He is disgusting in his personal habits, and he is drawn to Leventhal physically; there are homosexual elements in this tangled and macabre relationship.

Why must Leventhal feel the moral responsibility for rehabilitating this dreadful specimen of his people's historic enemy; why does he come to believe some of the worst charges of anti-Semitism that Allbee levels at him? What burden of guilt does he carry in his heavy, sweating, panting, hairy black carcass? He feels responsible, too, for the death of his brother's child—the brother he hardly knows, who has abandoned his own family—and for his Catholic sister-in-law. His only pride comes from doing his job well in the business magazine office where he works. His only solace is in the love and care of his missing wife Mary, who is, however, barely more than a shadow in the story. The memory of his mad mother, his ineffectual father, haunts him also; his own delicate, hypochondriacal physical system periodically erupts into storms of hysteria.

Yet we feel all this spiritual agony in *The Victim*, and we know there is a certain justice in it. Leventhal is the eternal Jew, accepting his moral responsibility for a world he never made. And, overcome by illness, treachery, and malice in the social air around him, struggling desperately, not indeed to "get ahead" but simply to survive, he is also, in Bellow's view, a typical product of modern urban life. He is the Dangling Man, as it were, at last coming to grips with life. He is in part heroic in meeting all these commonplace disasters of the poor—the white-collar poor—and as pure fiction, this novel is effective. We feel both the world of commercial journalism—dingy, drab, snide—in which the distraught Leventhal has achieved a tiny niche, and the inner psychological world of the novel, where all of Leventhal's precarious security is suddenly threatened by "some freakish, insane process," which yet has some curious inner logic. The account of Leventhal's neurotic symptoms in meeting this threat is a psychosomatic drama in itself.

This is indeed the fable of the persecuted Jewish spirit that now must embrace and revive the fallen image of its would-be persecutors. Yet as in *Dangling Man*, the hero's friends are still the same group of "assimilated"—that is to say, of decultured and deracinated Jewish souls. In this close, narrow, joyless lower middle-class environment, indeed, the element of almost stifling domestic piety is all that thus remains to these people of their cultural heritage. It is only the old Yiddish journalist Schlossberg who breathes that other air, that other source of life and culture —literary, artistic, Bohemian, intellectual, often atheist, radical, or socialist—which, rather than the dwindling orthodox religious tradition, marked the true contribution of the Jewish immigrants to American society around the turn of the century.

But Schlossberg, alas, has also turned from his passionate love of the theater to more modern "scientific topics." His successor is the Hollywood agent, Shifcart, or the anglicized Jew Harkavy. And Leventhal thinks of his own father to whom nothing mattered except to be freed by money from the power of his enemies. "And who were the enemies? The world, everyone. They were imaginary. There was no advantage. He carried on like a merchant prince among his bolts and remnants, and was willing to be a pack rat in order to become a lion. There was no advantage; he never became a lion. It gave Leventhal pain to think about his father's sense of these things."

> *"Ruf mir Yoshke, ruf mir Moshke,*
> *Aber gib mir die groschke"*

his father had cried.—"Call me Ikey, call me Moe, but give me the dough." No wonder the son had rejected and recoiled from his father's vision of things, just as he had repudiated, as Bellow himself does, the whole ethic of American success, power, and money: the fear of lagging, the dark climate within. Yet the father's generation had had its own form of defense, if only through hatred, arrogance, and cunning, against the evil world, and those "imaginary" enemies who were often actual enough. What is the real meaning then of the ogres and demons and succubi that continue to inhabit this harassed hero Leventhal's own world: these terrible fears and panics of inward collapse, these sudden and unexpected apparitions of outward evil and disaster, that the son can only accept and endure?

In a curious twist of the narrative, Allbee is more Jewish than Leventhal himself. He taunts this sweating hero with perverted references to Jewish folklore and history that Leventhal is ignorant of; he is almost the symbol of the cultural heritage that the Bellow spokesman has cast aside unconsciously, and that now returns to strangle him in this twisted and evil form. Certainly Allbee is the odious "double" of Leventhal; and, in this modern melting pot of all religious modes, Leventhal seems to have inherited all the pain and suffering of his moral tradition with none of its resources. Is New York a "Jewish" city in his fevered imagination? But then it is a city in which, like olden Babel, no man can any longer speak to or understand another. And indeed the whole "Jewish" concept in this hero (and in the author?) is so close to paranoia and madness, so fraught with guilt, anxiety, and fear, so lacking in warmth, humor, and joy, that it is no longer, in the historic sense, Jewish. There is all the Jewish guilt without the Jewish pride, there is all the agony of life but no enjoyment, there is the heavy vestigial morality with none of the deep or wild human impulses which necessitated this morality.

One is reminded of nothing so much as that drab, dingy, and dreadful lower middle-class London world of George Orwell's (high above it the code of "gentlemanly" behavior, just below it the gaping social abyss), dying by inches of sheer spiritual malnutrition, but refined to the last: that world of genteel poverty in *Keep the Aspidistra Flying*, from which Orwell's hero took his own desperate plunge into the pit. This is the real background of Bellow's best-known and most popular book, *The Adventures of Augie March*, a bestseller in 1953, a Book-of-the-Month Club alternate selection, and then winner of the National Book Award as the best novel of the year. Was it? The *New York Times* critic, Robert Gorham Davis, compared it with John Dos Passos' *U.S.A.* Robert Penn Warren called it "rich, various, fascinating, and important." Other critics of contemporary fiction such as Harvey Swados and Harvey Curtis Webster agreed that it was "the most significant and remarkable novel to have been published in the United States in the past decade."

Well, it wasn't, not by a long shot. It was important perhaps only in the sense that Saul Bellow was now aware of, and was attempting to compensate for, the narrow world of solemn sorrow that he knew too well. It was a declaration of insight and intention, rather than a record of achievement. The novel's hero was a proletarian, not a middle-class figure: a symbol of joy, exuberance, experience, of Wolfean extravagance and the Comic Spirit, arising from the lower depths and touching the dizziest pinnacles of American success. That was the novel's plan, at least, and in Augie's Chicago origins, Bellow put himself where his sympathies had always lain: with the social realism school of Dreiser, of Thomas Wolfe himself, and of such later figures as Ira Wolfert, James T. Farrell, and Nelson Algren. The book reminds us that Bellow is indeed, by environment and inclination, another one of these few surviving figures of the 1930's who have not repudiated their heritage and their link with a central literary tradition of the past.

There were the battles, the defeats, and triumphs of civilian life too, in those days; whose echoes are dim and lost in the generation of World War II writers which moved only from adolescence to the martial orbit. (The true break in contemporary American literature occurred somewhere in the late 1940's and Fifties.) But one must add that if *Augie March* describes the range of Chicago slum life, poverty, and misery during the depression years well enough to evoke our sympathy, it does not really compel our interest. It is done from the outside, as though the writer had lived near, but never quite in this life, and knew all the traits of this society without knowing *it*. It is a literary survey, or an anthropological study—this belated proletarian picaresque account of the American social depths—which is accurate, informative, aware—everything but authentic. What is significant, too, is that the hero's immediate family is the weakest part of the book. The tyrannical Grandma Lausch from Odessa, the gentle, weak-willed mother abandoned by her husband, the idiot brother Georgie, the "successful" brother Simon: these are almost daguerreotypes, done by a conscientious but bored photographer.

The formative years of Augie's life as a slum kid, a petty criminal, an amateur lothario, are simply dull. The prose, almost the only time in Bellow's work, is turgid and wooden. Only with Einhorn, the crippled sensualist who becomes Augie's foster father, does the narrative pick up. From here Augie wanders on to become the protégé of Mrs. Renling (who also wants to adopt him), and then meets the intense if empty-minded "upper-class" siren, Thea Fenchel, while he is in love with her sister. Escaping this snare of wealth and society for the moment, he descends to crime with the killer Joe Gorman, and then finds his true milieu stealing books in order to attend the University of Chicago. Meanwhile the family has gone to ruin: the mother as well as the half-witted brother have been placed in an institution, and the cynical Simon stakes his all on a marriage with the bovine coal princess, Charlotte Magnus. The Magnus tribe, as symbols of crude, ignorant, solid material power, are well done; the savage frenzy of Simon on the way "up" in the family business is one of the high spots in the novel.

Augie, too, has a Magnus daughter lined up for him, but again he evades the trap of success in life, and drifts into a quixotic love for the emancipated little working girl Mimi. (Perhaps this is his single real relationship in the narrative.) But there is also his little Sophie. Sexual love, free, open, generous, is Augie's yearning here, just as it has been the single great area of life which has been missing in Bellow's previous novels. ("Does anyone faint from pleasure?" says the apartment-house superintendent in The Victim about his dog Smoke; but this ecstasy has been confined to the animal kingdom.) And then there comes that curious and prolonged episode in the novel where Thea Fenchel returns to Augie, overwhelms him with her desire, transports him to Mexico, and develops a subterranean passion for snakes.

Thus the novel which opens in the Chicago slums ends with the exotics and expatriates of Mexico and Europe: which is also a curious parable of the course of American literary realism during the last half-century. But what can we really make of all this? Perhaps the only compelling episode in the last half of Augie March is that of the cowardly eagle, Caligula, who simply refuses to play out his Darwinian and Hemingwayish role as an eagle. And with *Seize the Day*, in 1956 Bellow himself returned to more familiar territory.

The surface of this short novel, the brilliance of texture which marks all of Bellow's work except perhaps the Chicago tale itself, is even more impressive here. The upper West-Side New York scene is brilliantly described from the huge and gloomy hotels to the barbershops, the steam baths for the tired, flabby businessmen, and the local branch of the stock market which is the nerve center of this overdressed and overfed segment of middle-class urban society. With his marvelously acute details of social observation, Bellow has almost reached, in his own area, the gloss of a Scott Fitzgerald, a John O'Hara, or a J. P. Marquand. And this whole New York City scene is of course an ironic parody of American society as a whole; just as Tamkin, the "psychologist," is the poet, the philosopher, the "scientific observer," and the spokesman for this society. It is Tamkin who has a "calm rational approach" to the money-fever; who analyzes the "guilt-aggression cycles" behind the gambling in lard, who is full of atomic inventions, and who summarizes the new American credo. "The past is no good to us. The future is full of anxiety. Only the present is real—the here-and-now. Seize the day."

This nightmare vision of the upper West Side—a grotesque inferno of useless, pampered, empty, and ugly old age—is extended to the nation's metropolis itself, where money has replaced blood in human beings. "The money!" cries Tommy Wilhelm. "When I had it, I flowed money. They bled it away from me. I hemorrhaged money. But now it's almost all gone, and where am I supposed to turn for more?" Even more than to the agonized hero in *The Victim*, New York has become a Babel of isolated souls. "And it was the punishment of hell itself not to understand or be understood, not to know the crazy from the sane, the wise from the fools, the young from the old or the sick from the well. The fathers were no fathers and the sons no sons. You had to talk with yourself in the daytime and reason with yourself at night. Who else was there to talk to in a city like New York?"

This is indeed the mechanized lair of the lonely crowd, the fragmented individual. In the central figure of Tommy Wilhelm

himself, who has lost his job with the Rojax Company, whose
wife has abandoned him, whose children are strangers, and who
now lives on Unicap and Coca-Cola, there is Bellow's central
observation on the dark fear of "lagging" in the United States.
Yet in other respects Tommy Wilhelm is an odd protagonist to
personify this social concern. With his still boyish and impetuous manner, but his clumsy, overgrown, sloppy body, he is one of
the natural misfits, the "loose objects" on the social scene. He
has never finished college, he has had illusions of being a Hollywood star, his vanity has destroyed his career as a salesman. Now
a stock-market "speculator" under the spell of Tamkin (and the
electronic bookkeeping machines that do not allow you to get in
debt), he is in fact completely dependent on his father for financial and spiritual support. In this uneasy relationship of father
and son (as in the tangled sibling relation of the Jewish "oppressor" and the anti-Semitic "victim," earlier) we reach the psycho-
center of *Seize the Day*.

But it is easier to say this, and to feel it, than quite to understand it, with the perhaps deliberately ambiguous material
that the novelist has recorded. Tommy's father, Dr. Adler, is another instance of those respectable, conventional, "assimilated"
Jews in Bellow's work. He is a retired professional man, emi-
nently correct, fashionable, and successful. He is also selfish,
vain, and cold. Disowning both his children, in effect, after his
wife has conveniently died, he simply wants to live out his self-
centered, narcissistic, comfort-loving existence in peace. He is
ashamed of his son, not because Tommy has Americanized his
name and life to an even further degree, but because he has
failed. And what the son wants from this narrow, proper, hard-
hearted father is not money, after all, but the paternal love he
thinks he has never had.

Is this at base a sociological issue of the immigrant folk
cultures adapting to the old, hard, abstract success pattern of
American society?* Or is there a still deeper question of a psycho-

---

* There is no doubt that the children of the foreign-born in the United
States are "mother-protected" against the pressures of a strange and hostile
society; and to some degree they carry on the softness of the dominant
mother image in most older cultures out into the harsh patriarchal power
patterns of American culture—where, in turn, the father image has been
succeeded by the dollar sign.

biological nature, oedipal in essence, which lies at the base of Bellow's work, as it has in the case of so many other writers of the Western world? Certainly the panting frenzy of Tommy Wilhelm's search for love is beautifully done in *Seize the Day*, clumsy, grotesque, self-defeating as it is. And one remembers the other panting, yearning, panicky and defeated heroes in his previous work, or the solitary, brooding, loveless, and self-imposed human exile of the dangling man: two facets of the same psychological projection. Even the superman *schlemihl*, Augie March, is an orphan in his own thoughts, with recurrent fantasies of noble adopted parents, who seeks refuge with the foster father Einhorn, or the foster mother, Mrs. Renling. One parent or another is always missing in Bellow's human chronicles; or in effect they both are.

Here it is the mother that Tommy mourns ("As though he didn't know the year, the month, the day, the very hour of his mother's death."), just as the image of the mad mother haunts the consciousness of the victim Leventhal. But the father is lost also, that is the true and present sorrow, just as the father has deserted Augie March's family, and as Leventhal's own brother has deserted his family. Surely Tommy Wilhelm is seeking to re-create his lost, his imaginary family (though he in turn has abandoned his own wife and children) while the earlier Leventhal also takes on an assumed, a contrived paternal role by assuming the responsibility and the guilt for his brother's child. In a larger sense one feels that this shifting, ambiguous parental pattern at the base of Bellow's work is itself somewhat artificial and even false: as though the writer were seeking it out almost too consciously, feeling its absence, knowing its importance, and putting together the plausible and yet not the true parts.

Or as though the true issues in this tormented constellation of contrived parental and sibling relationships had not yet been resolved. For the hatreds, jealousies, angers, and desires, illicit, amoral, and profound, that also mark and accompany the oedipal complex of emotions, are curiously missing in Bellow's work, just as they are missing in, and as they delimit, his whole artistic vision of life. The suffering, the humility, the moral goodness in his books, the honest and ironic realization of human weakness: these are the traits that appeal to us. But this note of resignation, of acceptance, does not appear in Bellow's work after the violence and passions of life, as it commonly does in the work of major artists. It appears in Bellow's fiction *instead of* the emotional storm and stress it should transcend. The central image of the hero in his novels and stories is not indeed that of the rebellious son, but of the suffering, the tormented, and the conforming son.

To use the phraseology of Salinger, this hero is the good boy, the sad sack; or to use the terms of depth psychology, he is the castrated son. There is that curious scene in *Seize the Day* when the desperate and frantic Tommy searches for his father in the steam bath and there sees the proud young athlete with the virile curve in his sexual organ and the cruel smile on his lips. (Rejecting the sadistic aspects of the cult of masculine virility, Bellow also denies, in effect, its legitimate, normal, organic, pleasure-seeking, and luxury-loving function.) There is the deliberately ambiguous ending to the tale where Tommy first sees the crowds of ordinary people in the streets (those Dreiserian and Whitmanesque masses that this highly sensitive and withdrawn artist has always yearned to link himself with):

> And the great, great crowd, the inexhaustible current of millions of every race and kind pouring out, pressing round, of every age, of every genius, possessors of every human secret, antique and future, in every face the refinement of one particular motive or essence—*I labor, I spend, I strive, I design, I love, I cling, I uphold, I give way, I envy, I long, I scorn, I die, I hide, I want.* Faster, much faster than any man could make the tally.

And then when Tommy joins the funeral of the stranger, and bursts into hysterical sobbing at the sight of the corpse:

> The flowers and lights fused ecstatically in Wilhelm's blind, wet eyes; the heavy sea-like music came up to his ears. It poured into him where he had hidden himself in the center of a crowd by the great and happy oblivion of tears. He heard it and sank deeper than sorrow through torn sobs and cries toward the consummation of his heart's ultimate need.

Now here Bellow's peculiarly lyric cry of compassion finds perfect utterance. But what really is that consummation of this hero's ultimate need beyond the depths of sorrow and self-pity? Does the anonymous corpse represent himself? Or his father, whom he might indeed have wished to kill if he had ever allowed his feelings their true expression? Or simply the fate of all men—though Tommy Wilhelm in this tale only lives the life of a belated adolescent? Just as the central psychological issue in Bellow's fiction is left unresolved at the end of his most recent story, so too we realize that the "Jewish" issue, which is partly a mask for and a cultural projection of the human issue, has become more evasive in proportion as it has become more dominant. Does old Dr. Adler also despise his *schlemihlish* son because he has carried the process of "assimilation" one step farther, the final step, by changing his family name for the purposes of Hollywood—that is to say, of "American" society today?

The father still calls the son Wilky, the diminutive of his real name; but to Tommy, aware dimly that he has two selves, Wilky only means failure, not affection, and he is ashamed of it. And behind that there are echoes of his old Jewish name, Velvel, by which his grandfather had called him: his third, buried, and perhaps true soul. But this soul, too, Tommy never attempts to meet and understand; it is an uneasy ghost from the past, rather than a source of life. Just as Bellow himself has always stressed the narrowest part of the Orthodox Jewish religious tradition—rather than the flowering of secular Jewish culture and art in the New World—so, too, all his heroes continue to be ashamed of and to repudiate their true religious heritage. Judaism in Bellow's work is a source of nostalgia, but also of guilt and anxiety rather than of pride and pleasure. It is a constrictive and disturbing, rather than an enlarging or emancipating force.

Yet saying all this, we cannot deny the accuracy of this social picture either, in so far as it relates to the assimilating of all immigrant cultures within the stereotypes of modern American society; while it is from the moral burden of a specifically Jewish heritage that Bellow himself has been able to assess the outlines of this society. What is the real business of life, his last hero asks himself, if not "to carry his peculiar burden, to feel shame and impotence, to taste those quelled tears. . . . Maybe the making of mistakes expressed the very purpose of his life and the essence of his being here." Yes, one may still wish that the business of life in Bellow's fiction could go beyond this shame and impotence, these quelled tears. One notices that even his vision of the great, great crowd (the matrix of humanity) excludes the motives of I *lust* or I *desire, I enjoy, I give pleasure and take pleasure;* or better yet, that *we* do all these things together which are good for life, which express life, and which alone often make it bearable or pleasant. But still we must not deny the value of Bellow's humanitarian view in an epoch of the utmost social savagery; nor yet the peculiar lyric sweetness of what seems to be the essence of a pure soul.

There is something in Bellow's accent that may remind us of the innocent and childlike spirit of a Stephen Crane, consumed as the earlier writer was also by the flames of his own oedipal and religious conflict. If I have already made the comparison with another Jewish writer in the popular field, it should be clear, too, that Saul Bellow is genuinely concerned with, and even oppressed by, the moral values of his heritage—that he suffers from them—while Herman Wouk has cashed in on them.

3·THE ADVENTURES OF SAUL BELLOW: Progress of a Novelist

WITH THE PUBLICATION of *Henderson the Rain King* (Viking, $4.50), Saul Bellow confirms one's impression that he is just about the best novelist of his generation. The new book has faults; it is uneven, it is sometimes diffuse. And besides the liability of its real faults, it makes its appeal to literary qualities which, although very much in the American tradition, Serious Readers have learned during the last decades to scorn. For much of its length *Henderson* is a "romance" rather than a "novel." It forfeits some of the virtues of the novel (realism, plausibility, specificity), but gains some of the virtues of romance (abstraction, freedom of movement, extreme expressions of pathos, beauty, and terror). The book is sometimes farcical, melodramatic, zany —qualities that Serious Readers know, know all too well, are inferior to Realism and Tragedy. But *Henderson* has realism and tragedy too, although not so much as some of Bellow's other writings.

Bellow has chosen a fertile subject—a demented American aristocrat at loose ends and in search of his soul. This is a subject which, before *Henderson the Rain King*, few if any American novelists had thought of using, except at the relatively low level of imaginative intensity that characterizes the polite novel of manners. In the brutal, loony, yet finally ennobled Henderson we have a character who for dire realism and significant modernity far surpasses in dramatic intensity the frustrated aristocrats portrayed by writers like Edith Wharton and J. P. Marquand. It is interesting, by the way, that of the few reviewers of *Henderson* I have read, none mentioned the patrician heritage of the hero, although this heritage is of cardinal importance in understanding him. It is as if the reviewers still regard "an aristocrat" as nothing but a walking collection of manners and therefore unsuitable for portraiture in anything but a novel of manners. Yet even in democratic America the well-born may receive as part of their birthright a certain dynamism, a distortion of character, a tendency to extreme behavior, or other qualities not easily expressed by a novel of manners.

One praises *Henderson the Rain King* in spite of the fact that in some ways it is not up to the high level Bellow set in *The Adventures of Augie March* and in the short novel *Seize the Day*, the best single piece Bellow has written. It is a thinner brew than *Augie* (but what novel isn't?) and less sustained and concentrated in its impact than *Seize the Day*. After the wonderful first forty pages or so, during which we see Henderson on his home grounds, Connecticut and New York, there is a distinct falling off. We doubt whether Bellow should have sent him off so soon to Africa, where most of his adventures occur. We perceive that the author is not always able to make his highly imaginative Africa into an adequate setting for his hero. We fear that Bellow is in danger of confusing Henderson with another pilgrim to Africa, Hemingway. We feel that the book wanders uncertainly for a bad hour or so in the middle. But then it begins to pull itself together again, overcomes the threadbare plot, and triumphantly concludes in a mad moment of tragi-comedy.

The book's shortcomings, along with certain qualities that strike me as real virtues, have led some Bellow devotees to put *Henderson* down as a failure or at best a misguided lark in a never-never land (if *Augie* is Bellow's *Huck Finn*, is not *Henderson* his *Connecticut Yankee in King Arthur's Court?*). But these adverse judgments are wrong. Bellow still works in a comic tradition that is greater than farce or the comedy of manners. He has not only farce and wit but also humor—a richer thing, being permeated with realism, emotion, and love of human temperament. His imagination is fecund and resourceful. His tradition, at a hazard, includes, besides the naturalistic novel, Mark Twain, Walt Whitman, Joyce, and Yiddish humor.

Over the years Bellow's writing has shown a great deal of flexibility and power of development. He did not start off with the big Thomas Wolfe attempt at an autobiographical first novel. He saved that subject until his third book, *Augie March*, and by doing so possibly avoided the fate of many young writers who have a special story to tell, such as that of being brought up in an immigrant family in an American city, but who find that after the story has been told, they have nothing else to say. True, Bellow's first novel, *Dangling Man*, was ostensibly autobiographical and in some of its passages it caught the experience of a young intellectual in the uncertain days of our involvement in World War II. Yet the story was told with so much reticence as to give a thin, claustral quality to the whole. Bellow's second novel, *The Victim*, was one of those books published in the years just after the war that seemed to promise a resurgence of American writing (and yet how many new writers of those days have failed to fulfill themselves!). As compared with *Dangling Man*, *The Victim* was notable for its increase in objectivity and drama, and for its picture of the complicated relations between a disorderly, drunken, middle-class Gentile and a hapless but morally self-directing Jew in search of a precarious status. Here Bellow was dealing with what was to be his favorite theme—the impulse of human beings to subject others to their own fate, to enlist others in an allegiance to their own moral view and version of reality. In *The Victim* it is the Jew Leventhal who must resist the attempt of the anti-Semitic Allbee to involve him in his fate. This theme gets its fullest treatment in *Augie March*, but finds its ultimate significance in *Seize the Day*.

The Adventures of Augie March first acquainted us with the formidable music Bellow can make when he pulls out all the stops. Like many other fine American books, it astonishes us first as a piece of language. There are the rather dizzy medleys of colloquial and literary words. For example, Grandma Lausch, the picturesque tyrant of the family in which Augie is brought up, is said to be "mindful always of her duty to wise us up, one more animadversion on the trusting, loving, and simple surrounded by the cunning hearted and the tough." "Not," says Augie, "that I can see my big, gentle, dilapidated, scrubbing, and lugging mother as a fugitive of immense beauty from such classy wrath." There is no doubt that Augie, who tells the whole story in the first person, is right in describing himself as "gabby." A wayward adolescent, almost a juvenile delinquent, he sometimes seems to resemble Marlon Brando. But he is not sullen and inarticulate in the modern style of American youth—far from it. Like any Rabelais, Whitman, Melville, or Joyce, he loves to catalog things, such as the people in the Chicago City Hall: "bigshots and operators, commissioners, grabbers, heelers, tipsters, hoodlums, wolves, fixers, plaintiffs, flatfeet, men in Western hats and women in lizard shoes and fur coats, hothouse and arctic drafts mixed up, brute things and airs of sex, evidence of heavy feeding and systematic shaving, of calculations, grief, not-caring, and hopes of tremendous millions in concrete to be poured or whole Mississippis of bootleg whisky and beer."

Augie is a real poet and lover of the tongue which his immigrant race has only just learned to speak. He loves to explore its resources. And we don't complain much if he is sometimes a bit on the flashy side, a little pretentious and word-besotted in the language he hurls at our heads. Often he is perfectly simple and as appealing as Huckleberry Finn, whom he sometimes reminds us of, while he is still a boy and beset by odd illusions. If Mark Twain had been willing to use the four-letter word, he might have made Huck say, as Augie does, "I understand that British aristocrats are still legally entitled to piss, if they should care to, on the hind wheels of carriages."

Augie is hard to characterize, and of course that is the point about him. He declines the gambit of the young man in an immigrant family; he does not have the drive to succeed or establish himself in a profession. Believing that to commit oneself to any sort of function in the going concern of society is a form of death, he remains unattached and free, although to what end we never fully learn. He is a little of everything: a student, a petty thief, adopted son, tramp, lover, apprentice to assorted people and trades, a would-be intellectual in the purlieus of the University of Chicago, a suppositious Trotskyite, an eagle tamer, a merchant seaman. He is protean, malleable, "larky and boisterous," vain, strong, vital, and also a bit of a fall-guy, in fact "something of a schlemiel." The plot of *Augie March* is that of Whitman's *Song of Myself*—the eluding of all of the identities proffered to one by the world, by one's past, and by one's friends. Augie calls himself "varietistic," just as Whitman says, "I resist anything better than my own diversity." "What I assume, you shall assume," writes Whitman. And Augie reflects on "what very seldom mattered to me, namely, where I came from, parentage, and other history, things I had never much thought of as difficulties, being democratic in temperament, available to everybody and assuming about others what I assumed about myself." Augie remains elusive and diverse. His fate is not that of any of the memorable people he knows: Grandma Lausch, his brother Simon, Mrs. Renling, Einhorn, Sylvester, Clem Tambow, Mimi, Thea, Stella.

Not that Augie is entirely happy about himself, or sure in his own mind that varietism and freedom from ties will lead him to individual autonomy. Bellow seems to leave him wavering as the novel draws to a close. At one point Augie calls for autonomy, for the unattached individual—"a man who can stand before the terrible appearances" without subjecting himself to any of them. He wants to take the "unsafe" road and be a "personality" rather than take the safe road and be a "type." He resists being "recruited" to other people's versions of reality and significance. And yet Augie strikes us as being puzzled, as we are, by the questions: What *is* his personality, what *is* his version of reality and significance? At any rate we find him wishing that his fate "was more evident, and that I could quit this pilgrimage of mine." At the end he is married and in Paris, "in the bondage of strangeness for a time still," yet oddly wishing that he could return to the States and have children. But even the idea of paternity is not allowed to thwart his desire for unattached selfhood. Where, he asks, is character made? And he answers that "It's internally done . . . in yourself you labor, you wage and combat, settle scores, remember insults, fight, reply, deny, blab, denounce, triumph, outwit, overcome, vindicate, cry, persist, absolve, die and rise again. All by yourself! Where is everybody? Inside your breast and skin, the entire cast." But all this sounds less like an autonomous personality than a man far gone in solipsism and illusion. Augie's concluding words belie

the "oath of unsusceptibility" he has taken. At the end he ex-
claims, "Why I am a sort of Columbus of those near-at-hand
and believe you can come to them in this immediate *terra incognita* that spreads out in every gaze." Augie's wish that people
could "come to" each other entirely without any ulterior motive or aggression is praiseworthy, but we share his doubts that
they ever can.

"A man's character is his fate," Augie says at the beginning
and end of his story. But the question, What is his character?
is not answered. The idea of character in *Augie March* is contradictory. Bellow is, from one point of view, in the line of the
naturalistic novelists (Norris, Dreiser, and Farrell—who have
also written about Chicago), and he therefore conceives of character deterministically as the product of heredity and environment. "All the influences were lined up waiting for me," says
Augie. "I was born and there they were to form me, which is why
I tell you more of them than of myself." On the other hand, as
I said above, Bellow follows the Whitman tradition which
believes that character is the autonomous self, the given transcendent fact which no amount of natural conditioning can
fundamentally change. The naturalistic account is incomplete
because it tries to describe only what *produces* character, the
transcendentalist account is vague, however liberating and in-
spiring it may be. A logical difficulty or a moral or metaphysical
anomaly doesn't necessarily spoil a fiction. And in fact it strikes
me that it is exactly Bellow's mixture of attitudes toward character that makes his novel such a rich experience.

What Augie fears is the death of the self, and his judgment
of the contemporary world is that it is terribly resourceful in its
stratagems for destroying the self. In *Seize the Day* Tommy Wilhelm comes to understand the death of the self in a harrowing
scene in a funeral parlor, a scene more profound and moving
than anything the bumptious Augie undergoes. Wilhelm, mid-
dle-aging, an unemployed salesman, separated from his wife and
two children, is on the ebb tide of his fortunes. The scene is in
and about a hotel on Broadway and not the least value of the
story is the accuracy with which Bellow has reproduced the bleak
gerontocracy which has gathered there from all parts of New

York and Europe—the "senior citizens," as our culture calls them, the forlorn octogenarians, the wistful widowers, the grimy, furtive old women. One of the aged is Wilhelm's father, a retired doctor with a professional sense of success and rectitude, who regards his hesitant romantic son as "a slob." Malleable like Augie, but less resilient, Wilhelm allows his career to be spoiled at the outset by putting himself under the guidance of Maurice Venice, who promises to get him a job as a movie star but turns out to be a pimp. He has lost, or given up, his job as a salesman of baby furniture, and now is at the mercy of the recriminations directed at him by his father and his wife. Of course, they have their point, but Wilhelm is not entirely wrong in thinking that there is something sinister and inhumanly aggressive in their nagging insistence that (as Augie would say) he allow himself to be recruited to *their* versions of reality.

But in trying to escape from his father and his wife, Wilhelm comes under the influence of Dr. Tamkin, who, whatever else we may think of him, is certainly one of Bellow's most glorious creations. Reminiscing, Augie March had exclaimed, "Why did I always have to fall among theoreticians!" It is a poignant question, suggesting that in a world where no one is certain about truth, everyone is a theoretician. And to the fastest theorizer goes the power; he is the one who can "seize the day." Dr. Tamkin, investor, alleged psychiatrist, poet, philosopher, mystic, confidence man, is one of the fast talkers. He is an adept in the wildly eclectic world of semi-enlightenment and semi-literacy which constitutes the modern mass mind when it expresses itself in ideas, the crazy world of half-knowledge, journalistic clichés, popularized science, and occultism, the rags and tatters of the world's great intellectual and religious heritages. Bellow is a master at describing this state of mind, and a sound moralist in suggesting that a Dr. Tamkin would be less reprehensible if he were merely greedy and materialistic, like the characters in naturalistic novels—but, no, he must also be a mystic, a psychiatrist, and a theoretician. And so Wilhelm, the well meaning, not too bright ordinary man, is all the more bewildered and devastated when the seven hundred dollars he has given Tamkin to invest in lard is lost and he is ruined.

Wandering the streets in search of Tamkin, who seems to

appear and disappear in the crowds like a ghost, Wilhelm is jostled by a group of mourners into a funeral parlor where, standing by the coffin of a man he does not know, he weeps uncontrollably for his own symbolic death, the death of the self. In this scene we have in its deepest expression one side of the meaning (as I understand the difficult idea) of Augie's apothegm: "Well, given time, we all catch up with legends, more or less." The same idea is expressed in the odd English of the somewhat incredible King Dahfu in Bellow's new novel: "The career of our specie is evidence that one imagination after another grows literal. . . . Imagination! It converts to actual. It sustains, it alters, it redeems! . . . What Homo sapiens imagines, he may slowly convert himself to." But the human power of actualizing the imaginary is a two-edged sword, which can destroy as well as redeem. We can be destroyed if, as in his moment of final anguish and illumination Wilhelm understands he has done, we allow ourselves to be recruited to, allow ourselves to become actualizations of, other people's versions of reality. Yet catching up with the legend or realizing the imaginary can also be liberating and redemptive. So we gather at the moment when Wilhelm catches up with the legend of his own death—a legend that has been entertained by himself and by those he has known—while he gazes, with the great revelation, at the stranger in the coffin.

Thus it appears that although Bellow's insistence on being free is not a complete view of human destiny, neither is it simply a piece of naïveté or moral irresponsibility, as has sometimes been suggested. He believes that if we ever define our character and our fate it will be because we have caught up with our own legend, realized our own imagination. Bellow's fertile sense of the ever-possible conversion of reality and imagination, fact and legend, into each other is the source of the richness and significance of his writing. He differs in this respect from the traditional practice of American prose romance, which forces the real and imaginary far apart and finds that there is no circuit of life between them. (On this point see my book, *The American Novel and Its Tradition*.) Bellow differs, too, from the pure realist, who describes human growth as a simple progress away from legend and toward fact, and from the naturalistic novelist, who conceives of circumstance as always defeating the human impulse of further thrusts toward autonomy. Which is merely to say that Bellow's sense of the conversion of reality and imagination is something he shares with the greatest novelists.

Bellow gives the light treatment to some of his favorite themes in *Henderson the Rain King,* although there are tragicomic moments which for the extreme expression of degradation and exaltation surpass anything in the previous books. With a fatal predictability, the conventional reviewers, often in the midst of encomia, have reproved Bellow for "descending" to farce, as well as to melodrama and fantasy. It does no good to ask where writers so different as Mark Twain, Dickens, Molière, Joyce, and Aristophanes would be without farce.

This is Bellow's first novel with no Jewish characters (although we hear at the beginning of a soldier named Nicky Goldstein, who told Henderson that after the war he was going to raise mink; with characteristic sensibility, Henderson decides on the spot that he will raise pigs). Perhaps in selecting for his hero a tag-end aristocrat, Bellow is responding in reverse to Henry Adams's statement at the beginning of the *Education* that as a patrician born out of his time he might as well have been born Israel Cohen. At any rate we find Henderson ruefully reflecting that despite the past eminence of his family, "Nobody truly occupies a station in life any more. . . . There are displaced persons everywhere." As Henderson at fifty-five freely admits, he has always behaved "like a bum." His father, though, had been an impressive example of rectitude; he had known Henry Adams and Henry James; the family eminence goes back at least to Federal times. His father had followed the traditional life of public service. He had written books of social and literary criticism, defended persecuted Negroes, and in general regarded it as his inherited duty to help guide the national taste, opinion, and conduct in his day.

As for Henderson himself, he cheerfully admits that he is one of the "loony" members of the family—like the one that "got mixed up in the Boxer Rebellion, believing he was an Oriental" or the one that "was carried away in a balloon while publicizing the suffrage movement." Yet he still affirms—to

the point of rainmaking for the parched inhabitants of Africa—
the "service ideal" that "exists in our family." Like Wilhelm in
Seize the Day, he has faced death, not in the war but while
gazing at the soft white head of an octopus in an aquarium.
"This is my last day," he thought on that occasion. "Death is
giving me notice." But Henderson is strong, brutal, willful, with
great stature and a big belly. Very much a creature of his time,
he "seeks wisdom," believing that earlier generations have performed all the more practical tasks—"white Protestantism and
the Constitution and the Civil War and capitalism and winning
the West," all these things have been accomplished. But, he
goes on, "that left the biggest problem of all, which was to encounter death. We've just got to do something about it . . .
it's the destiny of my generation of Americans to go out into
the world and try to find the wisdom of life." True, Henderson
is often retrospective. He has moments of family nostalgia and
piety, when he tries to get in touch with his dead father and
mother. For this purpose he goes to the cellar and plays a violin
(a genuine Guarnerius, of course) that had belonged to his
father. He croons, "Ma, this is 'Humoresque' for you" and "Pa,
listen—'Meditation from Thaïs.' " As we see, Henderson is not
only musical but occult. He is "spell-prone . . . highly medium-
istic and attuned."

But Henderson does not find fulfillment in such activities.
He is bored and dissatisfied with his disorderly wife. Like most
moderns he loves and pursues "reality" and yet he is just as
strongly drawn to the mythic and the magical. He is alternately
depressed and exalted by his inchoate notions, in describing
which Bellow shows himself again to be an inspired interpreter
of the eclectic, semi-literate mind of contemporary culture. Henderson needs new realms to discover, new opportunities of service and redemption. And so he is off to Africa, an Africa which
is sometimes that of fantasy ("those were wild asses maybe, or
zebras flying around in herds") and sometimes that of Sir James
Frazer and Frobenius.

He finds in Africa that there is a curse upon the land. A
terrible drought is killing the cattle of the first tribe he encounters, for although the cistern is full of water, the water is
infested with frogs, which frighten the cattle away and which

the natives have a taboo against killing. Henderson improvises a grenade to blow up the frogs, but blows up the whole cistern too. This is unfortunate because things had been going well for him. For example, Henderson had been absorbing animal magnetism from the natives, as when he ceremonially kisses the fat queen's belly: "I kissed, giving a shiver at the heat I encountered. The knot of the lion skin was pushed aside by my face, which sank inward. I was aware of the old lady's navel and her internal organs as they made sounds of submergence. I felt as though I were riding in a balloon above the Spice Islands, soaring in hot clouds while exotic odors rose from below."

But it is with the next tribe, the Wariri, that his most significant adventures occur. Here Henderson performs the ritual of moving the ponderous statue of the Rain Goddess, whereupon he is made Rain King, stripped naked, flayed, and thrown into the mud of the cattle pond, in the midst of the downpour he has summoned from heaven by his act. Humiliated, abject, yet gigantic, triumphant, visionary, an Ivy-League medicine man smeared with blood and dirt, Henderson dances on his bare feet through the cruel, hilarious scene. "Yes, here he is," cries our hero,

> the mover of Mummah, the champion, the Sungo. Here comes Henderson of the U.S.A.—Captain Henderson, Purple Heart, veteran of North Africa, Sicily, Monte Cassino, etc., a giant shadow, a man of flesh and blood, a restless seeker, pitiful and rude, a stubborn old lush with broken bridgework, threatening death and suicide. Oh, you rulers of heaven! Oh, you dooming powers! . . . And with all my heart I yelled, "Mercy, have mercy!" And after that I yelled, "No justice!" And after that I changed my mind and cried, "No, no, truth, truth!" And then, "Thy will be done! Not my will but Thy will!" This pitiful rude man, this poor stumbling bully, lifting up his call to heaven for truth. Do you hear that?"

There ensue several lengthy conversations on life and human destiny between Henderson and the philosophical King Dahfu—a somewhat pathetic monarch whom we often see surrounded by his demanding harem of naked women. He has read books like William James's *Principles of Psychology* and believes that when he dies his soul will be reborn in a lion, the totem animal of the tribe. Like the naturalistic novelists, Bellow is fond of characterizing people by analogies with animals. But Bellow, like Swift, follows the greater comic traditions of animal imagery. Tommy Wilhelm caricatures himself as a hippopotamus, yet the effect is to make him more human, more understandable, more complicated, rather than less so.

What might be called Bellow's totemistic style of comedy and character drawing gets a full workout in *Henderson*. A raiser of pigs and a self-proclaimed bum, Henderson has thought of himself as a pig. King Dahfu believes that what Henderson needs is rehabilitation in the image of the lion totem, and he therefore puts our hero through a course of what can only be described as lion-therapy, complete with psychiatric terms like "resistance" and "transference." This takes place in a cage under the palace, where the king keeps a magnificent lioness. The therapy consists in repeated exposures to the lioness, first getting Henderson to try to quell his fears of her and finally getting him to imitate the lioness, on his hands and knees, growling and roaring, so that by sympathetic magic he can absorb lionlike qualities. The scene in which he is finally able to roar satisfactorily, though still terrified, is a great comic moment. The king and the lioness watch Henderson "as though they were attending an opera performance." Henderson describes the roar he lets out as one which

> summarized my entire course on this earth, from birth to Africa; and certain words crept into my roars, like "God," "Help," "Lord have mercy," only they came out "Hoolp!" "Moooorcy!" It's funny what words sprang forth. "Au secours," which was "Secoooooor" and also "De Profooondis," plus snatches from the "Messiah" (He was despised and rejected, a man of sorrows, etcetera). Unbidden, French sometimes came back to me, the language in which I used to taunt my little friend François about his sister.

In this abject, ridiculous, and yet eloquent roar we are impressed with the full pathos, the utter humiliation, and also the odd marginal grandeur of Henderson. After this he writes a letter to his wife directing her to apply for his admission to the Medical Center, signing the application "Leo E. Henderson" (although his name is Eugene). For now he is resolved to become the M.D. he has always dreamed of being since, as a boy, he had been inspired by the example of Sir Wilfred Grenfell. Of course the letter never arrives.

Henderson escapes from the Wariri after King Dahfu has been killed trying to capture the lion who is his father. One need hardly bother about the plot—the conniving witch doctor, the escape from prison, the hazardous flight of Henderson. It is all pleasant enough in the reading.

But the end is magnificent. Here we have Henderson walking around the blank, wintry airport in Newfoundland, where his plane has put down for refueling. He is paternally carrying in his arms an American child who speaks only Persian and is being sent alone to Nevada. He remembers how his own father had been angry at him once when he was a boy and how he had hitchhiked to Canada, where he had got a job at a fair. His task was to accompany and care for an aged, toothless, and forlorn trained bear who was ending his days of performing by taking rides on a roller-coaster, though paralyzed by fear and vertigo and occasionally wetting himself, for the delectation of the crowds who watched from below. "We hugged each other, the bear and I, with something greater than terror and flew in those gilded cars. I shut my eyes in his wretched, time-abused fur. He held me in his arms and gave me comfort. And the great thing is that he didn't blame me. He had seen too much of life, and somewhere in his huge head he had worked it out that for creatures there is nothing that ever runs unmingled." Henderson the boy is long dead; Henderson the lion has disappeared, so has Henderson the pig. Henderson the bear remains, "longsuffering, age-worn, tragic, and discolored." Still a rather preposterous clown, he has nevertheless achieved a certain nobility by his way of "mingling" in the common fate of creatures. Will he remain Henderson the bear? Not if he can live up to the declarations of freedom and growth he made earlier in the book. "I am Man . . . and Man has many times tricked life when life thought it had him taped." And, though saddened, he had agreed with King Dahfu that "Nature is a deep imitator. And as man is the prince of organisms he is the master of adaptations. He is the artist of suggestions. He himself is his principal work of art, in the body, working in the flesh. What miracle! What triumph! Also, what disaster! What tears are to be shed!"

The king's words strike Bellow's "note." His main characters—Augie, Tommy Wilhelm, Henderson—are adept at imitation and at adaptation. They are different, to be sure. Augie remains young, strong, charming, yet emotionally soft. Wilhelm is wistful, unstable, romantic. Henderson is wild, brutal, a clown. But they are all malleable, emergent, pragmatic, and protean; they love freedom, development, pleasure, and change. They seek both natural and transcendent experiences that are expressive of their way of life.

What is so far chiefly missing in Bellow's writing is an account of what his heroes want to be free *from*. As Bellow is always showing, their very adaptability lays them open to forms of tyranny—social convention, a job, a father, a lover, a wife, their children, everyone who may want to prey upon them. And all of these forms of tyranny, fraud, and emotional expropriation Bellow describes brilliantly. But only in *Seize the Day* is there a fully adequate, dramatically concentrated image of what the central figure is up against—the institutional, family, and personal fate that he must define himself by, as heroes in the greatest literature define themselves. *Augie March* is prodigiously circumstantial, but the circumstances are never marshaled into a controlling image, and Henderson is bundled off to Africa before we see enough of him in his native habitat to know fully, by understanding the circumstances of his life, what his character and his fate are. But who can complain when, once he is in Africa, we see him in episodes which make us think him the momentary equal, for tragi-comic madness, for divine insanity, of the greatest heroes of comic fiction?

J. C. Levenson

4·BELLOW'S DANGLING MEN

> Dangle . . .3. in *grammar*, to lack clear connection with
> the proper substantive. . . . *New World Dictionary.*

AMERICAN LITERATURE is full of dangling men whose loose connection with actual, rooted institutions is what first lets them
move into a story and whose easy uncommitted relation to specific ideals keeps the plot going. Often the social context of
their fictive action is so vaguely represented that it can be said
hardly to exist. The true dangler wants to read all the terms of
the covenant, study the clauses in fine print, before he signs the
social compact. (If he ever does sign—for sometimes the free
hero declines, questioning not merely whether he will join society, but even whether he will join the universe.) Although no
one perfectly realizes the type, Natty Bumppo and Daniel
Boone, Hester Prynne and Ahab, Daisy Miller and Huckleberry
Finn march in the same direction even if they do not always
keep step; at a later hour, Jake Barnes joins the irregular parade
and laconically talks of wounds with raging Ahab, Jay Gatsby
in engaging Oxford tones puts a question or two to the Jamesian
contingent, Ike McCaslin humbly takes his place with the
foraging party. They are free spirits all, and yet they seem to
gravitate to the same open road. The classic American pattern
of individualism and uniformity is as evident in literature as in
society. The writer's problem is whether there may not be some
new way to be free, whether there must not be—when the fish
and game have all but disappeared, and illusions are hard to
come by, and society itself has sustained wounds from which it
may never recover—a new turn for the imagination to take.

After Buchenwald and Hiroshima, fiction can hardly remain the same, and in the most interesting of our postwar novelists, it has indeed changed. For while the persistent character of Saul Bellow's novels is the dangling man, the old American hero has been reborn in a new time and a new situation; he dangles differently.

One aspect of the difference may be suggested by the notion that Bellow's America has joined the world while his characters are still trying to decide whether or not they will join America. The American side of his subject is indisputable: Richard Chase has quite rightly declared that Whitman and Mark Twain stand benevolently looking over Bellow's shoulder as he writes; their energy, exuberance, and wonder are continued in him, and so is their determination to extricate their freedom whenever they may be caught "on the verge of a usual mistake." But Nietzsche and Dostoyevsky are equally the familiars of Bellow's imaginative world: the international theater of his imagination consists primarily in that. The new combinations which can be made out of the infinite possibilities of art are what give delight even in Bellow's earliest novel of 1944, *Dangling Man*—the story of a young man waiting indefinitely for the draft call; his number having come up, there is no chance of finding a job, only endless waiting and the indefiniteness of life without purpose. Joseph began with the Whitman endowment of equanimity, in which "judgment is second to wonder, to speculation on men, drugged or clear, jealous, ambitious, good, tempted, curious, each in his own time and with his customs and motives, and bearing the imprint of strangeness in the world." And he had the old hopefulness which looked toward "a 'colony of the spirit,' or a group whose covenants forbade spite, bloodiness, and cruelty. To hack, to tear, to murder was for those in whom the sense of the temporariness of life had shrunk. The world was crude and it was dangerous and, if no measures were taken, existence could indeed become . . . 'nasty, brutish, short.' " But when war and the machinery of the state have thrown a barrier across his open road, he falters. American attitudes, however warmly and deeply held, cannot exempt a man from the European, the human condition of limited choice. His sanguine detachment becomes aloneness, isolation from others and even from his own true self. To hope for a colony of the spirit has been to hope too much for the way he can shape his life, and when the hope fails, he gradually becomes disengaged from all connections of love and all capacity for purpose. The blank wall in his path is as absolute as two plus two makes four, and for him there is neither the noble transcendence of Isabel Archer's accommodation to destiny nor Huck Finn's simple (and spurious) detour to the territory ahead. Confronted by the wall, he goes underground.

But Bellow's Joseph is not altogether Dostoyevsky's man, for he dangles in the "crater of the spirit," he does not drown. His vitality wanes until in his boredom with the world and himself he gets to be the man who picks fights, who looks for danger, who is "tired of having to identify a day as 'the day I asked for a second cup of coffee,' or 'the day the waitress refused to take back the burned toast,' and so want[s] to blaze it more sharply, regardless of the consequences. Perhaps, eager for the consequences." To this point, the pattern of ennui in Bellow's novels runs parallel to that of *Notes from the Underground*, in which "luxurious inertia" and the "voluptuous pleasure" of morbid self-exploration provide our clue to the leading character. But the answer to Robert Frost's sardonic question, "How are we to write The Russian novel in America/As long as life goes so unterribly?" has not been simply to rewrite Dostoyevsky in a new place. The theme of Bellow's fiction is the reverse of his model's, for the drama enacted *through* his characters makes it clear that if we do not find ourselves, we are likely to lose ourselves. The sick soul is the same anywhere, but what the Bellow hero seeks is recovery, not rebirth. Joseph's friend, who can look into the dark with the eyes of a cat and yet not collapse at the sight of the truth, is the ideal: ". . . In spite of the calamity, the lies and moral buggery, the odium, the detritus of wrong and sorrow dropped on every heart, in spite of these, he can keep a measure of cleanliness and freedom." The friend survives, however, because he faces the outward more than the inner dark. Bellow puts little emphasis on the point simply because his hero has to learn this for himself, but the point exists to suggest an interpretation of Joseph's agonized cry about the way "we throw ourselves away"—"When what we really want is to stop living so exclusively and vainly for our own sake, impure and unknowing, turning inward and self-fastened." Joseph finally breaks out of his "six-sided box" by asking his draft board for an immediate call.

One of the reviewers of *Dangling Man* expressed a low opinion of the ending in which Joseph concludes his notes with his last sentiments as a civilian: "I am in other hands, relieved of self-determination, freedom canceled. Hurray for regular hours! And for the supervision of the spirit! Long live regimentation!" But I doubt that the irony stops at the suggestion that mankind cannot long stand freedom, and I do not think that Bellow is simply translating the Underground Man's morbid "Hurray for the underground." The act of choice implies an affirmation of freedom as well as the loss of it. Why not believe Joseph when he claims to understand the virtue of preserving oneself—not one's skin, but one's humanity? The cheerful interpretation, to be sure, can be argued from nothing less than the whole context of the novel. But at the very beginning, Joseph's notes cite Goethe:

> "All comfort in life is based upon a regular occurrence of external phenomena. The changes of the day and night, of the seasons, of flowers and fruits, and all other recurring pleasures that come to us, that we may and should enjoy them—these are the mainsprings of our earthly life. The more open we are to these enjoyments, the happier we are; but if these changing phenomena unfold themselves and we take no interest in them, if we are insensible to such fair solicitations, then comes on the sorest evil, the heaviest disease—we regard life as a loathsome burden. It is said of an Englishman that he hanged himself that he might no longer have to dress and undress himself every day." (18)*

The Englishman who hanged himself from ennui is immediately coupled in Joseph's mind with Shakespeare's Barnardine in *Measure for Measure* "whose contempt for life equaled his contempt for death, so that he would not come out of his cell to be executed." Despite Joseph's fixing upon Barnardine's insensitivity, the coupling in his mind is really right because of contrast rather than likeness: the drunken convict who with comic vitality will not consent to die is an alternative to the enfeebled slave of boredom. Such comicality belongs to the dangling man also,

---

* All pages references are to the first editions of the novels.

who, when he is not passively suffering, explodes by making scenes. The explosions are painful but also hilarious, for Joseph does what an inhibited reader might like to do and his outrageous conduct relieves our embarrassing impulses vicariously. But our pleasure in the assertion of vitality is never free of a lurking sense of danger until Joseph finally asserts himself constructively—not against society, but with it. And the irony with which his joining the army is treated strikes me as truly proper; as Barbara Deming showed in her study of the movies in wartime, the popular pattern would have the hero, whom circumstance has made us doubt, turn out to have been a patriot all along; Joseph, aware that "certain blood will be given for half-certain reasons, as in all wars," obviously cannot rally the "irresponsibles" as well as Humphrey Bogart. Moral necessity demands a social act rather than a simple patriotic reflex, and if in conduct these two seem to come down to the same thing, in attitude there is a world of difference: Joseph laughs at himself.

Bellow's first novel prefigures the themes if not the amazing variety of his later work. Not that the later heroes all have to join the world by signing up with the United States Army; but time after time the inward and self-fastened man, the "apprentice in suffering" like Joseph, must learn if he can the Whitman lesson that agonies are one of our changes of garments. I think this is true even of his least inward, most Whitman-like character, Augie March, who describes himself as "democratic in temperament, available to everybody and assuming about others what I assumed about myself." *The Adventures of Augie March* (1953) seems to invert the pattern, since Augie's impulse is to explore the outer world and his chief adventure is to look for greatness, but the inward measure is still the means by which he ultimately preserves the self. He who looks will find, of course; and Augie can find greatness in the unlikeliest of spots, in a minor real-estate operator, a crippled apartment-house owner in one of the drabber parts of Chicago:

William Einhorn was the first superior person I knew. He had a brain and many enterprises, real directing power, philosophical capacity, and if I were methodical enough to take thought before an important and practical decision and also (N. B.) if I were really his disciple and not what I am, I'd ask myself, "What would Caesar suffer in this case? What would Machiavelli advise or Ulysses do? What would Einhorn think?" (60)

In the ironic contrasts we also have a magnification of Einhorn himself, even when his young lieutenant Augie must carry him on his shoulders into a brothel: "He used to talk about himself as the Old Man of the Sea riding Sinbad. But there was Aeneas too, who carried his old dad Anchises in the burning of Troy, and *that* old man had been picked by Venus to be her lover . . ." We catch our sight of greatness here because of the liveliness and reach of Bellow's (and Augie's) language, and we retain our safe distance of detachment because of Augie's (and Bellow's) remembering that he is *not* a disciple, but an admirer. When Augie loses his detachment, he illustrates the varieties of lostness in the modern city as well as Joseph ever did. There is always the trap of ideology, for one; as Augie puts it, "God knows, there are abandoned and hungry principles enough flowing free and looking for attachment." And if principles can swallow up a man, so can people—unless the man asks as Augie asks, "Why should I become like these people who do not even know what they are themselves?" Augie learns the lesson early and often. He is "available" to so many principles and people that he makes us think, not altogether admiringly, that Walt Whitman has turned into Moll Flanders. Two hundred pages later than he ought to, he understands the repeated lesson and comes to a resolve: "I will never force the hand of fate to create a better Augie March, nor change the time to any age of gold." The resolution, I grudgingly admit, needs perhaps most of the repetition of adventures, for the "moral," as I read it, goes beyond the acceptance of oneself: the resilience of the true self is a necessary means of survival.

Not that Bellow deals in survivors only. After *Augie March*, he turned from finders to losers and presented a story of utter lostness. In *Seize the Day* (1956) we have the bitter comedy of another kind of urban character. Tommy Wilhelm is completely a part of the modern, urban system and its artificialities; he lives off a dwindling fortune, has failed equally as movie actor and as salesman, frequents the lobbies of brokerage houses following the ups and downs of the commodities on which his last speculations ride. Estranged from father, wife, children, he has very little self left to hold in contempt, and yet even in his misery he is funny. With his face shoved hard against the blank wall of his existence, he prays: "Oh, God. . . . Let me out of my trouble. Let me out of my thoughts, and let me do something better with myself. For all the time I have wasted I am very sorry. Let me out of this clutch and into a different life. For I am all balled up. Have mercy."

Tommy Wilhelm dangles and finally drops, but his pathos is but one aspect of Bellow's picture of the modern city, even in this novel: the brilliant language which Bellow found in *Augie March* and the wonderful comic muse whom he first openly invited in that work, are both still present. What makes *Seize the Day* so compelling is an extraordinary villain, the devil who beguiles Tommy Wilhelm, takes his last seven hundred dollars to invest in rye and lard just when rye and lard are about to go down, and at the end lets Wilhelm keep him company at lunch and of course pick up the check. Dr. Tamkin is a psychologist, salesman, poet, and general purveyor of all the false or questionable or merely specious cures for what ails Wilhelm. Charlatan and chameleon, he can, when Wilhelm waxes maudlin, invent a wife to be sad about himself:

> "I was married to a lush," said Tamkin. ". . . But I loved her deeply. She was the most spiritual woman of my entire experience.
> "Where is she now?"
> "Drowned," said Tamkin. "At Provincetown, Cape Cod. It must have been a suicide. She was that way—suicidal. I tried everything in my power to cure her. Because," said Tamkin, "my real calling is to be a healer. I get wounded. I suffer from it. I would like to escape from the sicknesses of others, but I can't. I am only on loan to myself, so to speak. I belong to humanity."
> Liar! Wilhelm inwardly called him. Nasty lies. He invented a woman and killed her off and then called himself a healer, and made himself so earnest he looked like a bad-natured sheep. He's a puffed up little bogus and humbug with smelly feet. A doctor! A doctor would wash himself. He believes he's making a terrific impression, and he practically invites you to take off your hat when he talks about himself; and he thinks he has an imagination, but he hasn't, neither is he smart.
> Then what am I doing with him here, and why did I give him the seven hundred dollars? thought Wilhelm. (95-96)

The power of imagination from which humanity and humor stem has passed like Wilhelm's money to the enemy of life, so that nothing can any longer save the protagonist from spiritual bankruptcy. At the end he stumbles into a stranger's funeral and gives way to sobbing, the one passionate mourner, grieving for himself—sloppy, pathetic, and horrifying.

Wilhelm's yielding himself to the bands of death would be only grim if it were not for the crucial scene in the cafeteria when he passes judgment just as firmly as if he said with Conrad's Kurtz, "The horror! The horror!" The moment of self-recognition gives moral perspective to the whole story, but the fact of perception is no more important than the manner: Wilhelm sees himself as ludicrous, not horrible. Even a split second of comic vision testifies to a vitality that elsewhere in the story we see as only waning. The question, What am I doing here?, is funny, but it is not a joke. It is the very question which Bellow rephrased twice, within a year after *Seize the Day*, in an essay called "Distractions of a Fiction Writer." When the novelist, faltering momentarily, faces the blank wall of his solitude, he may ask himself:

> "The whole world is in motion, blazing. And what are you doing? You're doing nothing commensurate. Only sitting here alone, oddly faithful to things you learned as a boy. They taught you the Palmer method in school, so here you are still covering pages with words. You go on about men and women, families and marriages, divorces, crime and flight, murders, weddings, wars, rises and declines, simplicities and complexities, blessedness and agony, and it's all largely imaginary. Who asks you to write such things? What the devil are you doing here? What's all this about dead and non-existent people—Priams and Hecubas? Who is this Hecuba anyway and what are you to her?"

The doubter may wonder why he writes; the doubter's question is good enough for Hamlet or Job's tempters. And it is good enough for all civilized humanity, too, for the essay returns to it when the writer has taken off his comic mask:

> Why were we born? What are we doing here? Where are we going? In its eternal naïveté the imagination keeps coming back to these things.

The comic turn which Bellow puts upon his crucial situations is no doubt partly an American response. He knows that writers everywhere have been concerned in our time with men in impossible fixes; he is thoroughly aware of the grave, not to say morbid, sense of the "absurd," that watchword of postwar European letters. Yet an American writer has reason to be less surprised than his European fellows at finding the traditional props of human values to have fallen. "When so much is left out," Henry James long ago observed of American culture, what pre-eminently remains to the writer is "his national gift, that 'American humor' of which of late years we have heard so much." And certainly Bellow is not alone in seeing the absurdity of the absurd, the ridiculousness of the serious: two other writers who come to mind are Ralph Ellison and James Powers. The Negro, the Catholic, and the Jew have in present generation joined the Southerner in discovering the advantage of being in a conscious minority; if the politicians and authors of textbooks had not been saying so for so long, one might speculate that this is one of the most viable ways to be an American. Writers are always in minorities of one, to be sure; but the life of the mind needs company too, and history and caste have created in America rich bi-cultural traditions for those who can possess them. Despite everyone's proper worry about the tyranny of the majority, no nation is richer than America in the saving variety at its disposal. Scholars can refine their classification of Southern, Negro, Jewish, Irish humor, but each tradition has its dual status in the federal system of our literature.

The case of Bellow is very much to the point. He can present Dostoyevsky's blank wall with humor partly because local tradition makes humor come easily; after all, it is the wall of Melville's Bartleby, too, and the alienated dangler is as American as Henry Adams. But Bellow's native grounds, while they are local, are not singly or narrowly so: my guess is that for every chuckle he has had from Mark Twain, he has had half a dozen at least from the Yiddish humorists whom Mark Twain admired. From the Russia which produced Dostoyevsky came this other literary tradition which expresses the humor rather than the despair and exaltation of the Insulted and Injured. Yet it is in America that the two strains have been combined. That Amer-

ica's curious freedom from the European past can work thus is
not unusual: I take my notion from Louise Bogan's observation
that Miss Marianne Moore combines in a peculiarly American
way the Puritan and Baroque traditions, the Reformation and
the Counter-Reformation. Surely the organic blending of Dostoyevsky and Yiddish humor is not less remarkable, nor less a
subject for patriotic self-congratulation.

The interanimation of American and Jewish strains is a matter of gesture, language, and conception. Tommy Wilhelm's
ludicrous self-pity at being all balled up puts him just a step
away from the hero of *Henderson the Rain King* (1959), who
sums up his personal history: "In my own way I worked very
hard. Violent suffering is labor, and often I was drunk before
lunch." If not the character, then the author himself makes us
see the comical aspect of agonies. And when Augie March in-
dulges in his wintry speculations, he applies the dangling-man
psychology to culture, whereby blank walls initiate new beginnings. "It was now full winter, and barbarous how raw," he
says; and he goes on to reflect on the Chicago landscape:

> There haven't been civilizations without cities. But what about
> cities without civilizations? An inhuman thing, if possible, to
> have so many people together who beget nothing on one an-
> other. No, but it is not possible, and the dreary begets its own
> fire, and so this never happens.

The live imagination cannot finally yield to the belief in total
disaster, and the supple language indicates its own live sources:
for in setting the time—"It was now full winter, and barbarous
how raw"—Bellow has linked a classically pure literary diction
with a phrase that sounds like speech, an idiom which is Yiddish-
American in a way that Hemingway's idiom is sometimes Span-
ish-American, a phrase heard nowhere perhaps but made for the
ear. Bellow's voice and imagination are his own, but language is
a social thing.

For Bellow's humanism, which takes us from the texture of
his writing to underlying conceptions, there is ample precedent
in American writers and in the European writers on whom Americans are educated. The idea that genuine freedom includes the
acceptance of necessity and that life can only proceed by renew-

ing itself seems the more valid in that it is not original. Yet the
bi-cultural dimension, the looming presence of Jewish humor, is
essential in Bellow's particular formulation. The best evidence of
this is in Bellow's second novel, *The Victim* (1947). This most
neatly composed of Bellow's works shows least his comic profu-
sion or his humorous observation. The absurdity in the chain of
victimizations seems not at all laughable, and the plot itself is
the story of a dangler caught in the embrace of a drowner. The
Victim thinks his downward spiral began because an antisemitic
remark of his prompted the Jewish protagonist to revenge: when
Leventhal made a scene with Allbee's boss, didn't he act with
the malicious intent of getting Allbee fired? Suffering is con-
tagious, and Leventhal is almost persuaded that if there is a
victim, someone must be guilty—himself. Before chance and the
unpredictable assertion of vitality untie the knot, Leventhal
hears two versions of how suffering man may regard life. One is
from Allbee:

> "Now let me explain something to you. It's a Christian idea
> but I don't see why you shouldn't be able to understand it.
> 'Repent!' That's John the Baptist coming out of the desert.
> Change yourself, that's what he's saying, and be another man.
> . . . You have to get yourself so that you can't stand to keep on
> in the old way. . . . We're mulish; that's why we have to take
> such a beating. When we can't stand another lick without
> dying of it, then we change. And some people never do. They
> stand there until the last lick falls and die like animals. Others
> have the strength to change long before. But repent means
> *now*, this minute and forever, without wasting any more time."
> (227)

The other version he hears at a party which he forces himself to
attend when his spirits are sunken:

> "They tell a story about a little town in the old country. It was
> out of the way, in a valley, so the Jews were afraid the Messiah
> would come and miss them, and they built a high tower and
> hired one of the town beggars to sit in it all day long. A friend
> of his meets this beggar and he says, 'How do you like your job,
> Baruch?" So he says, 'It doesn't pay much, but I think it's
> steady work.' " (253-254)

In his own way, Bellow joins Emerson and Whitman in
admonishing us not to change, but to live, and like his predeces-

sors he does not intend us to live meanly. *Henderson the Rain King* gives one more proof of that. In the first place, Bellow's energetic, alienated, suffering, and remarkably unquiet hero enacts a fable against salvation by good works which puts Graham Greene's *Quiet American* in the shade. Exploring an Africa of the imagination in search of his own soul (does the idea come from Conrad—or from Thoreau?), the benevolent Henderson resolves to help the gentle cattle-people rid their water-supply of the taboo frogs which pollute it. Summoning to the cause of technical assistance all the inborn know-how he commands, he magnificently blasts the frogs out of existence and, incidentally, the dam and the water-supply as well. But Bellow's purpose goes beyond his demonstrating the superiority of American know-how in satirizing America. Henderson's main adventure is among the lion-people, among whom he learns both acceptance and aspiration. At home he had taken to pig-raising out of a gratuitous impulse to irritate a Jewish friend. Now with his porcine face and enormous body, he seems to prove that those who live among pigs will become like pigs. It is the lion-king who says so, but I think it takes little daring to suggest that behind the narrative is the *persona* of an old Yiddish story-teller. When Henderson returns to America at the end or, rather, alights from the airplane at Gander, the first landfall of the New World, he has a foundling child in his arms and a lion cub on a leash at his heels.

Some of the comment on *Henderson the Rain King* has complained that the reader is not shown how Henderson makes a life for himself in the United States after he has thus recovered his humanity, and perhaps Bellow himself, a gentle, choleric, humorous, and somewhat dangling man, wishes he knew. But that is another novel. Meanwhile the new beginning, looking westward this time with a sense of possibility less than infinite, is a good ending: it shows that the American imagination has rediscovered an old way to be free.

5·SAUL BELLOW: The Illusion of Environment

AFTER NEARLY two decades, the so-called "social novel" reappeared in the Nineteen-Fifties. At an unlikely time, a distinctive milieu fiction—urban and conscious of minorities, depression, and war—commanded critical attention: Ralph Ellison's *The Invisible Man*, Saul Bellow's *The Adventures of Augie March*, or Bernard Malamud's *The Assistant*. These novels express a generation which had been molded by the conditions of the Nineteen-Thirties that had made "social" fiction important. They also seek to come to terms with this tradition, ironically exploiting its most indigenous form for their reckoning. For these writers broke with their past through expansions and modifications of the "social novel" itself.

Socially conscious fiction of earlier generations had grown out of naturalism and of the older tradition of the political thesis novel. Indeed, books exploring or satirizing human experience as a social condition like *An American Tragedy, Man's Fate,* or even *1984,* have always suggested that at the heart of man's problem lies a dislocation of his social and political universe which he is hard put to set to rights. Political and social reality (or "environment") is a kind of metaphysical force; the hero, isolated and victimized, is usually defeated by this force. As a most obvious alternative, other novels have suggested that "reality" is by no means explained by man's physical surroundings and conditions, indeed, that environment is always at bottom symbolic. Although since Zola the naturalistic novel has used symbolic interpretations of facts to evoke man's struggle with his world, the purely symbolist novel has insisted on the

51

validity of symbolism as an end in itself. In Andre Gide's *The Immoralist* or in Virginia Woolf's *To the Lighthouse*, the hero refracts the world as a symbolic image. If naturalism proposes a novel in which man is unfree because he is determined by circumstances beyond his control, symbolism proposes a novel in which man is a mask, displaying, with pitiable circularity, reflections of his own condition.

Both these approaches appeal to polar but equally oppressive anxieties. The anxiety inherent in naturalism is prompted by man's fear of his own disintegration. The hero commands our sympathy not so much for his manner of rising against his fate as for the pathos of his dissolution. Moreover, even where his lack of freedom cannot be traced to any visible compulsion, it is always caused by the fact that man can be "explained." Like St. Augustine's God, the novelist foresees and, by foreseeing, foreordains. Symbolism to some extent relieves this anxiety. The hero himself is the seer. He is a romantic visionary whose symbolic knowledge is the only reality. Environment, deformed by this visionary, becomes a more truthful world, symbolic of the inner man. Even in a novel like Faulkner's *Light in August* (which uses environment also in a "naturalistic" sense), Joe Christmas' death is made meaningful not as a dissolution of the self, but, on the contrary, as a climactic recognition symbolically expressed through his world. But in relieving this anxiety about the preservation of the self, symbolism, in its most consistent forms, also created a new one. If the protagonist's world is an image of private experience recreated as art, its independent, palpable existence in life is fading. The world becomes a pretext for more pertinent inner visions, a state which, as a French critic has put it, is "always dissolving." Reduced to a mask functioning in no dependable world, man ultimately retreats from his mirrored double.

It is one of Saul Bellow's typical achievements that he used and exploited, lampooned and dissected both these anxieties. In his early novels—*The Dangling Man* (1944) and *The Victim* (1947)—Bellow's heroes were centers of consciousness as well as victims of a relentless environment. But when the first excerpts from *The Adventures of Augie March* (1953) began to appear in 1949, it soon became evident that the social novel had under-

gone an important transformation. Although the reader still
encountered familiar themes dealing with urban middle class
life and urban squalor, he found them in unexpected contexts
and configurations. Society was no longer only opposed to the
hero, whether knowing or blind. Rather, it ironically reflected
the hero's consciousness—functioning as his symbolic mirror
—while at the same time it also maintained its time-honored
place as the source and creator of his condition. In consequence,
hero and world became related to one another in a new, rather
light-hearted dialectic. A dialogue ensues between protagonist
and world, in which both prove to be equally evanescent as
well as equally stable, equally prone to interchanging their active
and passive states.

Bellow's novels of the later Nineteen-Fifties recreated the
perennial victim of the social novel as such an extension and
mockery of its environment. In *Seize the Day* (1956), Tommy
Wilhelm exacts our sympathy not because he was oppressed by
an irresistible social force, but because he had been pathetically
and farcically outwitted by a figure so indigenous to his environment that he emerged as an image of himself. In *Henderson the
Rain King* (1959), environment is created at will to suit the
hero's peculiar triumph and denouement. The protagonist-
victim is wholly absorbed by the picaro who outwits himself at
the same time as he dominates a surprisingly evanescent world.
Both in novels of awareness bearing the imprints of Gide and
Camus, and in picaresque novels of education, Bellow moved
towards a reinterpretation of reality. Gradually, the minute
examination of consciousness against the background of the
external world is supplanted by a human charade played against
the scenery of a spurious environment.

In his early novels, Bellow's exploration of "reality" evidently coincided with that of the outer world. In *The Victim*,
for example, his evocations of the city landscape constitute, as
critics have instantly perceived, the most striking features of
the novel:

> There was a still redness in the sky, like the flame at the back
> of a vast baker's oven; the day hung on, gaping fierily over the
> black Jersey shore.

In this sentence, the New York "landscape" is portrayed in a manner familiar from naturalistic novels: the colors symbolically evoke the *chiaroscuro* of a threatening city. The description obtains a further meaning, however, through the hero's conscious reflections:

> The Hudson had a low luster, and the sea was probably no more numbing in its cold, Leventhal imagined, than the subway under his feet was in its heat . . .

The "numbness," combining the upper and lower worlds, also expresses the contradictory impulses within the universe in which Asa Leventhal must find his way. His feelings are emphasized in the conclusion of the passage: ". . . the trains rushing by under the gratings and along the slanting brown rock walls seemed to set off charges of metal dust." [p. 22][1] This image is a combination of actual, remembered, and projected experience as it defines and manipulates the protagonist. Having apprehended his world, his conscious mind absorbs it into its own inner discourse.

Reality, described in this manner, evolves in *The Victim* both as the conventional protagonist of the naturalistic social novel and as an internal image, a content of consciousness, through which the hero and his plight are defined. In other words, causality is matched by self-definition. "Environment" serves as an index for the exploration of characters' attitudes towards themselves and their world and at the same time as an index for the definition of an external life. To explore this question of what is "real," Bellow begins by shifting his hero's environment, permitting a fantasy atmosphere to prevail as a result of the temporary absence of the protagonist's wife. This "unreality"—made apparent through changes in Leventhal's immediate environment like covered chairs, restaurant eating, and similar dislocations of his routinized life—issues in a dual plot: the "real" illness and death of a child, the son of Leventhal's estranged brother; the spurious subjection of the hero by his adversary and shadow, Kirby Allbee, and the equally spurious "death" which constitutes their denouement.

The careful introduction of change into an inherently stable environment is reminiscent of Kafka and Camus, of Swift and of a contemporary like William Golding. In Bellow's work it is general and objective at the same time as it is private and subjective. On the general level, in a manner far more fully developed in *Augie March*, the change is almost mythical in its proportions. In *The Victim* the familiar city is shrouded in an oppressive summer heat, interspersed by sharp tropical showers, which gives it an atmosphere of "unreality." In Leventhal's particular life it first manifests itself in a telephone call by his sister-in-law, calling him to her sick child. Leventhal's abrupt departure from his job disturbs the routine and evokes unpleasant comments from his employers. Similarly, after his return to his already empty apartment at home, the second motif—the appearance of Allbee —also makes itself felt through unexpected, partially spurious events in his environment. Allbee, his very name ironically suggesting allegorical connections, mysteriously appears in the familiar surroundings of the park, catapulting himself into a questionable reality.

The "change" which Bellow thus imposes on his character's world invariably turns from external fact to illusion or the hero's symbolic attempt to refashion the universe in accordance with his preconceptions. Leventhal's experience is abnormally acute (as, for example, when he writes his wife about the taxi ride to the hospital with the sick child [pp. 6–67]), but it is deformed by his projections. Yet he is not wholly caught in an egocentric predicament; his private understanding is always accompanied by the impact upon him of a causally effective world. Sharing this capacity with the antagonist, Allbee, he perceives the duality of this turn of mind in Allbee's projections. Although Leventhal had actually caused Allbee to lose his job during the depression, the motive the latter attributes to him (revenge for anti-Semitic remarks long since forgotten) is wholly spurious. Nor was Leventhal responsible for the chain of events leading to Allbee's desertion by his wife, her death, and his alcoholism. Yet the fact that the event causing this chain had actually occurred, combining with a deeply symbolic sense of personal guilt, leads Leventhal to accept Allbee's version, thereby becoming his victim. It also makes possible their symbolic contiguity despite their hostility in the world of "facts."

In the conception of characters and plot, the dual function

of environment—also portrayed through evocations of typical apartment houses, cafeterias, offices, and parks—appears as a coincidence of a social and a mythical-psychological theme. Society, Bellow suggests, emerges as both external "fact" and inner awareness. This double action of "others" on himself informs all of Leventhal's encounters: his Jewish friends and his non-Jewish colleagues, the superintendent's wife as well as people brawling in the street. It is most poignantly revealed by his attitude towards his physical brother who emerges as a counterpart in "fact" of the symbolic brother, Allbee; moreover, his recognition of the discrepancy between his own image of his brother's world and its simpler actuality reinforces the simultaneous presence of perception and "fact."

In this sense, the social theme, supported by Bellow's use of "environment," constitutes both a metaphysical and an epistemological motif. It acts with a metaphysical force, because it is a causal agent creating the protagonist's condition. But through his penetrating imagination, the world also becomes a symbolic creation. In this latter epistemological sense, the dual vision Bellow evokes cannot be attributed to a discrepancy in points of view. Remaining within Leventhal's peculiar perspective, experience is developed simultaneously as illusion and "fact," as content and object of consciousness. The resolution of the novel occurs through little Mickey's funeral and the denouement in Leventhal's apartment. The former is a "real" event; the latter a symbolic resolution. After having compulsively identified himself with Leventhal—from living in his home, seeking to share his friends, connections and letters from his wife, to bringing a woman to his marriage bed and seeking to gas himself in his kitchen—Allbee dissolves a symbolic relationship through a symbolic near-death.

In a sense, the problem of the *Doppelganger*, which underlies *The Victim*, could have been enacted through any theme. The pervasive use of the Jewish theme, therefore, compels a social interpretation. The dichotomies of American subcultures, present in the novel, are too numerous to be ignored: the marriage of Max Leventhal to an Italian wife with a disapproving mother; the derogating remarks about Jewishness at Leventhal's place of work; the conscious opposition of the non-Jewish benefactor, Williston, and his Jewish friends, all culminating in the hysterical relationship itself with Allbee. At a climactic moment, when Allbee seess himself as the perennial victim of Jews, the "oppressor" Leventhal reminds him of six million deaths. But in Bellow's dual method the two characters are simultaneously oppressors and victims, active and passive selves, "environment" and centers of awareness. This theme is linked, in the protagonist, with a particular Jewish condition: the acceptance of the anti-Semitic image of himself by the Jew makes the internal situation possible as a social theme. Ironically, therefore, the reconstruction of the "real" world is made possible through the individual's passive triumph over his inherent social condition.

Nearly a decade later—after the monumental task of *Augie March* had been confronted and overcome—Bellow re-examined an alienated Jewish consciousness once more in the pitiable image of Tommy Wilhelm in *Seize the Day*. In this short novel, the issue of Jewishness itself is no longer central but primarily acts as background for an individual's search for maturity and awareness. Although Tommy Wilhelm is still a Jew in a Jewish world, his problems are centered on a simultaneous need to preserve and to escape from this world. Asa Leventhal's compulsive Jewish guilt has been displaced by the motif of flight and of the frustration of flight. Far from being a "self-made" man, as in a sense Leventhal had been, Wilhelm is a perennial failure, the child of a wealthy home, overshadowed by a great, now aging father. But at the same time, the denial of social pressure through a spurious reconstruction of the world is pushed even further.

In many ways, the world of *Seize the Day* is a reproduction of the milieu of *The Victim* on a different social and economic level. The east-side walkup is replaced by the faded pseudo-continental splendor of west-side apartment hotels. The numerous playing children Leventhal constantly encounters are displaced by old men, living off the fruit of their past successes, preparing their beds to die. Into this world Wilhelm returns in his early middle age to plead from his father the paternity he had never been given in his youth. Physical descriptions underline the banality of both the world and the attempt:

Dr. Adler liked to sit in a corner that looked across Broadway down to the Hudson and New Jersey. On the other side of the street was a supermodern cafeteria with gold and purple mosaic columns. On the second floor a private-eye school, a dental laboratory, and a Hebrew school shared the space. The old man was sprinkling sugar on his strawberries. Small hoops of brilliance were cast by the water glasses on the white table cloths, despite a faint murkiness in the sunshine. It was early summer, and the long window was turned inward; a moth was on the pane; the putty was broken and the white enamel on the frames was streaming with wrinkles. [p. 31][2]

As in most of Bellow's novels, relationships in *Seize the Day* are made manifest in contrasting and complementing pairs through which the protagonist perceives himself and is, in turn, perceived by an external intelligence. Leventhal's relationships with the physical brother and the symbolic double are replaced by Wilhelm's relationship with his actual and his adopted father. But this dual situation once more demonstrates Bellow's approach. Having left his wife and children, incapable of exacting a divorce in his continued dependence on his wife, incapable therefore of remarrying, Wilhelm has turned to his father for succor. He is adamantly rejected; the way back to childhood is closed. But the substitute father, the spurious "psychologist" Dr. Tamkin, emerges to take the real father's place as other swindlers had done before in Wilhelm's life. Emerging from a world of changed circumstance—the deliberate disaffiliation in which Wilhelm had indulged—this phantom father relieves him not of his troubles but of his money. Left by this phantom of his environment—typifying the universe of manipulators which Wilhelm admired and in which he had fared so badly—the abandoned child is left to weep at the funeral of a stranger.

Seize the Day is a milieu as *The Victim* had been a milieu piece. On a less elemental level than the earlier novel, it deals with the perennial victim of social circumstances. But the great difference between the two novels can be attributed to the fact that the dialogue between hero and world in *Seize the Day* is treated pathetically and almost lightly. If Wilhelm is an exaggerated expression of his environment (in his self-pity, his failure, and his self-immolation), the environment created by Wilhelm's imagination is equally limited and pitifully distorted. Forces of causal efficacy are underplayed; instead, Bellow matches environment and person with one another in an interchange which, except for the recognition in the end, is pathetic and comic. This method is evident in many scenes: the details of the hotel, the flashbacks summarizing Wilhelm's life, his telephone conversation with his wife, the pathetic conversations with his father, mounting in intensity to the scenes of Wilhelm's abandonment. In these latter scenes, this dialogue is even more sharply enacted. The ticker-room where Wilhelm's fate is played like dice is a tour de force in matching a brilliant milieu satire with Wilhelm's dramatic and symbolic awareness. These scenes are all focused in the hero's consciousness while the reader observes the satanic destruction of the hero himself. The flight to Dr. Tamkin's hotel room concludes this bizarre comedy: the hero finds himself alone with the faded carpet, the chambermaid armed with a vacuum cleaner, and the professor's abandoned bathrobe. Self and scene confront one another at last in mutual failure. In the conclusion, of course, Wilhelm finds a larger resolution which is also both internal and external. Weeping at the funeral, he achieves a measure of insight not because he has been defeated by an omnipresent social force, but because he recognizes the death of his world—the decaying hotels, the banal glory of Dr. Adler, the defeated suburban ambitions—as *the* image of death. Having been wholly abandoned, he rises from self-pity to universal mourning and therefore a degree of self-transcendence. External and internal perception unite, as Wilhelm both recognizes and is recognized as a symbolic brother.

This notion of the function of society and environment can be ascribed to Bellow's more original approach following his experimentations with *Augie March*. Indeed, the more concrete and unique in his conception of character and scene Bellow became, the more generalized and symbolic became his conception of "reality" and world. This is evident even in the poorer short stories, as, for example, in the *New Yorker* story, "A Father-To-Be." Here a symbolic quest for paternity is accompanied by painfully evoked details of the urban milieu, encompassing a range of expediencies from typical smells in a delicatessen to typical faces in the subway. But the milieu, though evoked with clarity, is rendered impotent as a causal agent and becomes, instead, a symbolic image. The world which had stimulated the protagonist's desire for a son is dissolved in the obviously symbolic gesture of hair washing, administered by the solicitous fiancée, that dissolves present and past into a surrender of his claim to life. Action by the world has been displaced by the world as a functioning symbol.

Bellow's large novel, *The Adventures of Augie March*, constitutes the mainstay of his reputation not merely because of its bulk or the multitude of its themes, or even because of the unusual amount of favorable critical attention it has received, but primarily because of the freshness and innovations it has brought to the form of the novel. For this book has rendered a new, if not always convincing, reinterpretation of the social novel without entirely exploding the form of the social novel itself. Like *The Dangling Man* and *The Victim*, this "new" novel of the Fifties explores the life and consciousness of a disaffiliated urban hero. As in *The Victim*, the city is the principal landscape on which—with the significant exception of the Mexico sequence —the panorama of the novel unfolds. But, unlike any of his previous novels, Bellow develops a recognition of mid-century America into its Whitmanesque praise, epitomized by the well-known opening sentence: "I am an American, Chicago born." Far from seeming out of place when referring to a second generation Jew, this statement has been seen as altogether fitting. Augie March typifies mid-century America which has produced him. His pilgrimage through the Twenties and the depression, issuing in the confusion of the Second World War, is matched by his shifting life, his search for stability, his fluctuations between active and passive states, which express the trauma of our mobile, urbanized culture. Thus, Bellow succeeded in assimilating Asa Leventhal's problems into the American landscape as a whole. He did so by dissolving Leventhal as a discerning intelligence, by recreating him as a picaro for whom the world is always dissolving because it is of his creation and yet Leventhal remains throughout a typical product of that world. Rendering the familiar social theme as an interplay of object and of content of consciousness, Bellow created a fresh vision of environment as a symbolic motif in the novel.

The sense in which *The Adventures of Augie March* is both a social and a symbolic novel is too obvious to require detailed elucidation. Both critics and reviewers have shown that the "realism" of the novel is matched by a wealth of obvious symbolic significances which requires none of the symbol hunting Bellow has castigated in his article in the *New York Times*. But beneath this realism and this wealth of symbolic and allegorical references lies a further subtle conception of character and scene.

Themes and motifs in *The Adventures of Augie March* elaborate the notion of a simultaneously involved and detached self within a similarly involved and detached environment. Augie is outside society not only because he is a Jew but also because he is illegitimate. Footloose and isolated, he is a foundling like Tom Jones, learning "prudence," an outsider, yet attracted by the world, like the traditional *Eulenspiegel*. Throughout much of the novel Augie seeks to affiliate himself, to be "adopted," at the same time that he rejects affiliation. In this endeavor, which focuses on a search for relationships (as well as their rejection), he is more vulnerable than his brother Simon, who seeks affiliation with things (position and money), but also less prone to the latter's suffering. As a result, however, the carefree picaro always turns into the familiar victim. Up to the end, whatever Augie attempts to accomplish "goes wrong" after having first been "right," because in his endeavor to manipulate relationships he is actually manipulated himself. This contradiction expresses Augie's nature as a simultaneously active and passive hero, which is the source of his strength as well as of his comic failures. Only on the concluding page, in a fleeting reduction of the hero's life to rural simplicity, is this contradiction momentarily resolved.

Bellow's choice of the picaresque form is particularly fortunate, because through this form a "dialogue" of subject and object—of the hero as consciousness and as the victim of his world—can be most successfully portrayed. As a wanderer through space and time, the hero can absorb his world, converting scenes into images. Thus, the world which had produced Augie March acts upon him as a panorama in which significant scenes of a personal as well as a universal life are enacted. But at the same time the picaresque also establishes the wanderer and his world as distinct entities whose deliberate interactions provide the tragi-comic substance of the episodes. It is in this latter sense that Bellow used the picaresque form to portray the remorseless actions of the environment upon the hero and so preserved the outlines of the social novel.

The Adventures of Augie March exhibits this duality through its evocations of the different milieus with which the stages of the hero's progress are identified. In the childhood home, Augie minutely apprehends the figures which populate his life, figures which express his environment and, indirectly, himself, such as his idiot brother, the domineering lodger "Grandma" Lausch, or his more "affiliated" relatives. But Augie not only experiences these figures; he is also significantly determined by them, struggling at all cost to maintain his identity. The universe is both internal and symbolic, and separate and formative. This action is epitomized by the motif of the institution. The pathetic scene in which Augie takes "Grandma" Lausch to a Home for the Aged—after she had been instrumental in committing their brother George—stands out in clearly symbolic dimensions. But the institution is also a decisive social force which counteracts normal social affiliation and the epitome of displacement to which the decline of family might lead. The careful repetition of the "institution" motif—the early and later visits to George, the institutionalization of the mother—develops this theme in both its dimensions in carefully drawn scenes. A similar "world" is represented by the clan of the Einhorns, the urban politicians and manipulators falling and rising through their quixotic management of the depression. Later, different milieus act upon as well as express the hero. At various stages, he encounters different worlds, all minutely evoked, such as the suburbia of the Renlings, the Jewish business magnates, the Magnuses, into whose clan Simon marries, the fantastic psychological world of Thea Fenchel. These sequences symbolize Augie's attitudes, but they also contain encounters in which Augie ends up as a passive victim. They not only express particular states of mind, or of knowledge, but also assail the hero's integrity so that at one point he is led to exclaim that there could not be more for him to *endure*.

The recurrent dilemma of Augie March's search for his per-

sonal integrity is registered in this way through symbolic encounters in which his identity is constantly tested. From the
domineering image of his childhood, "Grandma" Lausch, to his
substitute father, Einhorn, Augie creates, and uses, symbolic
figures which also act upon him. In the fashion of the picaresque
Bildungsroman, a prototype of the romantic novel, Augie must
subject himself to these various "teacher" figures. His mentor
Einhorn, the crippled, self-styled Socrates, teaches Augie the
meaning of experience within the confines of their shared environment. Although Augie never learns Einhorn's business, or
displaces the natural son, he absorbs the idea of "manipulating"
—of the dialogue between the active and passive which is the
substance of Augie's quest. This fact is underlined by Einhorn's
enforced passivity which at the same time compels him to seek
sexual relations. Both in his function and in his nature, therefore, Einhorn impresses upon Augie the dual nature of his quest.

Augie's symbolization of and subjection by the figures of his
life is clarified particularly in his relations with women. His
search for the ideal image of love—as for the ideal parents—is
complemented by the comic love adventure, the inverse Casanova episodes in which he is always the loser. It is part of Augie's
nature that he cannot permit himself to be loved for himself
(The Greek working-class girl who does so is therefore only
casually accepted); he feels compelled to associate love with an
image. Moreover, each of the significant women in his life seeks
to convert Augie into her image, thus leading him to escape
when his identity is perversely endangered. But as each woman
suggests a particular ideal relevant to each particular station in
Augie's life, she also becomes a "reality" making him into her
"object." This attitude, which also extends into his marriage to
Stella, is clearly expressed by the Mexico episodes. Having allowed Thea Fenchel to rescue him from a chain of unhappy
circumstances, he falls in love with the image of "being taken"
and "taken care of." Learning to manipulate himself—extending
what Einhorn had taught him—he momentarily asserts his will
by making clear to his beloved that he is not the symbolic image
she had created but himself an originator of action, capable of
impressing his own image upon the world. This recognition,
which ultimately renders him useless to Thea, is naturally gained

through his manipulation of the eagle—his having learned to "hunt through others"—to which Thea has introduced him. Indeed, this episode is pivotal because it dissolves Augie's most typical relationship (to the feminine ideal, recreating him in her image) into a basic relation between human consciousness and a symbolic object which he learned to direct. Whatever symbolic associations the eagle Caligula may involve (about America or about cowardice or appearances), this mutual interaction, epitomized by the disastrous last hunt, between man and animal-object, leads Augie to a transitory resolution of his dual relationship with his world.

Distorted and made alive by the comic mode in which much of the novel is written, *Augie March* expresses the dialogue between self and world and their mutual interaction. Environment impresses itself upon Augie who is molded by his consciousness of it. In figurative language, raised in a symbolic plane, Bellow thus demonstrates the action of a universal world upon human consciousness of which it is also an emblem:

> Now there's a dark Westminster of a time when a multitude of objects cannot be clear; they're too dense and there's an island rain, North Sea lightlessness, the vein of the Thames. That darkness in which resolutions have to be made—it isn't merely local; it's the same darkness that exists in the fiercest clearnesses of torrid Messina. And what about the coldness of the rain? That doesn't deheat the foolishness in its residence of the human face, nor take away deception nor change defects, but this rain is the emblem of the shared condition of all. [p. 201][3]

In this universal way, the perennial condition of the external world signifies not only experience but also the human consciousness and physiognomy itself. An atmosphere, involving things and worlds, conditions actions while being also projected by the human mind. In this way, ultimately, all the figures in *Augie March* are also generalized figures: fathers, brothers, women, whose rootedness in particular social worlds reinforces their simultaneous function as a causal force.

This conception of the relationship between hero and world is put to a test in Bellow's most recent novel, *Henderson the Rain King*. A method similar to that of *Augie March* and attitudes toward theme and environment reminiscent of Bellow's earlier novels compel obvious comparisons. In *Henderson the Rain King*, we encounter a quixotic distortion of *Don Quixote*, an attempt to draw a hero whose search to transcend an environment symbolic of himself dissolves into a hoax.

Evidently, Bellow's latest novel was intended not merely as a more fantastic repetition of *Augie March*. To the extent that the book symbolizes and satirizes contemporary America, it is a continuation of *Augie March*; it deals with the landscape of the Fifties as the earlier novel dealt with the landscape of the depression and the war. Consequently, the terms have had to be changed. The child of the Twenties growing to the young man of the early war years is replaced by a man of middle age; the illegitimate Jewish child of a squalid Chicago lower middle class is transformed into a millionaire's son. The familiar social environment is changed into an affluent Connecticut suburbia. But these changes introduce a more deep-seated formal change: satire based on the social novel becomes wholly absorbed into a satire of manners.

In *Henderson the Rain King*, the "real" world of contemporary America and the "symbolic" world of Africa are juxtaposed. In the "real" episodes, we are led to expect clearly relevant satire, for through it the hero's search for commitment and meaning is to be defined. But the satire is disappointingly broad and generalized. Augie March's adventures in Einhorn's office, as a book thief and a union organizer, make sense because they are rooted in an environment which is evoked with great clarity. Henderson's quixotic journey to Europe, his domination by his first wife and ridiculous pursuit by the second, his attempts to find "meaning" through drinking, violin lessons, and pig breeding make less sense, because the environment is drawn with the glossy skill of a *New Yorker* formula. For this reason, Bellow's brilliant satiric inventions are left without a base. Lacking control of his world, Bellow is impatient to hurry on to his main task—the symbolic satire in the African setting. But Henderson's ridiculous safari into an unknown world—each encounter turning into a passive image of his quest—is an impressive inversion of Hemingway's journeys towards self-realization.

As in the early novels, Bellow produces his symbolic, and "illusory," vision through a convenient shift from one level of reality to another which coincides with the social and psychological theme of disaffiliation. Henderson escapes from Connecticut into the darkest Africa in order to find himself at last, to cease being outwitted and betrayed, by losing himself in a "reality" that might lead to self-transcendence. In this desire, which caricatures the aims of Augie March, he becomes the passive, symbolic hero of the romantic tradition. But it is one of Bellow's most comic paradoxes that he imposes such an intention upon a hero who is continually in motion. The result has been a farcical distortion of the conventional hero. The quixotic picaro and the symbolic disciple of the allegorical *Bildungsroman* are contracted into one.

As the world of affluent and frustrating contemporary America is coupled with the wholly symbolic world of "Africa," Bellow's dual intention, which had been distinctive of his work throughout his career, is clarified as well as reduced to absurdity. The inversions are manifold: Henderson, in his soiled jockey shorts with his green "rain king's" attire sitting at the feet of a sophisticated African king, is the American naif faced by the idealized version of his own longing for knowledge and sophistication. His very journey multiplies this inversion. As he sets out with his prayerful native guide—a satiric combination of Sancho Panza and Dante's Virgil—he enters into a world of symbolic way stations in which each significant episode leads him from being a spectator-percipient to being a mauled participant. In the first stage of his Progress—the "cattle" tribe of the Areiri —he passes a wrestling test with flying colors only to disgrace himself by blowing up the tribe's water supply in a vain effort to help them. In the main stage—the "lion" tribe of the Wariri —he seeks to erase this failure by making himself into a wholly ridiculous victim. The wrestling match is reproduced in a feat of great strength which Henderson performs to assist the tribe's rain-making; finding himself mauled in a powerful "ceremony," he inadvertently becomes the doomed rain-king. But far from obtaining an awareness of "reality" by acting responsibly for others of his own choice, Henderson ironically discovers that the whole show had been "rigged"; having been destined to be "rain-king" from the start, he merely followed a predetermined course. In this way, all the scenes deal with a victimization of the hero, his determination by forces beyond his control. But these forces also belong to a symbolic world of his own creation, for both "cattle" and "lion" people express definite stages of his condition and search.

Many of the motifs of *Augie March* are thus reproduced in *Henderson the Rain King* in a more clearly symbolic manner. For although the *terms* are different, their *relations* remain constant as an implicit dialogue between self and "other." This is true both of Henderson's basic relationships and of the symbolic events with which he deals. Augie's Casanova episodes are expressed farcically in his courtship and marriage to Lily in the "real" world. Augie's filial attachment to Einhorn ironically matches Henderson's friendship with the symbolic king Dahfu of the Wariri. This latter relationship, parenthetically mocking the spellbinding "transference" of modern psychoanalysis, chiefly satirizes the disciple's dependence on the symbolic teacher by which the *Bildungsroman* is defined. But the hero's progress toward commitment and "reality" amid symbolic encounters most fully suggests the parallel between the two books. The whole rain-making episode—and the attendant conversations with the king—explores the relationship between actuality ("scientific" fact) and symbolic meaning (the "ceremony"). It is also produced by the animal symbolism which pervades the novel. Caricaturing the Caligula episodes of *Augie March*, the various animal motifs suggest the notion that man's "reality" is expressed by his conversion into relevant animal types. It is enacted on all three stages: the hero's defiant pig-breeding in Connecticut, his encounter with the moistly affectionate cow-women of the Areiri, his experiences with the human Amazons and the lioness among the Wariri. The comically horrifying scene in which the untamed lioness sniffs at Henderson's crotch becomes also the epitome of his passive discipleship under the king's tutelage. In this way, he constantly finds "reality" in worlds dissolving into drastically symbolic events in which the hero—like the slain mentor himself—becomes the excruciated victim.

Henderson's symbolic wrestling with an illusory environment is perhaps best demonstrated by his ceremonious feat with the wooden goddess—a totem assuming the nature of a person

—and the tribe's action towards symbolic events as if they were causally efficacious. If he outwits all these figures and escapes to find his "reality" in the idea of a new commitment, this does not detract from the dual meaning of the episodes themselves. For the bracing walk out of the plane—armed with a symbolic lion-cub and a stray "son," with plans for medical school in his heart —merely opens the way to another chapter of Henderson's quixotic learning.

Whatever the measure of Bellow's success or failure in this latest tour de force, it most fully demonstrates the direction of his approach. In increasingly abstract terms—the comic and farcical modes reinforcing the abstraction—environment as an internal force and as an apparently external, conditioning force imposes itself on his novels producing thematic and emblematic motifs. But this dual action upon a passive hero, as an actor and as a focus of consciousness, is expressed not in "realistic" terms but in terms of an increasingly artificial illusion. The outlines of the social novel—its typical relations between self and world— are maintained, but the concrete nature of the environment is dissolved into an image. Bellow thus finally distorts a concept of fiction which had almost always been rooted in a particular social scene; yet he also distorts the purely symbolic use of the world by portraying its *reductio ad absurdum*. At a time when symbolism in literature has reached its apex, and perhaps also the beginning of its decline, Bellow has confronted the dissolu-tion of the self with a parallel dissolution of the world in a pertinently ironic dialogue.

Notes

1. *The Victim*. New York: Compass Books, 1956.
2. *Seize the Day*. New York: Popular Library, 1958.
3. *The Adventures of Augie March*. New York: Viking, 1953.

6·REALITY AND THE HERO:

Lolita and *Henderson the Rain King*

BOTH VLADIMIR NABOKOV's *Lolita* and Saul Bellow's *Henderson the Rain King* are important novels, important in theme and important in structure, important for what they reveal about contemporary reality and for what they demonstrate about the novel itself and its much-heralded crisis. Written by two of our finest novelists, problematical, tragi-comic, appearing at crucial moments in the careers of each writer, they put demands on our attention which we cannot ignore. Yet despite the respectful press each has received, the numerous reviews, and the best sellerdom of one of these novels, they remain baffling, original, and sportive books, leaving each critic with his own theory, each reader with his private experience. I would like to show how a reading of these books in conjunction might throw light on what they are "really about," and how, both as success and failure, each novel illuminates the problems of the contemporary novelist.

I

The aesthetic bankruptcy of naturalism is a twice-told tale; even the kind of realism we associate with the great nineteenth-century masterpieces of the novel, Russian, French, and English, no longer seems viable as a mode for our best novelists. After Joyce and Kafka, the novel, bitten by poetry and teased into symbolism and allegory, has withdrawn from a social milieu it can no longer describe or is no longer interested in. The newest experimental writing moves in one of two directions, toward the pure evocation of objects in a hero-less world, as in Robbe-Grillet and Nathalie Sarraute, or toward a withdrawal from objects into an isolate self, a hero without a world, feeding on himself as in Samuel Beckett. Beckett's heroes, indeed, have even lost the ability to communicate the role of self, the hero of *The Unnamable* confessing that

> the fact would seem to be, if in my situation one may speak of facts, not only that I shall have to speak of things of which I cannot speak, but also which is even more interesting, but also that I, which is if possible even more interesting, that I shall have to, I forget, no matter. At the same time I am obliged to speak. I shall never be silent. Never.[1]

The self collapses into incoherence here; the work of fiction exists only as a self-defeating triumph of method. But even when parody threatens to topple the whole enterprise, the formula of return to the world is suggested: "In the frenzy of utterance the concern with truth. Hence the interest of a possible deliverance by means of encounter. But not so fast. First dirty, then make clean" (15). The encounter which the self desires here is the experience of something real, the real being defined as that which is not the self; the method suggested is the familiar purgative rite of withdrawal and return, the return giving us back a world which the novelist may still communicate and describe, although in Beckett this description does not exist.

Humbert Humbert and Henderson are not pushed so far out by their creators and they are brought back closer to the reality they seem to evade. Yet, as first-person narrators, as characters whose individual reality dominates the books in which they appear, they come closer to the solipsistic protagonists of Beckett than they do to the characterless consciousness of the hero in Nathalie Sarraute's *Portrait of a Man Unknown*. At the same time, they must be distinguished from the picaresque heroes of Kingsley Amis and John Wain whose existences serve largely the purpose of setting forth a sharply realized milieu which is under attack or criticism. Yet, even here, as Raymond Williams has pointed out concerning these "realistic" novels, "for all their genuine relevance and records of actual feelings, their final version of reality is parodic and farcical."[2] *Lolita* and *Henderson the Rain King* begin with a version of reality that is parodic and farcical and end with a vision of parody overcome and farce turned to real anguish and real discovery. While we sense in Beckett's Malones and Molloys real anguish degenerating to unintentional farce and parody, in *Lolita* and *Henderson*, these traditional comic modes serve to exalt and define the potential reality the protagonist desires.

This, then, will be the grounds of our comparison: *Lolita* and *Henderson the Rain King* are novels about the quest for reality on the part of protagonists who completely fill the novels in which they appear but who are not satisfied with such a role. The nymphet Lolita stands in the same relation to Humbert Humbert that his symbolic African journey stands to Henderson; Africa and Lolita are realities which remain *outside* in the otherness which must be real because (1) the protagonist wants such reality, and (2) in the wanting, he discovers a world to live in. I would also suggest, without making it part of the subsequent analysis, that these novels are about the novelist himself wanting an actual world to describe.

Such an analysis as intended here must begin with the protagonists themselves, and, before we begin a reading of the content and structure of each book, it would do well to examine how Nabokov and Bellow set their protagonists in motion, and how their quests for reality, while comic in texture and incident, yet do not undergo satiric reduction.

Both Humbert Humbert and Henderson are characters *in extremis*, and both must face the charge of mental aberration; both admit this charge but in different ways. The great fun Nabokov has with psychoanalysis and psychiatry transcends mere personal pique: through this means Humbert resists the judgment of the fuddled normal. Who is there to judge him? Admitting that "I am writing under observation" and that "you have to be an artist or a madman" to perceive the reality of the nymphet, he presents himself with such complete knowledge of his condition that it is not possible for the reader to "interpret" his reality. This is emphasized in his re-enactment of the incident that presumably made him a pervert, the unconsummated seaside seduction of the earlier nymphet, Annabel, which he attempts to relive with Lolita, but, although he did look for a beach, he confesses "that even had we discovered a piece of sympathetic seaside somewhere, it would have come too late, since my real liberation had occurred much earlier."[3] The beauties of Lolita herself had so transcended any psychological fixation that the original cause, a cause apparently demanded by the Freudian-mongering reader, is lost in the present experience. We can find no *reasons* with which to classify Humbert's behavior, however insane and aberrant it may seem both to him and to us. He simply is, and as Eros, as desire, we accept him for what he is, for the sake of the projected reality of Nabokov's comedy.

Henderson also poses the problem of insanity. Unlike Humbert Humbert, he does have a background and history which might account for his behavior, and he worries about this: "I, too, am considered crazy, and with good reason—moody, rough, tyrannical and probably mad."[4] Henderson finds a familiar justification for his excesses: "Of course, in an age of madness, to be expected to be untouched by madness is a form of madness. But the pursuit of sanity can be a form of madness too" (25). He can also plead hereditary excuses:

> Now, I come from a stock that has been damned and derided for more than a hundred years, and when I sat smashing bottles by the eternal sea it wasn't only my great ancestors, the ambassadors and statesmen, that people were recalling but the loony ones as well. One got himself mixed up in the Boxer Rebellion, believing he was an Oriental; one was taken for $300,000 by an Italian actress; one was carried away in a balloon while publicizing the suffrage movement. There have been plenty of impulsive or imbecile parties in our family. (86)

Although Henderson characteristically worries about his mental condition more than does Humbert Humbert, and, although he spends most of the novel in a fever as much psychic as physical, no possibility for dismissing him arises from this situation; like Humbert Humbert he remains wholly defended through the expedient of admitting everything. No judgment can be made because there is no one to judge him, least of all, the hidden voice of the author.

Yet, we do have in these novels two protagonists who commit actions and express thoughts generally adjudged insane. How, then, do Bellow and Nabokov get us to accept the reality each desires? The reality of these novels, the social texture, the analogous "real" world each moves through does not exist, or, at least, does not come into being in the way this world normally comes to life in the novel. These novels are less about an actualized and possessed reality than they are about that area of experience between the potential and the actual, between dream and waking where all of us are partial madmen and comic Fausts. Between the potential and the actual falls the wish, and the most familiar form of the wish is the dream. Humbert Humbert and Eugene Henderson are scapegoats for everyman's grandiose desires and private itches; they live our dream, but they live this dream in a world they want and expect to be real, a theme which since Don Quixote, at least, has been more a subject for comedy than tragedy. As Erich Auerbach has pointed out in *Mimesis*, the reality of Cervantes' novel is not problematical: we know always where we are—the real is that which the Don has to make unreal; Cervantes never loses his ironic perspective. But, in the novels under discussion, the reality which may exist beyond the wish-engendered fantasies of Humbert and Henderson is not at all clear. Their presumed insanity or abnormality does *not* lead us to a countering rational world; like their heroes, we must discover a reality through their wishes, and we must participate in their serious dreams. Only the excessively confident reader could do otherwise, and these novels are not written for confident readers. As a result, below the comic surface of each book, a desperate tone emerges, and a serious purgation takes place. This process can best be described by a separate examination of the course of each book.

II

Lolita is certainly the more problematical of the two books. Among other things, it has been described as a satire on America, a parody of the romantic novel, a contribution to the *roman noir*, one of the last love stories, and by John Ray, Ph.D., as a "poignant personal study in which there lurks a general lesson" (7). Mr. Lionel Trilling, in perhaps the best essay yet written on the book,[5] does justice to its seriousness by reading it as a contribution to the tradition of passion-love seen through a comic and parodic perspective which does not reduce its actual intensity. But Mr. Trilling, like other critics and reviewers, expresses puzzlement and uneasiness over the shifts in tone which seem to occur in the novel, passages in which Nabokov seems to be either pulling the reader's leg or trying to exalt his novel into something it has not been, for example:

> I loved you. I was a pentapod monster, but I loved you. I was despicable and brutal and turpid, and everything, *mais je t'aimais, je t'aimais!* And there were times when I knew how you felt, and it was hell to know it, my little one. Lolita girl, brave Dolly Schiller. (286)

Apparently, it is not easy to laugh at this passage, not because the basic incongruity is forgotten—middle-aged Humbert and the gum-chewing nymphet—but because this intensity, coupled with our knowledge that soon Humbert dies of a heart attack and Lolita fails to survive childbirth, leaves a comic response open to the charge of callousness. The intensity of the feeling here seems to overcome both comedy and satire, reminding us of Keats's remark that "the excellence of every art is its intensity, capable of making all disagreeables evaporate from their being in close relationship with Beauty and Truth."[6] That this witty, acerb, even slapdash and high-jinked book might have anything to do with Keatsian Beauty and Truth seems unlikely, yet the growing intensity of the novel is undeniable, and either we must regard this as misplaced or as part of an intention beyond the satiric and the funny. In a perceptive remark about the book, F. W. Dupee recognizes this duality: "*Lolita* is partly a masterpiece of grotesque comedy, partly an unsubdued wilderness where the wolf howls—a real wolf howling for a real Red Riding Hood."[7]

The development of Humbert's sentimental education is a progress from fantasy to reality, in which the content of the wish remains the same, while the object of the wish slips away, leaving the desirer with the recognition of his self-induced folly. Whatever the content of his specific sexual perversion (and there is no psychological interest attached to it by Nabokov), Humbert's world, in which Lolita remains the sole content, arises *in spite of* tawdry surroundings and absurd misadventures, so much does the hero hunger to exist in a real world. Upon his arrival in Ramsdale, he learns that the house in which he was to stay has burned down, "possibly owing to the synchronous conflagration that had been raging all night in my veins" (37). A joke, of course, but this internal conflagration is about to find its proper outlet. Humbert meets Lolita for the first time and experiences the epiphany which never leaves him.

Although, with the self-admitted naiveté of the pervert and like the tragi-comic hero of romance, Humbert is shocked to discover that his mistress is not chaste, the progress of Humbert's nympholepsy is self-induced, not self-deceived. The actual method by which Dolores Haze becomes Lolita is not a helpless reflex of perversion: "She was Lo, plain Lo, in the morning, standing four feet ten in one sock. She was Lola in slacks. She was Dolly at school. She was Dolores on the dotted line. But in my arms she was always Lolita" (11). In Humbert's words, he *incarnates* her as all nympholepts apparently incarnate their nymphets. The process is part of a cunning epistemology: "It is a question of focal adjustment, of a certain distance that the inner eye thrills to surmount, and a certain contrast that the mind perceives with a gasp of perverse delight" (19). Yet, paradoxically, Humbert would like to claim much for Lolita's external reality. Contrasting his memory of Annabel with the memory of Lolita, he writes:

> I see Annabel in such general terms as: "honey-colored skin," "thin arms," "brown bobbed hair," "long lashes," "big bright mouth;" and the other when you instantly evoke, with shut eyes, on the dark innerside of your eyelids, the objective, absolutely optical replica of a beloved face, a little ghost in natural colors (and this is how I see Lolita). (13)

This adjustment is not perfect; and, in fact, the novel is the history of its increasing difficulty as Lolita ages into adolescence and Humbert's lust turns to love. The self-created vision nearly fails early in his quest when, seeing her at the summer camp where he has gone to pick her up after the death of her mother, he has to perform some mental and visual gymnastics to recover his vision. But the possibility of "a sound education and a healthy and happy girlhood" soon disappears. " 'In a wink,' as the Germans say, the angelic line of conduct was erased, and I overtook my prey (time moves ahead of our fancies!) and she was my Lolita again—in fact, more my Lolita than ever" (113).

That the real Lolita, or Lolita as someone else might conceive her, constantly threatens to break into Humbert's self-induced reality makes his journey an unhappy one, and I think it worth noting how little satisfaction Humbert gets from his delirious enchantment. He seems most triumphant after his initial sexual encounter with Lolita on the couch which, however perverse, has preserved her supposed purity.

The safety Humbert feels here is not mere safety from the police, but the safety one feels in preserving a wish intact; the experience has not diminished the wish because the *construction* remains standing: Lolita is still a controllable reality. Yet Humbert Humbert cannot remain in this blissful vestibule of being, for, though he claims shortly before he is seduced by Lolita in *The Enchanted Hunters* that "I had gradually eliminated all the superfluous blur, and by stacking level upon level of translucent vision, had evolved a final picture" (127)—the comic anti-climax of his sexual plot introduces a new element into his carefully contrived world: the element of resistant chance, and as choice turns to chance, dream turns to nightmare.

At this point in the novel, the comedy of the basic situation darkens, although some of the funniest parts of the book still lie ahead: the parody of motels and highways, the monstrous Miss Pratt of the Beardsley School For Girls, and the climactic killing of Quilty. Humbert's increasingly agonized possession of Lolita begins to transcend its literary and parodic origins and becomes something more important. As usual, Humbert himself is fully aware of what is happening and gives us a later clue. When Lolita has left him, he finds that his perversion remains intact and that his greatest *pleasure* comes from unconsummated imaginings and visions, "the great rosegray never to be had," yet upon getting Lolita's letter asking for money, he doesn't hesitate to put away his dreams and set out again for the reality Lolita has become.

Two elements complicate the satiric and the comic perspective from which the book starts out, and both these elements are presented seriously by Nabokov because they belong to the underlying seriousness of the theme and not to the comic surface. One is the passage of time and the other is the related moral problem which surprisingly and superbly makes its appearance just when the joke *qua* joke threatens to become tiresome. Of course, Humbert, in his guise as perverted comic hero, is ready to meet the fact of Lolita's aging with his wildest and grandest flight.

But such bravado cannot sustain him. Like an Elizabethan sonneteer, he fears and fights against time's ravages of his lady-love: "I perceived at once how much she had changed since I first met her two years ago." And, as he enumerates how the approach of adolescence coarsens her and sickens him, he still must recognize that "everything about her was of the same impenetrable order." No matter how he has prepared himself for the decline of his nymphet and her resulting abandonment, he continues to love her even when "my alembics told me she should stop being a nymphet" (241).

The reader must now make a commitment to the characterization of Lolita that he neither expected nor thought possible. Humbert Humbert's concern and compassion undeniably involve the reader in a way he has not been involved before. Although she is not a "real" character in the usual novelistic sense, if we have been caught up in the cunning comic rhythm of the whole, we cannot help lending our sympathy to the unwinding of the plot. Until now, we have known two Lolitas 1) the gum-chewing, unindividualized comic caricature, and 2) the conscious romantic distortion of her constructed by Humbert Humbert. Now we meet a third Lolita, who is no more real than the first two, but in whom we recognize the anguish of the narrator. Nabokov does not bring Lolita to characterized "life"; rather, he brings his hero to a deep awareness of her human situation. The comedy resulting from the incongruity of Lolita One and Lolita Two gives way to the pathos of Lolita Three, without, however, affecting the basic disparity of the first two. The important point to recognize is that Humbert Humbert remains in control of the reality of the novel; the reader still does not know any Lolita apart from him—he does not know any Lolita at all; he responds wholly to the development in the narrator, and this development, without destroying the comic surface, suddenly presents us with the traditional moral problem of the novel: what is the individual and social reality and how should we respond to it? Nabokov has achieved a considerable feat here:

the subsequent disquieting passages referred to before now take their place in the whole—we have been prepared for them, not only by the increasing intensity of the novel but by the thinning out of the shocking joke which has borne us along this far. Suddenly, the real wolf emerges and the real Red Riding Hood demands our sympathy.

When I speak of "moral problems," I am not referring to the legal aspects of Humbert's perversion, although there are numerous satiric passages dealing with the harmless pervert he thinks himself to be. The satire is effective here, although Humbert is, as he says, writing under observation, and although the audience, as jury, is constantly present, the social judgment does not much concern Humbert or his creator. In the key passage of the book, in which parody and satire come to suspension, Humbert commits himself to the reality and thus to the moral problem which Lolita has become for him, a reality not the product of his fantasy but of actual remembered experience.

Who wants to prove that life is a joke? Here Humbert's world is invulnerable to laughter. Lolita has becomes Dolores Haze, and whoever *she* is, she is not Humbert Humbert, and therefore has actually happened to him and is real. In the masterly scene in which Humbert Humbert visits the now married and pregnant Lolita all the devices are there: parody, wordplay, comic situation, and the marvelous excess characteristic of the whole, but the scene comes through with a new-found power; we attend to the scene with *both* comic detachment and the sympathy essential to pathos. And, because of our relation to the protagonist, our own sense of reality is called into question. What has been real in their relationship? As he later muses on their final meeting: "I was to her not a boy friend, not a glamour man, not a pal, not even a person at all, but just two eyes and a foot of engorged brawn" (285). Lolita's reality is not in question here, but the reality of Humbert himself, and because of his complete control of the reality in the novel, *our* own sense of reality undergoes scrutiny and anxiety. For Lolita's reality has come into being through the perversion and fantasy of Humbert's genuine love. This progression is almost muffled by the verbal gymnastics and parodic situation of the whole, but the emergent theme cannot be ignored. It even makes an explicit appearance, though in typically disguised spoof. The play written by Humbert's rival, Clare Quilty, and in which Lolita makes her schoolgirl appearance, is described contemptuously by Humbert as a plot in which "barefooted Dolores was to lead check-trousered Mona to the paternal farm behind the Perilous Forest to prove to the braggard she was not a poet's fancy, but a rustic, down-to-brown-earth lass, and a last-minute kiss was to enforce the play's profound message, namely, that mirage and reality merge in love" (203).

We are well aware that parody has its serious uses, that in satire from Petronius onward it can serve the severest purposes. But the relation of serious parody to comedy is more problematical. *Lolita* is a genuinely funny book at the same time that it is a serious comedy; part of its parody serves obvious enough satiric functions, whether Nabokov is lampooning psychoanalysis or American tourism, but its parody has an ultimately more important purpose because *Lolita*, paradoxically enough, is more serious in its comedy than in its satire. The satire is largely a matter of filling out the comic texture, while the basic parody of the love-novel relates to the serious comedy at the core of Nabokov's conception. As Northrop Frye points out, in the typical serious parody of apocalyptic symbolism, "the demonic erotic relation becomes a fierce destructive passion that works against loyalty and frustrates the one who possesses it."[8] This is what happens in *Lolita*, but through a comic reversal, because we cannot at first take Lolita herself seriously as the harlot, witch, or siren of such forms. We have reached that decline in the form where the convention itself turns to irony. Yet, this very parody, through Humbert's developing relation to the reality of love, gives us back the value we thought we had lost. *Lolita* is a serious comedy because the value which the comedy threatened to reduce is maintained, is finally, and in spite of everything, upheld.

Mr. Trilling touches closely on the true theme of *Lolita* when he writes that the novel is not about sex at all, but about love. However, only the possibility of love is suggested, the beginning world of relationship. The novel is about the lover's quest for reality, a reality which he first creates out of himself, but which then is discovered to have an actual existence beyond him. We attend to this discovery because the form of the book is the form of discovery, and the reality, which appears in difficult splintered guises in modern fiction, here finds committed representation. The world of *Lolita*, then, is far more real than the Winchellian peepings of O'Hara or Cozzens; it is also more real, because more whole, than the highly intellectualized constructs of Robbe-Grillet and Sarraute. In this book, Beckett's underground man finds a possible way of relating to the world. That world itself does not emerge. We must look at another underground man of contemporary fiction to find a world that is closer to being born.

III

As *Lolita* uses the familiar progress of passion-love, seen through an unfamiliar parodic perspective, to discover a reality, so *Henderson the Rain King* uses the familiar rituals of quest and initiation, also from a comic perspective, to lay bare its reality. There is not the problem of mood in *Henderson* that there is in *Lolita*; for all the comedy and farce in the novel there is never any question that we must attend seriously to Henderson himself; we do not stand outside to judge him any more than we fail to give our confidence to Falstaff and other large comic heroes who fill the world in which they appear. Neither is the theme elusive in *Henderson*, although its ultimate working out requires an understanding of its structure. Through Henderson's own, eventually repetitive, assertions, the theme comes clear: he is searching for a reality, a reality which, like Humbert's, can be shown conclusively to be something other than himself. Such a reality has nothing to do with adjustment or the small and orderly world in which mediocrity lives. Henderson makes huge claims on reality and reality answers him hugely back.

Henderson's relation to reality can be best approached through the argument which he has with his wife early in the book and which recurs to him throughout the novel. Having been told by her that she is glad that he seems more able to accept reality, he blusters back: "I know more about reality than you'll ever know. I am on damned good terms with reality, and don't you forget it" (36). This boast sets up the familiar enactment of *hubris*, but Henderson is not easily cured. He does make large demands on the world, as the brilliant first fifty pages show, and his passionate sense of the real gives him the right to his boast. Later, when he is sitting with King Dahfu, he asserts that, while Lily neither likes nor loves reality,

> Me, I love the old bitch just as she is and I like to think I am always prepared for even the very worst she has to show me. I am a true adorer of life, and if I can't reach as high as the face of it, I plant my kiss somewhere lower down. (150)

Henderson as *alazon* goes through several phases, largely as a result of his relationship with the philosopher—king Dahfu. To his inborn and passionate sense of the real, Henderson adds spirit and imagination admitting that what we often call reality is nothing but pedantry and that he needn't have quarreled with his wife: "The world of facts is real all right, and not to be altered. The physical is all there, and it belongs to science. But then there is the noumenal department, and there we create and create and create" (167).

The theme of a supra-reality finds its fullest expression in Dahfu's own paean to the imagination and how it becomes actualized in experience, one of Henderson's profoundest and most necessary lessons:

> Birds flew, harpies flew, angels flew, Daedalus and son flew. And see here, it is no longer dreaming and story, for literally there is flying. You flew here, into Africa. All human accomplishment has this same origin, identically. Imagination is a force of nature. Is this not enough to make a person full of ecstasy? Imagination, imagination, imagination! It converts to actual. It sustains, it alters, it redeems! (271)

Henderson's reality is complete when he encounters the lion Gmilo with Dahfu on the climactic lion-hunt. Even though Henderson has been trained by Dahfu to meet this contingency, even though he has assumed lionlike characteristics, it becomes apparent to him that, until now, he has not experienced true reality:

> The snarling of this animal was indeed the voice of death. And I thought how I had boasted to my dear Lily how I loved real-

ity. . . . But oh, unreality, unreality, unreality! That has been
my scheme for a troubled but eternal life. But now I was
blasted away from this practice by the throat of the lion. His
voice was like a blow at the back of my head. (307)

The lion completes Henderson's quest; we understand that
Henderson has come to know a truth because of the connection
between suffering and knowledge insisted on throughout the
novel. But what is this knowledge? What reality has Henderson
discovered?

This discovery can only be described by an examination of
the organization of the book itself. Paradoxically enough, though
this is a novel about reality and the need for its rebirth, the world
it presents is most akin to a dream. One almost expects Henderson to wake up at the end of the book and come down to breakfast with his wife and children. But it would be precisely this
breakfast that would defeat the structure of the novel. We do
not see Henderson "return"; the emphasis is on the content of
the dream itself, not on the world which it abstracts, though
Bellow tries to give the book the dimensions of a coherent world.
As Henderson himself admits, "Still, an explanation is necessary,
for living proof of something of the highest importance has been
presented to me so I am obliged to communicate it. And not
the least of the difficulties is that it happened as in a dream"
(32). A further complication to a realistic texture is the fact that
Henderson's dream is both wish and prophecy. Bellow suggests
the dual nature of his plot in the lightly-held identification of
Henderson with Joseph. The wizened figure who leads Henderson and Romilayu into the trap set by the Wariri is identified
with the figure who led Joseph into the trap set by his brothers.
"Then the brothers saw Joseph and said, 'Behold the dreamer
cometh.' Everybody should read the Bible" (171).

Henderson's pursuit of reality arises from no scientific or
philosophical impulse; as the development of the book shows,
he is seeking the real because he is seeking salvation and he believes that the real will set him free. Through the ritual of
initiation (and every incident in the book is either a prelude to
initiation or the act itself) Henderson is successively reborn and
brought closer to the truth. The quest is a successful one since
he returns from his symbolic Africa in presumed possession of

the selfhood he went to seek. But what success means here and how he has achieved it can be best understood by what his symbolic adventures and misadventures achieve. An actual process and method, akin to a religious experience, must be undergone.

In the beginning, a kind of stripping, a psychic and physical reduction, is necessary. Daniel's remark to Nebuchadnezzar, referred to throughout the novel, gives us the clue: "They shall drive thee from among men, and thy dwelling shall be with beasts of the field." This reduction (or exaltation) to the animal defines Henderson's characteristic experience. He begins as a breeder of pigs and returns with a lion cub; in between he suffers degradation in faintly parodic imitation of Lear, who is also forced to the animal and undergoes an actual and symbolic stripping. Yet Henderson's degradation began long before his African adventure. When he was in the Army during the Second World War, he was stripped by Army medics because he caught the crabs and was left naked in the middle of a crossroads, swearing and roaring revenge. Again, after he has been made Rain-King, he is stripped by the village women and forced to accompany them on the Rain-King's rounds. " 'No, No!' I said, but by that time the underpants were already down around my knees. The worst had happened" (197). In this state, poor bare forked Henderson is able to consummate the ritual that brings on the required rain. Again and again, Bellow calls attention to Henderson's tragi-comic seminudity. With dragging drawers and sweaty T-shirt, he goes about his salvation, even losing his bridgework, an occurrence which causes him more pain and agony than anything that happens to him. In the end, like Lear, he is re-clothed. On his return from Africa he stops in Italy. "On Friday I got to Rome. I bought a corduroy outfit, burgundy colored, and an alpine hat with Bersagliere feathers, plus a shirt and underpants" (332). The martial feathers provide an outward sign of Henderson's triumph, a hero's return. But first he had to become naked.

The stripping is the first step in the initiation, but the tests that follow actually do drive Henderson from men and force him to dwell with the beasts of the field. From bear to pig to cow to frog to lion, Henderson comes into successful or disastrous relationship with other forms of life. The tribe of his first encounter, the Arnewi, are a mild, pacific people who raise and worship cattle. Henderson, in his guise as a parody of Moses, attempts to rid the Arnewi of frogs who have infested their water-supply by blowing them from the water. But he suffers his first crushing defeat in Africa by blowing up the reservoir and losing what water the tribe already had. This is a directly personal failure: "That cistern of problem water with its algae and its frogs had entered me, occupying a square place in my interiors, and sloshing around as I moved" (61).

Other tests on Henderson are met more successfully, tests which usually involve his impressive physical strength. He defeats Itelo, king of the Arnewi, in required wrestling; he carries away the body of the dead Rain-King of the vigorous Wariri; he lifts the stone idol Mummah, thereby becoming Rain-King himself. All these are of interest in examining the novel, but we only have room to discuss the key test: his relation to Dahfu's lion and to Dahfu himself, the king of the Wariri.

Dahfu, a problematic tutor in Henderson's fantasy, stands at Henderson's side, advising, cajoling, and warning him. This figure of the "prophet" is a familiar one in Bellow's novels, sometimes appearing as a threatening charlatan as well as a beneficent advisor to the hero; one thinks of Allbee and Shifcart in their relation to Leventhal in The Victim, of Tamkin in relation to Tommy Wilhelm in Seize The Day, of Einhorn and Mintouchian in relation to Augie March in his Adventures. Dahfu, as a climax to these symbolic prophets, shares their characteristics: he possesses their eccentric knowledge, he is partly comic, and he is excessive in thought and deed. Above all, like his forebears, there is an essential mystery about him. Dahfu is the most benign of these personages, and, in fact, undergoes a sacrificial death that Henderson may assume his characteristics. Indeed, the lion cub Henderson brings back with him from Africa is the symbolic representation of the dead king. But what does the king himself symbolize?

As with any resonant poetic symbol, no linear meaning can be attributed to the lion and lion-king of this novel. Indeed, this is a symbol wholly integrated with Henderson's quest, thus forming an interesting contrast with the eagle-ritual that Augie March undergoes in a partly real, partly symbolic Mexico. In

the earlier novel, the symbol of the eagle, for all the brilliance
of the writing, appears as a strange excrescence, but in Bellow's
new book, the ordeal-by-lion does not put symbolic strain on a
realistic content since the latter has only a tenuous existence
in the novel anyway; moreover, the symbol gathers force and
meaning throughout the whole novel. Henderson's relation to it
begins in a characteristically daft comic manner when he tries
to shoot the cat left by his disgruntled tenants; later, he sees
Dahfu's insistence on his leonine education as a revenge plotted
by the cat family. It soon becomes apparent that the lion kept
under the throne by Dahfu is precisely what Henderson is not,
something external, powerful, real. For all his boasting about
reality, Henderson must undergo a savage encounter with something entirely foreign, and from this discover reality in himself.
He asks, "How shall a man be broken for whom reality has no
fixed dwelling?" (211). By an encounter with the Other in the
form of a lion.

The lion which Henderson encounters through Dahfu is
actually a substitute for a second lion the king must capture in
order to solidify his position, the uncaptured lion being the representative of Dahfu's father, the former king. His "practice
runs" with the lion-surrogate annoy his councillors and, in fact,
suggest that Dahfu himself, for all his magnificence, does not
maintain a perfect relation to the real; indeed, Henderson must
complete Dahfu's role after the latter's death. The lion will help
him, as Dahfu explains:

> You ask, what can she do for you? Many things. First she is
> unavoidable. Test it, and you will find she is unavoidable. And
> this is what you need, as you are an avoider. Oh, you have ac-
> complished momentous avoidances. But she will change that.
> She will make consciousness to shine. She will burnish you.
> She will force the present moment upon you. Second, lions are
> experiencers. But not in haste. They experience with deliberate
> luxury. The poet says, "The tigers of wrath are wiser than the
> horses of instruction." Let us embrace lions also in the same
> view. (260)

This test proves the hardest for Henderson. On all fours in
the posture of the comic and the beast, he fulfills the prophecy
of Daniel, yet even this comes out in a comic guise. "Certain

words crept into my roars, like 'God,' 'Help,' 'Lord have mercy,'
only they came out 'Hoolp!' 'Mooorcy!' It's funny what words
sprang forth. 'Au secours,' which was 'Secooooor' and also 'De
profoooondis,' plus snatches from the 'Messiah'" (274). Yet
Henderson preserves as much dignity as he can and comes upon
his truth and his reality. In a letter to his wife just before he
marches out with Dahfu to the climactic lion-hunt, he suggests
one part of the answer: "I had a voice that said I want! *I* want?
I? It should have told me *she* wants, *he* wants, *they* want. And
moreover, it's love that makes reality reality. The opposite makes
the opposite" (286).

In his encounter wth Gmilo, Dahfu's symbolic lion-father,
Henderson meets his ultimate reality in the passage already
cited. He moves from a life-long unreality to an immediate truth,
for the lion symbolizes death. This confrontation, added to his
insight into love quoted above (not unlike *Lolita's* buried theme
of mirage and reality merging into love) completes his education.
The rest of the novel: the escape from the mausoleum with the
lion cub, the flight homeward with the American Persian waif
Henderson picks up in a symbolic reversal of the earlier rejection
of the Negro foundling brought home by his daughter Ricey,
the joyous arrival in Newfoundland—all these complete Henderson's dreaming triumph, but add nothing essential to the
theme or to the reality already discovered. However, we do not
begrudge a Henderson triumphant; he has spent most of the
novel in defeat.

I have used the word "symbol" frequently in discussing
Henderson and there is no doubt that the novel cannot be understood without reference to the symbolic references and relationships established in the novel. Yet, the symbolism of *Henderson* is best described as light-hearted,[9] though this characterization does not indicate a casual reading. Henderson himself
calls up, either directly or in a parodic mode, Oedipus, Moses,
Joseph, Jacob, Falstaff, Lear, etc., and his entire quest has a
familiar mythic pattern. But the novel never sinks under its airy
symbolic weight; as in *Lolita* the prevailing comic texture provides an atmosphere in which the serious symbol appears trans-
parent, not as a revelation of inner meaning, but as a useful reference which, more often than not, increases the comedy.

Yet this comedy nowhere debases the symbol because Bellow's comedy is not ultimately critical of its protagonist. As in the presentation of Humbert Humbert, there is nothing in the novel with which Henderson is compared unfavorably. It is true that some of the comedy is less serious than the theme demands. Indeed, in its inheritance from *Gulliver's Travels* and *The Connecticut Yankee*, it sometimes sprawls into conventional aimlessness: a blustering American companioned by a wise but strangely articulate African, who, of course, knows more of the world than he does. But Henderson is a nobler comic hero than this. In the larger forms of comedy, as Northrop Frye says, "the comic hero will get his triumph whether what he has done is sensible or silly, honest or rascally."[10] Henderson is doubly rewarded, both as a comic hero and as a hero putting his comedy behind him. He contains both *alazon* and *eiron* in himself; while he blusters, he suffers, and though he proves his own ironist, he never loses the huge sense of himself so necessary to his quest. When he discovers his reality, we attend seriously because we have the same doubleness in ourselves and rejoice to see it fulfill a pattern.

IV

I have argued that the two novels under discussion, using the devices of comedy, parody, and satire, still do not reduce their heroes to victims of emotionless observation; rather, we follow their return to reality with seriousness and sympathy. But how far this "return" takes us, how far a fused individual and social reality is restored to the novel form through these strategies remains to be seen. The complete circuit is not made for a variety of reasons. *Lolita* sometimes tends to fight off the serious bite reality has made in its parodic structure; the rather slick humor found in some of Nabokov's other stories and novels makes an appearance here in occasional aimless puns, undirected satire, and a certain thinness of event. At times the novelist seems weary of the whole idea, but with the abduction of Lolita the pace again quickens and the theme emerges strongly. Yet the reported death of Lolita in childbirth and Humbert's heart failure before trial seem expedients for closing out a troublesome situation. The artistic impulse has completed its cycle, but, as often in first-rate fiction, reverberations echo beyond the closed form. Of particular concern would be Humbert Humbert's subsequent mentality (we would not expect him to change his habits), the mind that wrote his manuscript, the impulse that made him an artist. Nabokov himself sees *Lolita* as rounding its effect: "For me a work of fiction exists only insofar as it affords me what I shall bluntly call aesthetic bliss, that is, a sense of being somehow, somewhere, connected with other states of being where art (curiosity, tenderness, kindness, ecstasy) is the norm" (316-317). This attitude toward art can be related to Humbert's peroration: "I am thinking of aurochs and angels, the secret of durable pigments, prophetic sonnets, the refuge of art. And this is the only immortality you and I may share, my Lolita" (311). Nevertheless, we are left in this novel with a compassionate murderer and pervert who has discovered the nature of reality. If we consider what the novel form still might be capable of, given such an astonishing possibility, the abrupt end must seem a disappointment. And if we accept Kenneth Burke's definition of form as the satisfaction of aroused desire, *Lolita* does not complete its structure. Like Humbert Humbert, we are left hungering for the reality he has finally begun to experience.

Henderson the Rain King appears similarly short-circuited. Bellow's unwillingness to show Henderson back in the society from which he fled makes his discovery and triumph less forceful. *Henderson* has the kind of comic structure which leads us to expect some kind of reintegration of the hero with his society. It is right that Huck Finn lights out for the territory, but it is not right that Henderson's drama, however brilliantly it may be rendered in terms of symbol and dream, remain wholly within the fantasy-world. The first four chapters of the novel are among the most striking in contemporary fiction for the manner in which the realistic life of a huge and suffering comic hero is presented. The flight to a symbolic Africa is inevitable, but so, according to the rhythmic expectation, is Henderson's return. Of course, the narrative problems of such a return are enormous, and I have no prescriptions to suggest. Neither am I suggesting that *Henderson* should complete the "moral closure" which Edwin Honig sees as characteristic of traditional allegory.[11] Yet, Bellow is not writing satire, and a Gulliver-like withdrawal to the stables is not indicated, for Henderson seems about to begin where Gulliver leaves off. The ending in which Henderson runs around the grounded airplane in Newfoundland with his foundling by his side is unsatisfactory because the symbol consummates only Henderson's wish and not the reality he is about to re-enter: "I guess I felt it was my turn now to move, and so went running—leaping, leaping, pounding, and tingling over the pure white lining of the gray Arctic silence" (341). Earlier in the novel, Henderson had experimented in living at home in an igloo and had dreamed of going to the Arctic like his boyhood hero Wilfred Grenfell. "But I don't think I would have found what I was looking for there. In that case, I would have overwhelmed the world from the North with my trampling" (282). He is now ready for the Arctic silences, the same whiteness that disturbs Augie March at the end of his *Adventures* and which seems to represent pure potentiality in Bellow's world. But if Henderson is free to add his colors to the world we do not get a chance to see him do it.

A further problem in the representation of reality has to do with the texture of each novel. Elizabeth Hardwick has written of *Henderson*, "The scenery is too unreal for picaresque comedy; the events have too little resonance for symbolic fantasy."[12] I think this criticism is too harsh because the area between picaresque comedy and symbolic fantasy is precisely the area Bellow is interested in depicting, and this is manifestly the area of the wish. But there is an undeniable thinness of texture in *Henderson* and in *Lolita* as well. This is surprising in view of the very rich texture we normally associate with these writers; indeed, Nabokov's short stories are often little more than exercises in texture, and *Augie March* is perhaps the richest of all American novels. There are exceptions, set pieces like the marvelous description of Lolita's tennis game or Henderson's experience with the sunlight on the wall of his hut before his battle with the frogs, but, for books so deeply concerned with reality, there is an insufficient concern with sensation in each novel: a world dense with sensory possibility and actuality is not built up as fully as the subject seems to demand. However, sensation as personal pain, shock, or withdrawal is constantly present in both books and that may be all that is needed.

When we turn back to the novels of Beckett, Sarraute, and other experimenters with the modern forms of the novel, we find parody, just as we do in Bellow and Nabokov. But parody in these writers is directed toward the destruction of the novel form as we understand it and involves a satirical and nihilistic view of reality. It is possible, as Erich Heller avers in discussing Mann's *Doctor Faustus,* that "the artist is condemned to the sphere of higher parody, the only thing that is still left when the 'real thing' has become impossible."[13] But this "higher parody" need not take the nihilistic road of Beckett nor join in the desperate metaphysical jokes of Kafka. Mann's *Felix Krull* can be taken as a prototype of the kind of modern comic parody that is restorative as well as destructive, restorative of the form and the experience which the form encloses. *Lolita* and *Henderson the Rain King* are essentially serious parodies of comic parody itself because the initial value which the parody is meant to question is restored and with this restoration the unique reality of the experience sought reveals itself: we come into love in *Lolita* and into selfhood in *Henderson.* We are familiar with such a doubleness in an earlier writer like Stendhal: Fabrizio del Dongo, in particular, has this in common with Humbert Humbert and Henderson: the external reality in which he finds himself is less real than his sense of himself, is not large or various enough for his completest expression. As a result, many of his adventures and misadventures appear comic, but Fabrizio himself is always regarded with affection and sympathy: he discovers a world after all. Nabokov and Bellow do not possess, indeed, cannot afford, Stendhal's superb mixture of the tragic and the satirical, the comic and the pathetic. But the final effect of their novels is not unlike the mood of Stendhal's work, in which one not only comes into possession of the realist cake, but is also able to discover its inner romantic richness.

Of course, as I have said, neither of these novels comes back all the way into reality. Humbert Humbert and Lolita die conveniently and Henderson is left in his symbolic Newfoundland. These novels do not restore a full-bodied reality, but they encourage us to continue our search for one.

Notes

1. Samuel Beckett, *The Unnamable* (New York, 1958), p. 4.
2. "Realism and The Contemporary Novel," *Partisan Review*, XXVI, 3 (Spring 1959), 208.
3. Vladimir Nabokov, *Lolita* (New York), p. 169.
4. Saul Bellow, *Henderson the Rain King* (New York, 1959), p. 4.
5. "The Last Lover," *Encounter*, XI, 4 (October 1959), 9-19.
6. *The Selected Letters of John Keats*, ed. Lionel Trilling (New York, 1951), pp. 91-92.
7. "A Preface to *Lolita*," *The Anchor Review*, No. 2 (1957), 13.
8. *Anatomy of Criticism* (Princeton, 1957), p. 149.
9. Bellow's much-noted essay attacking excessive symbolic reading— "Deep Readers of the World, Beware!" *New York Times Book Review*, LXIV (Feb. 15, 1959), 1, 34—may be best understood as a defense of the tone of his novel.
10. *Anatomy of Criticism*, p. 43.
11. *Dark Conceit* (Evanston, 1959), p. 68.
12. "A Fantastic Voyage," *Partisan Review*, XXVI, 2 (Spring 1959), 302.
13. *The Ironic German: A Study of Thomas Mann* (Boston, 1958), p. 272.

7 · A DISCIPLINE OF NOBILITY:
Saul Bellow's Fiction

IN THE 1950s the sensible hero journeyed from a position of alienation to one of accommodation. Accommodation to the happy middling community of those years, to the suburbs, to the new wealth and the corporate conscience, to the fat gods. But the accommodation was aware of itself and, for the spirit's ease, it saved a tic of nonconformity. That was the substance of David Riesman's lessons in autonomy, and no social prescription of the decade was so well-liked as his. The journey was the *reisemotif*, so to speak, of serious American fiction in the decade, and of less serious American fiction, too. When the retrieved awareness was small, as often happened, when Marjorie Morningstar accepted Mamaroneck and Sloan Wilson his tailor, when, that is, the progress toward accommodation was most successful, accommodation looked most like retreat.

Saul Bellow's novels, altogether the most exciting fiction of those years, worked too—quite beyond any question of Bellow's intentions—within the motion from alienation to accommodation. Indeed, from a certain distance Bellow's novels find their definition as a systematic exploration of the concerns of all the Wilsons and the Wouks. Only—and of course it makes all the difference—they were more aware, more imaginative, and more severe. Bellow's characters, despite the variousness of mood and style of his work, remain much the same: a youth and a fat man, with a quirky philosopher loitering nearby. And they face problems which are reducible to a single problem: to meet with a strong sense of self the sacrifice of self demanded by social circumstance. Alienation, the sense of separate and unconciliating identity, must travel to accommodation. Bellow's inspiration is finally in other, deeper sources, but as the novels have worked themselves out they have dealt in the terms presented by the history in which they have found themselves. The dialogue between alienation and accommodation is what first of all they are about.

Dangling Man, published in the mid-1940s, took its terms from the '40s and pushed a dour hero over the arc from the impossibility of alienation to the death in accommodation. Joseph in his idiopathic freedom is functionless and unbearably isolated, but when, by hurrying his draft call, he seeks accommodation, he sacrifices the freedom of the self. The problem, whose formal construction Bellow perhaps borrowed from debates in *Partisan Review*, is insoluble, and in Bellow's next book, *The Victim*, it yields to a more tangible problem in responsibility. Asa Leventhal must balance what he owes a man who is at once his persecutor, his victim, and also his companion in this universe against what he owes himself. He discovers that he has a moral obligation in each direction—and that the issue is not only a moral one. Life is a battle in which each engagement suggests the necessity of disengagement, and *vice-versa*.

It may be a comic battle. This is a proposition which all of the dozens of high adventures of Augie March will want, serially, to prove, and which Augie finally will want to preserve intact. Except that it can't be preserved. There is too much running and brawling in the proposition, and no possibility of real freedom or community or love. For that reason *Augie March* never really ends.

In *Seize the Day* Bellow suddenly made the problem and his fiction severe by bringing to the last extremity a hero who can run and brawl no longer, who must find a principle of life in this world that has beaten him—or die. Tommy Wilhelm (together with Bellow) manages it, though he just manages it, in his last, desperate, resonating adventure. He finds himself weeping at the bier of a stranger, and in the same motion discovers that he is moving "toward the consummation of his heart's ultimate need." That need, the whole of the novel comes to reveal, is the need not to die. At the moment of death, his motion is toward existence, the vitality that defines and unites everyone, and his weeping is an acceptance of it and therefore an act of love toward life.

What has been caught, but just caught, is a progress of the soul through its freedom, from isolation to affirmation of ordinary life in the world. The affirmation is made again in the first movement of *Henderson the Rain King*. "Grun-tu-molani," man-want-to-live, an ancient African queen whispers to Henderson, and his heart fills with joy. But Henderson is ridden by high energies and lofty ambitions, and equipped therefore for the discovery that the principle of reconciliation is not enough. He needs further adventures, as the principle needs extension. Man wants to live, but in what shape and form? The communal principle fails Henderson as soon as he learns it when, in an impetuous gesture of good will, attempting to rid a cistern of frogs, he blows up his host's water supply. The idea of community imposes the idea of service, and Henderson possesses that idea fiercely. He would make men better, and free them from the law of decay. But his passion for service must be chastened and trained, and his further adventures under the tutelage of Dahfu, an African king who is part Wilhelm Reich, part Zarathustra, and part King David, provide him with just that spiritual exercise. He is put to lessons in self-transcendence. He must learn to contain humiliations. He must overcome fear. Like Zarathustra, he must empty himself in order to become a man again. Having done so, he can return to his home in Connecticut, to his wife, and he can make plans to enter medical school.

It is to these Nietzschean terms that the dialogue of *Dangling Man*, between alienation and accommodation, has come. The terms now, well over a decade later, are in no close sense the same terms at all. Bellow has got beyond them. But they are clearly consonant with their originals. They refer to the same problem, and the five novels show a strict struggle with it. What is remarkable is that Bellow has played it all by ear. The orderliness of his progress, and the intellectual unity, have after all been the wonderful accident of his commitment. The novels, with perhaps the exception of *The Victim*, are not even well-made. They spill over on themselves; they work themselves out according to the demands of character and frequently, one feels, out of the demands of gimmicks. They exhibit novelistic failures: *Dangling Man* is enclosed and short of action; Augie's exuberance runs down in the middle and becomes repetitive; Henderson suffers turgidity among his other sufferings. But they are shaped, and that is the excitement one feels in them, by an energy of total commitment, by an imagination that will confront human needs and greeds as they spill all over themselves and yield to clarity only after heavy labor.

A large and suffering appreciation of maelstrom, of personality filled with its own chaos and set down in the chaotic circumstances and the obscure obligations of the ordinary world, has shaped the novels and made them into a coherent vision. Bellow's alienated hero before he is alienated is a terribly oppressed individual, and it is with the feeling of his oppression that the fiction no doubt begins. Human beings crowd upon Bellow's hero and attempt to subjugate him. Human beings become burdensome to him. And it is not only those others who directly assault him who threaten his freedom. He begins in a condition of individuality imperiled, and his career is a series of adventures through a metropolis of perils. Bellow's hero lives among clutter, boredom, distraction, things. "Things done by man overshadow us," says Augie. "And this is true also of meat on the table, heat in the pipes, print on the paper, sounds in the air, so that all matters are alike, of the same weight, of the same rank, the caldron of God's wrath on page one and Wieboldt's sale on page two." Augie's complaint is diagnosed as *moha*, opposition of the finite, a curious complaint which is the start in fact of all the Bellovian protagonists.

It is the sheer weight of chaotic existence that first of all defines them. "The novelist is distracted," Bellow says in one of his discursive pieces. ". . . there are more things that solicit the attention of the mind than there ever were before." The novelist is menaced with "death by distraction," and not only the novelist: everyone on every level is exposed to the danger. We are menaced by the sheer distraction of sheer wealth. "The world is too much with us, and there has never been so much world," Bellow has said elsewhere. There is so much money now and there are so many possessions. "Love, duty, principle, thought, significance, everything is being sucked into a fatty and nerveless state of 'well-being.' " The fat gods of the new materialism are all about us demanding our energies.

We are menaced, distracted, and overborne by the sheer clutter of things. And of course it is to the point that Bellow, unlike the past masters, Hemingway and Faulkner, is entirely a city writer. (*Henderson* takes place mostly in Africa, to be sure, but not in the green hills of Africa. It is an Africa teeming with people and political intrigue, and with furniture; an Africa urbanized.) In the city there is much more to contend with. Things and others both are close and thick in Bellow's novels, and though Bellow is not without affection for nature, there is no escape into rural simplicities. In urban circumstances the rites of love are enormously difficult. Bellow's cities—Chicago and New York—are dense with neighbors and noise, with streetcars, subways, families, friends, soot, and filth. Joseph, living in a six-sided box within a Chicago rooming house, is victimized by the old man next door who coughs all night, leaves the door to the toilet open, steals socks, and throws empty whiskey bottles into the alley. *The Victim* begins: "On some nights New York is as hot as Bangkok," and all the gagging heaviness of a New York summer, the light of the sun like "the yellow revealed in the slit of the eye of a wild animal," the subways, the sweat, the listless crowds in the parks, the invincible dirt, the struggle for air, is brought upon Asa Leventhal's moral burden. Augie's Chicago, while it spawns heroic vitalists, is what he calls it in his first sentence, a "somber city." Those vitalists are all Machiavellians, omnipresent, dangerous, reaching out with too many clever hands. The somber city provides neither a recollection of Edenic childhood nor expectation of heaven. Augie is set down into "deep city vexation" and "forced early into deep city aims," and "what," he wants to know, "can that lead to of the highest?" His initiation into love is of the kind the city affords, love paid for and second hand. "That's what city life is. And so it *didn't* have the luster is should have had, and there *wasn't* any epithalamium of gentle lovers . . ." The character and the fate which are Augie's study are located first in his response to the enormousness and complexity of Chicago. "Crusoe," he says, "alone with nature, under heaven, had a busy, complicated time of it with the unhuman itself, and I am in a crowd that yields results with much more difficulty and reluctance and am part of it myself."

The clutter of the city weighs upon the shapes Tommy Wilhelm and Eugene Henderson, too. His existence lies upon Tommy Wilhelm like a hump, he is "assigned to be the carrier of a load which was his own self," but it makes a difference that he must carry it along upper Broadway on a summer's day. On a day after a sleepless, noisy New York night. Through the dust of the street and the fumes of the buses, through "push-carts, accordion and fiddle, shoeshine, begging, the dust going round like a woman on stilts," talking to himself because there is no one else to talk to among the millions of a city like New York. "The traffic seemed to come down Broadway out of the sky, where the hot spokes of the sun rolled from the south. Hot, stony odors rose from the subway grating in the street." And when Dr. Tamkin, the tutelary confidence man of the novel, a deity of this inferno, tells Tommy that the world is full of murderers, Tommy answers helplessly that "there are also kind, ordinary, helpful people. They're—out in the country."

Henderson goes out in the country, first as gentleman pig farmer, then as an African explorer, but the spirit, the heat, the humanity, and the junk of the city are always at his back. His farm, become a pig kingdom, swarms with grunting animals. The city's steaming pavement becomes the strange, obscurely threatening "calcareous" rocks of King Dahfu's country. The heat of the city becomes the boiling African sun, felt as the jungle fever which oppresses Henderson throughout his spiritual adventuring. Tamkin is recreated in King Dahfu, Henderson's guiding spirit, king of the warlike Wariri, another prince of darkness. The clotted Broadway crowd becomes the frenzied savages who batter Henderson to his knees in the ceremony in which he is made the Rain King.

Henderson abandons things and people to make the trip to Africa. It is the notion of junk that is the immediate motive of his going. Climbing through the rooms of an old lady just dead, he is overwhelmed by her collected rubbish: "Bottles, lamps, old butter dishes, and chandeliers were on the floor, shopping bags filled with string and rags, and pronged openers that the dairies used to give away to lift the paper tops from milk bottles; and bushel baskets full of buttons and china door knobs." And he thinks, "Henderson, put forth effort. You, too, will die of this pestilence. Death will annihilate you and nothing will remain, and there will be nothing left but junk." He puts forth effort to escape, but the city stays with him nonetheless. In Africa he talks city talk: "Now listen, Your Highness, don't sell me down the river. You know what I mean? I thought you liked me." He thinks, in Africa, in city metaphors and of city events; the city maintains its pressure, and alive within his other speculations is the city idea of people, nameless, faceless, with whom no communication is possible. Tommy Wilhelm was condemned to talk to himself in a city where every other man spoke a language entirely his own, and Henderson is brought to the vision of Babel raised to include the universe: "This planet has billions of passengers on it, and those were preceded by infinite billions and there are vaster billions to come, and none of these, no, not one, can I hope ever to understand. Never!" He goes on to reflect that this matter of quantity, come upon in another view, need not bury you alive, that it is marvelous and not depressing—but the reflection comes of his struggle and not of his primary condition.

Under the mass of such quantity and confronted by such chaos in the external world, Bellow's hero in his first motion moves toward unburdening and sloughing off. Civil society is too much, and indeed in extreme moments even the cultural accumulations, the very history and wisdom of civilization, are too much and are rejected. Most emphatically by the aging wise man, another Zarathustrian prophet, of Bellow's monologue called "Address by Gooley MacDowell to the Hasbeens Club of Chicago":

> Around our heads we have a dome of thought as thick as atmosphere to breathe. And what's about? One thought leads to another as breath leads to breath. By pulling [it] into universal consciousness, can [we] explain everything from Democritus to Bikini? But a person can no longer keep up, and plenty are dying of good ideas. We have them in the millions, in compilations, from the *Zend Avesta* to now, all on file with the best advice for [one] and all human occasions. . . . Look at us, deafened, hampered, obstructed, impeded, impaired and bowel-glutted with wise counsel and good precept, and the more plen-

tiful our ideas the worse our headaches. So we ask, will some good creature pull out the plug and ease our disgusted hearts a little?

It is a prayer Augie, too, records: "Anyway, there's too much of everything of this kind, *that's* come home to me, too much history and culture to keep track of, too many details, too much news, too much example, too much influence, too many guys who tell you to be as they are, and all this hugeness, abundance, turbulence, Niagara Falls torrent. Which who is supposed to interpret? Me?" And Tommy Wilhelm is overcome by the sheer information in Tamkin's discourses, and Henderson, an overwhelmed millionaire, under the spur of a similar impulse fills beautiful pieces of architecture with pigs and then, seeking Eden, makes a safari to the precivilized past, "the real past," he says, "no history or junk like that." And if all history and culture are rejected in a style that borrows widely from the world's accumulation of literature, that fact is more than irony. Bellow's style, which beginning with *Augie March* has become a racy vehicle bearing great freights of knowledge, is a thing that simultaneously admits and dismisses clutter. All its process of literary echoing goes to lend the rejection authority.

The matter has become more and more apparent, but since the beginning all Bellow's heroes have started in a gesture of escape from burdens, an extreme romantic gesture. It is a gesture which in its extremity brings Bellow into touch with one of the defining impulses of American character, into touch with at least all the classic Redskins of American letters, from Leatherstocking to Whitman to Mark Twain to Hemingway, all those who light out for the woods, the open road, the Territory, and into touch perhaps with the Palefaces, too. (The extreme need to escape burdens, to be free of all the clutter, is certainly as well a distinction of Hawthorne and Henry James.) Bellow's hero is tempted frequently to epiphanies of love for mankind in general, though never for things, and his motion is brought to various thematic significances, but he is in the first instance activated by the need to rid himself of the weight of the chaos.

He can escape from under that weight into harmony with

natural laws vaguely realized as beneficent, or he can escape into himself, locate all value and reality in his person, or he can in various ways attempt to reconcile himself with external existence in all its chaos. And it is out of those three possibilities, the first two stretching toward the last, that the action and the total thematic construct of Bellow's novels have come.

Neither as a metaphysical conception nor in the pleasantness of its phenomena is Nature ever dominant as a motif, though it has become more emphatic as the novels have succeeded each other. Bellow's city imagination is not comfortable with the Natural Laws. He has little nature to bring to them. But his hero entertains a yearning for them and a provisional trust that they are good, because the circumscription of the possibility of escape demands it. Joseph dismisses "nature" when it is presented to him by a friend who complains of the treelessness and too-human deadness of New York, dismisses it as nostalgic sentimentality. Nevertheless his whole struggle toward what he calls the "facts of simple existence" is involved in a turn of the seasons toward fruitful harmony. The chaotic winter submits to spring. Joseph begins his journal in the dark Chicago December and surrenders himself, relieves himself of his freedom, in April. Bellow accents the matter by having Joseph look forward throughout his winter to walking in the park in his spring coat on the 21st of March, and he shifts the mood of the novel toward resolution with the coming spring.

Asa Leventhal, locked in New York's inhuman heat, has moments of freshness and deep breathing at sea on the Staten Island ferry, and the plot of the novel moves him toward the relief that will come with Labor Day. The attempted suicide of his antagonist, Allbee, on the eve of that day makes possible Leventhal's birth into a possible world, and the day itself brings cooling breezes. Nature as transcendent reality brushes Leventhal lightly once—for a brief moment of half-sleep he feels the whole world present to him and about to offer him a mysterious, it would seem redeeming, discovery. But the discovery blows by him and at the end of his action, having abandoned ultimate questioning and now re-entering a darkened theatre with his wife, he is no closer to a notion of reality.

But Augie comes, if not conclusively, at least wholeheartedly to the natural laws, his "axial lines" called "Truth, love, peace, bounty, usefulness, harmony!" which, he says, quiver right through him when striving stops. They excite him in the moment after his perception of them to pastoral ambitions. He wants to own and settle on a Midwestern farm, to marry, and to teach orphans. His adventures carry him, however, into complexities which won't permit cessation of striving. The axial lines, he says, are "not imaginary stuff . . . because I bring my entire life to the test." There is no doubting his sincerity, but this is one of the moments when Augie's hopefulness becomes shrill. His whole life does not validate the perception. The novel does not earn that leap into faith. In fact the novel is honest beyond Augie's knowing and it does not permit him so easy an escape. Nor is it an escape that Tommy Wilhelm, so strictly confined by authentic troubles, can practically afford to take. Not, anyway, in its romantic simplicity. Tamkin does offer him nature. "Creative is nature," he says. "Rapid. Lavish. Inspirational. It shapes leaves. . . . You don't know what you've got within you." But it is no solace to a middle-aged slob rapidly and lavishly dying in the middle of New York City. Tommy is simply confused by the offer.

It is Henderson who most clearly moves toward harmony with the natural laws. He goes among noble savages and to live with the beasts in the field—and if his Africa has the feel of Chicago and the smell of New York, that is apparently despite Bellow's first intention. Moreover it is Henderson who most clearly demonstrates the naïveté of the escape into nature. He makes a journey into the heart of darkness to discover the horror of it. He goes to Africa to discover Reality. A voice within him says constantly, "I want," and that is what it ultimately wants. "Truth" and "Reality" are ambitions always at his lips. His soul's progress is marked by a succession of emblematic beasts. First a porcine pig farmer in a sty of piggish phenomena, he comes in the first stage of his journey upon a motley tribe of pious cow-worshipers and then he tries to do what none of them will do, to deal at first hand with a plague of frogs. He fails, but in failing he has pursued nature to a certain depth. His next, and most important, stop, with a tribe of lion-worshipers, brings him face to face with the thing itself. Under the tutelage of Dahfu—himself a refugee from civilization come home to meet Reality—Henderson is put to the task (following disciplines derived from the somatic psychology of Wilhelm Reich) of assuming and absorbing Dahfu's pet lioness. She is all lion, Dahfu observes. "Does not take issue with the inherent. Is one hundred per cent within the given." She is the way to Being, the end of Becoming, the unchanging truth prior to the cycle of desire and fear. She will force Henderson to the present moment. "She will make consciousness to shine. She will burnish you." She *is* Being—or, as it turns out, penultimate Being—itself. (Being, of course, not seen as daffodils. Bellow is never so lacking in severity as that.) And Henderson has some small success in overcoming his fear of the lioness and then in absorbing lion-ness. He meets the inhuman thing. In the same way, it happens, and within the same image as previous Bellow heroes have met it—Asa saw the yellow of the sun like that in the slit of the eye of a wild animal, "say a lion, something inhuman that didn't care about anything human and yet was implanted in every human being, too," and Augie had adventures with the lion's American equivalent, an eagle with a "pressed-down head, the killing eye, the deep life of its feathers." But Henderson goes further. The lion is pure fire, he says, forcing him to close his eyes. So are the stars pure fire, he realizes, and not small gold objects. He develops his consciousness of the matter beyond ways that are permitted Asa and Augie. He discovers that the inhuman fire is at the center of his humanity, too.

With that discovery he should achieve harmony. Here is the very principle of Augie's axial lines. But Henderson is hurried to a further pitch of Reality. Dahfu's lion is a pet lioness after all. Henderson is now made to confront the authentic lion, male and wild:

Then, at the very door of consciousness, there was a snarl and I looked down from this straw perch . . . into the big, angry, hair-framed face of the lion. It was all wrinkled, contracted; within those wrinkles was the darkness of murder. The lips were drawn away from the gums, and the breath of the animal came over me, hot as oblivion, raw as blood. I started to speak aloud. I said, "Oh, my God, whatever You think of me, let me not fall under this butcher shop. . . ." And to this, as a rider, the thought added itself that this was all mankind needed, to be conditioned into the image of a ferocious animal like the one below.

That lion castrates and kills King Dahfu. The voice of the lion is the voice of death itself. And this Real, far from being the escape from chaos, is chaos and old night itself. To submit to the harmony it offers, on the principle that the lion outside is inside, too, would be to accept the inhumanity of the inhuman Real. Henderson had in one of his discourses with Dahfu parried Eliot by saying that humankind could not stand too much unreality, but Eliot wins the point. Henderson now reflects on the great inescapable rhythms of life, Augie's axial lines once again, but he reflects that he can't afford to worry about them. The old queen's advice, "Grun-tu-molani," man-want-to-live, comes to mean going about the business of living despite the death-dealing, chaotic Real.

That is very much, if not explicitly, the ground upon which Augie finally mounts his optimism. If Augie is only incidentally concerned with the nature of the real Real, he is completely engaged with the natural laws as they impinge on his larky and boisterous freedom, and the *animal ridens* rises in him *despite* their influences. His adventures are escapes from all determinisms, human and suprahuman. And that is the ground upon which Tommy Wilhelm, finally made to confront death as ultimate reality, can choose to live. The escape from under the weight of external chaos into the natural laws does not work. It is no escape at all. At the center of the universe are violence and death. The vague yearning for the natural laws lucent in the earlier novels is quite extinguished when the fiction works it out to the test.

There is an alternative dodge for Bellow's oppressed hero in the assertion of his own character as the locus of reality and value. In the face of cluttering chaos and with a swagger, he can assert personality broadly. "A man's character is his fate, says Heraclitus," says Augie with relishing approval, and if at the end he learns that a man's fate is his character, why, that is a fate good enough for him. Tamkin advises Tommy:

> Seek ye then that which art not there
> In thine own glory let thyself rest.
> Witness. Thy power is not bare.
> Thou art King. Thou art at thy best.

It is advice under which Tommy staggers. The hero of one of Bellow's short stories, "The Trip to Galena," a young man engaged in a war against the overburdening boredom of things and people, proposes that "a man is bound to do everything in his lifetime." He will conduct war by the simple exertion of personality. And Henderson, whose person is explicitly reflected in his body, is great and joyous in his body. His very suffering delights him because it is an exercise of personality. At the center of the universe, then, in this action, is the individual self. The self constantly threatened, however, and presenting an obligation. The Bellovian hero will protect his personality from the outside or, because he can't live in a nutshell, insinuate it in and out of chaotic experience; but he will maintain it, attempt to maintain it, always unbroken.

At the end the assertion is merely a dodge, and the escape is blocked precisely because the inhuman outside *is* within— that, finally, is why "alienation" is impossible. Nor can personality remain untouched. The attempt at self-preservation raises severe moral problems. And at the end the person must indeed be broken in order to achieve life. But the motion of the escape meanwhile irradiates Bellow's writing. It is the inspiration of his comedy. Because the need is desperate, the assertion of the person is extreme—with *Augie March* and thereafter, though there are hints of the mood before, the assertion is raised in various characters to burlesque. Bellow's personalist hero yelps, quite the gamecock of a new, urban wilderness, quite like his backwoodsman prototype impelled to brashness by dispossession and inadequacy and the feeling of threatening powers everywhere. He sings himself with quite the same nervy insolence with which Walt Whitman met the world, and like that witty comedian he makes a great gesture of including the whole world in himself, but then he adopts shifts and evasions and contrarieties to keep free of it. And like Whitman, he celebrates himself by the exercise of a free-wheeling, inclusive, cataloguing rhetoric, gripping great bunches of facts in sentences that just manage to balance, racing through various levels of diction, saying with every turn, "Look at me, going everywhere!" It is a gaudy fireworks of a style, in itself a brilliant affirmation of the self. At the same time it performs the ironic function, by its calculated indiscriminateness (in Bellow and in Walt Whitman, too), of discarding everything it picks up. It is therefore the perfect expression of the dynamic, disengaging, mock hero.

Dahfu accuses Henderson of being a great avoider, and the same accusation may be made against all of Bellow's personalists. Augie is the clearest instance. His famous "availability" is the flamboyant self-asserting part of him, but it is perfectly and in every engagement countered by his "opposition." At the end he still has all his availability; his great appetite for life and engagement is intact precisely because he has spent it in no experience. He is presented taking what amounts to still another oath of unsusceptibility to all the "big personalities, destiny molders, and heavy-water brains, Machiavellis and wizard evildoers, bigwheels and imposers-upon, absolutists." The oath is redundant, for his unsusceptibility is continuous. Indeed it is a moral failing, and one which Augie is made to realize. The one advice by his many advisers which cuts deep is that he can't be hurt enough by the fate of other people. That is a failing in love, and the most strenuous part of Augie's action is in the problem it poses. It is a failing he never rectifies, for to do so would stop him cold.

Augie is a kind of Huck Finn, with his something adoptional about him, his participation in a linear series of adventures, his resilience, his mounting good humor. The comparison has been noted. But he is like Huck, too, in his reluctance to be civilized. He eludes. He is not to be caught by the shaping influences. He won't be determined. Moreover, he is Huck confined to a city populated by endless duplications of the King, the Duke, and Colonel Sellers. No matter that his adventures take him over two continents, he is always in Chicago, without a Territory to light out for—and so he is put to more muscular shifts of duplicity. What the Mississippi and the Territory could do for Huck, Augie must do for himself. His only territory is his personality, which he must keep free. Life is dramatic for Augie, it is process, and the process is that kind of evasion that keeps all events and the person from settling.

A new discipline and another notion of the possibilities of freedom will be needed by the personalist hero who is to avoid evasion and be hurt enough by the fate of other people.

Bellow comes to it, but after *Augie* as before the strong assertion of independent personality secures all of his lyricism, and without restriction to the personalist protagonists. Radical self-assertion, assertion of the real, untypical self, is an act of courage in Bellow's squeezing world. There is glamor in it which just for itself for the moment transvalues all moral obligations. It commands Bellow's love even for the very Machiavellians he loathes—sometimes, it should be added, with the disastrous result of turning them quaint.

Almost in the very beginning, in 1942 with his second published story, "The Mexican General," there appeared the first in Bellow's line of resolutely vital knaves. The General is a provincial opportunist who has secured his opportunity with the assassination of Trotsky. He is an arrogant ghoul, well-mistressed, a vile entrepreneur at the funeral of the Revolution, and he is made to bear a moral of political corruption. But he is also equipped with Lawrentian innuendoes of personality— he has Indian vigor, he is alive, he has personal force, he is an *Übermensch* just not yet attained to moral transcendence, and the pale moral sophisticate of the story is reduced by him to a fascinated helplessness. There is no doubt that the Mexican General is intended as a villain, but, perhaps despite his intentions, Bellow celebrates him. There will be many like him, with variations in virtue: Kirby Allbee and (also in *The Victim*) incidental chieftains, the patriarch Schlossberg; the matriarch Mrs. Harkavy; then Augie's Grandma Lausch and his "first superior man," William Einhorn—and indeed every one of the thirty-odd Machiavellians in his adventures; then Dr. Tamkin; then King Dahfu with his "strong gift of life" and his extra shadow-casting intensity, and Henderson himself. All of them are, if not reincarnations of the General, at least apparently related to him. The descendants inhabit Bellow's shorter pieces as well: plays, stories, monologues, and a curious and festive interview (published in *The Reporter*) with Joe "Yellow Kid" Weil, an aged oligarch among the Chicago confidence men and among the Chicago intellectuals of Bughouse Square, "an elegant and old-fashioned gentleman" of "round phrases and leisurely speech," a reader of Nietzsche and Herbert Spencer, a masterful man who has refused to be society's obedient slave.

The virtue in the exercise of personality for its own sake is clearly a virtue derived from necessity. It is derived as well, seemingly, from the lessons in necessity inherent in one tradition of Yiddish literature, the tradition of what has been called *dos kleine menschele,* the little man of the Eastern European ghetto, the *stetl,* who is forced by the presence of perils everywhere to ingenious ways of personal survival. One of those ways is in mock-heroism. Yiddish conversation itself, a vessel of the spirit that produced *dos kleine menschele,* is, Bellow himself has said,

> full of the grandest historical, mythological, and religious allusions. The Creation, the Fall, the Flood, Egypt, Alexander, Titus, Napoleon, the Rothschilds, the sages, and the Laws may get into the discussion of an egg, a clothesline, or a pair of pants.

The conversation of Augie and his major successors is full of the same, sprouting comparative references to heroes from Jacob to Caesar to John Dillinger to Sir Wilfred Grenfell, to epical events from the Diaspora to the campaigning events of World War II. This manner of living on terms of familiarity with greatness, Bellow goes on to say, contributed to the ghetto's sense of the ridiculous. It also performed a more delicate feat of irony, and one to which Bellow is sensitive. On the one hand, the mock-heroics of the little man render all conventional heroism absurd. Mock-heroism in Bellow's fiction serves that function. But the mock-heroics of Bellow's protagonists and antagonists (both) are far from those of tradition—the tradition of Chaucer and Rabelais and Swift. They are not practiced with such broad and easy security. On the other hand, the acts themselves constitute real heroism, a mode of strong self-assertion in a community that disallows the self. Given the prison of restrictive circumstances of the *stetl,* and then those of Bellow's city, it is the only mode by which personal identity can be emphasized. Augie's mythical mouthfuls provide rough fun; they burlesque his own bravado and dilute all pretension. At the same time they call Julius Caesar and John Dillinger to witness. There is courage in the insolence of it. The bravado is a thin mask for the bravery, rather than vice versa. Augie's frisky speech is the power he puts forth to win from all oppressive circumstances a right to exist.

The exercise of personality is everywhere in Bellow's world an act of courage. The salvation of the self, whether by defiance or evasion, is an honored behavior. The self is where felt reality is, and where meaning may be. But the rocks upon which simple exulting personality would founder were discovered at the beginning. Joseph, whose whole struggle was for the means by which the self might be preserved in a time of death, comes upon the disappointing fact of his own baseness and then on the necessity of goodness in community. Alone and allowed to test his dreadful freedom, he becomes irritable, self-indulgent, oversensitive, quarrelsome. Perhaps he has not achieved the highest freedom. Freedom should be the condition of dignity. But, meanwhile, he does not know what to do with the freedom he has. His free self becomes burdensome to him, and he has a continuous lesson in the end of ordinary free self-hood in Vanaker, the lonely, disgusting old man next door, grunting, hacking, thieving, and smelling away his existence. It is when Joseph sees a rat scurrying through some garbage that he resolves to give up his freedom and his self. The self he has held so dear is an "imprisoning self," and the end of his speculation about "ideal constructions" is that the highest of them is that which *unlocks* the imprisoning self. Alienation is not to be made into a doctrine. The other side of freedom is isolation. Alienation is, moreover, morally reprehensible. "What we really want," Joseph discovers, "is to stop living so exclusively and vainly for our own sake, impure and unknowing, turning inward and self-fastened." Joseph's talent is "for being a citizen, or what is today called, most apologetically, a good man," and "goodness," he is forced to know, "is achieved not in a vacuum, but in the company of other men, attended by love."

The notions of inherent baseness, of human nature sharing the bestiality of nature itself, and of love as an imperative lurk everywhere for the personalist hero. At some point in his adventuring each of Bellow's heroes finds the beast within. Asa Leventhal must wrestle with his own inhumanity. Augie, rich in spirit and rowdy as he is, is unable to stay with his purest feelings. He is confronted by the last of his many advisers with a vision of the human soul as composed of secrets, lies, and diseases. Tommy Wilhelm is confronted by Tamkin's notion of a corrupting "pretender soul" turning all human beings into murderers.

("Yes, I think so too," says Tommy. "But personally . . . I don't feel like a murderer. I always try to lay off. It's the others who get me.") Henderson sees himself as a bargain basement of deformities, his whole existence proposed in metaphors of beasts. And in one short lyrical instance, in an Easter sermon by one of Bellow's quacky truth-telling rejuvenators, cannibalism is imploded as the law of life. "The Sermon of Dr. Pep" begins in a protest against hamburger for the bad conscience in its disguise of the slain beast and ends in a protest against the suicide by which a gentle humanity disguises its murders. Men must eat, and murder is the cost of civilization.

But that statement is merely ecstatic. Bellow's major heroes, compelled to live beyond the lyrical moment, confront the beast within and the human propensity to murder, and they cannot rest in their perception. They must—each of them—as well confront the moral conditions of civilization, the cost of which would seem to be precisely the self.

Each of the major protagonists is forced, like Augie, to suffer confusion between love and an independent fate. Not only that, he must strain to reconcile those impossible opposites. That is what the struggle for accommodation comes to. Joseph strains and fails—or he ends not quite in failure but in a desperate attempt to reacquaint himself with ordinary communal reality. Asa Leventhal, a self-enclosed, self-righteous victim, is assaulted by the imperative of brotherhood, which at the end he cannot accept. But he does reach a large idea of what it is to be exactly human. An old man in the lavatory of a movie theatre tells him that Boris Karloff is a law unto himself. One wouldn't be Boris Karloff. To be neither more nor less than human, Asa discovers, is to be "accountable in spite of many weaknesses," and with that discovery he achieves a tentative goodness. Augie, not hurt enough by the fate of other people, particularly fails the severe test of romantic love. The test, his affair with Thea, is most particularly rich in confusion —not only for Augie; Bellow too has groped his way through it. Thea's love is murderous. But it is real love, a way of discovering other people. If it is strange to Augie, then, Augie himself comes to admit, that is his own fault. The struggle for Augie is to make it less strange. And Tommy Wilhelm and Henderson, too, struggle to admit love to their freedom, to be themselves and at the same time to have a place in the human community.

Tommy Wilhelm at the last extremity of his need seizes the day and moves toward the consummation of his heart's ultimate need. But it is with *Henderson* that the consummation is first achieved and rendered, achieved by a Nietzschean notion of heroic self-transcendence based on freedom, a notion that has been hinted at in all the previous novels.

Despite all circumstances of oppression, despite the violence of nature and the violence of men, despite the cocky, assertive "I," despite all determinisms and despite finitude and death, the individual *is* free and free to choose. He can become better. Joseph felt that by some transcendent means human beings could distinguish themselves from brute things and he considered that the universal quest was for pure freedom, but the practical means to transcendence were not at hand. In *The Victim* the patriarch Schlossberg suggests as equal possibilities that man is "lousy and cheap" and that he has "greatness and beauty." But if those are equal possibilities, then one *can choose*. The means of transcendence are at hand. And what would one choose? "Have dignity, you understand me?" he says. "Choose dignity." But for Asa there are practical difficulties. Augie's Einhorn preaches a similar doctrine of self-transformation, as does Augie himself, in passing. And Tamkin strenuously offers Tommy Wilhelm the possibility of choice. Tommy *can* seize the day and thereby choose life. But not yet nobility, a word much favored by Bellow and meaning the coalescence of selflessness and selfhood. The individual who would exert his freedom toward such transcendence will need great spiritual capabilities to begin with, and then hard discipline.

Henderson is the man, and, in terms of a succession of metamorphoses, he gets such discipline.

By Bellow's own inspiration or by astonishing coincidence, Henderson's career follows with great closeness, with only one initial deviation, that of the spirit in the first parable of *Thus Spake Zarathustra*. Says Zarathustra:

> Of three metamorphoses of the spirit I tell you: how the spirit becomes a camel; and the camel, a lion; and the lion, finally, a child.

There is much that is difficult for the spirit, the strong reverent spirit that would bear much: but the difficult and the most difficult are what its strength demands.

What is difficult? asks the spirit that would bear much, and kneels down like a camel wanting to be well loaded. What is most difficult, O heroes, asks the spirit that would bear much, that I may take it upon myself and exult in my strength? Is it not humbling oneself to wound one's haughtiness? Letting one's folly shine to mock one's wisdom?

Or is it this: feeding on the acorns and grass of knowledge and, for the sake of the truth, suffering hunger in one's soul?

Or is it this: stepping into filthy waters when they are the waters of truth, and not repulsing cold frogs and hot toads?

Or is it this: loving those who despise us and offering a hand to the ghost that would frighten us?

*[Walter Kaufmann translation]**

Henderson is not a camel—he is a Connecticut millionaire, not a Bedouin, and so without that opportunity—but he is a strenuous spirit who would bear much and who demands the extremest test of his strength. He engages the Zarathustrian burdens of humility and folly. If he does not feed on acorns and grass, he raises and identifies with pigs that do, and he suffers hunger in his soul. He does precisely, among the first of his African tribes, meet the test of frogs in the filthy waters, but without humility, and it is to his sorrow that he repulses them. And he strains to love those who despise and reject him.

Says Zarathustra:

All these most difficult things the spirit that would bear much takes upon itself: like the camel that, burdened, speeds into the desert, thus the spirit speeds into its desert.

In the loneliest desert, however, the second metamorphosis occurs: here the spirit becomes a lion who would conquer his freedom and be master in his own desert. Here he seeks out his last master: he wants to fight him and his last god; for ultimate victory he wants to fight with the great dragon.

Who is the great dragon whom the spirit will no longer call lord and god? "Thou shalt" is the name of the great dragon. But the spirit of the lion says, "I will." "Thou shalt" lies in his

* All excerpts from *Thus Spake Zarathustra* are quoted with permission from *The Portable Nietzsche*, trans. by Walter Kaufmann. Copyright 1954 by The Viking Press, Inc.

way, sparkling like gold, an animal covered with scales; and on every scale shines a golden "thou shalt."

My brothers, why is there a need in the spirit for the lion? Why is not the beast of burden, which renounces and is reverent, enough?

To create new values—that even the lion cannot do; but the creation of freedom for oneself for new creation—that is within the power of the lion. The creation of freedom for oneself and a sacred "No" even to duty—for that, my brothers, the lion is needed. To assume the right to new values—that is the most terrifying assumption for a reverent spirit that would bear much. Verily, to him it is preying, and a matter for a beast of prey. He once loved "thou shalt" as most sacred: now he must find illusion and caprice even in the most sacred, that freedom from his love may become his prey: the lion is needed for such prey.

Henderson speeds from the meek, reverent, cow-worshiping Arnewi into the desert. There he destroys himself, body and soul, in order to become a lion, and in the very process he learns something about the possibilities of self-transformation. He learns, moreover, what it is to contain one's freedom. The lion, Dahfu tells him, is pure Being. It is entirely itself, it is all unobliging will, and, heavy with the clutter of existence, on all sides oppressed, Henderson secures from it a way of confronting the oppressing, death-dealing universe. The lion is for Henderson, and Dahfu, the intensity of the self beyond all reverence, the avatar of freedom, and Henderson, as lion, looks forward to new creation.

Says Zarathustra:

But say, my brothers, what can the child do that even the lion could not do? Why must the preying lion still become a child? The child is innocence and forgetting, a new beginning, a game, a self-propelled wheel, a first movement, a sacred "Yes." For the game of creation, my brothers, a sacred "Yes" is needed: the spirit now wills his own will, and he who had been lost to the world now conquers his own world.

Of three metamorphoses of the spirit I have told you: how the spirit became a camel; and the camel, a lion; and the lion, finally, a child.

The last of Henderson's tutelary spirits is the child he adopts on his plane back to America. The airplane makes a fueling stop and he runs with the child in his arms around the airport in Newfoundland. What, specifically, Henderson has newly found is his way back, after he had been lost to the world, to his ordinary life, but he comes back now in a new movement with a new will to creation: "I guess I felt it was my turn now to move, and so went running—leaping, leaping, pounding, and tingling over the pure white lining of the gray Arctic silence." A self-propelled wheel. And he is provided with a sacred "Yes." He has always had a "service ideal." It had been crushed, but now it has been newly invented, he will enter medical school, and his suicidal violence has been transformed to love.

Thus spake Zarathustra, and it is perhaps of note that Zarathustra at that time sojourned in the town that is called The Motley Cow.

That is not to suggest anything programmatic about *Henderson*. The novel is not a manual for living. If the Nietzschean parable is at the center of it, the parable is elaborated, indeed sportively elaborated. It is a funny book and it goes off all sorts of ways. Nor is it to suggest that *Henderson* is the summit of a mountain of thought up which Bellow has been scrabbling the years thus far of his novelist's career. Bellow, too, has been disorderly and boisterous, full of strong assertions and apothegms which have the finality only of the fullest fiction, which crack on the next turn of events and mood.

And there will be more events.

But the novels have, all this while, been going somewhere—not, of course, toward any summit at all, nor toward any solution to anything. Bellow's domain for investigation is nothing less than the bases of all moral behavior, wherein one expects no solutions except by fiat or by sermon. Fiction is only the jittery act of reaching. When the goal is sufficient, as in Bellow's fiction it is, and when in spite of jitters the reach is serious and long and one can see that it is reaching, fiction becomes crucial. As in Bellow's case it has.

8 · CALIBAN ON PROSPERO:

A Psychoanalytic Study on the Novel
Seize the Day, by Saul Bellow

SAUL BELLOW's novel *Seize the Day*[1] represents, I believe, an extraordinary contribution to the relationship between father and son as a theme in fiction. The father-son relationship is an area of experience which the artist shares to a larger degree than he does any other kind of experience with the cultural historian, the moral philosopher, and more recently with the psychologist, particularly the psychoanalyst.

The relationship has always been the nuclear symbol for the artist-mythologist when he attempts to place himself or his race within its proper *Weltanschauung*. Time, in literature, defines itself as the recurrent clashing of generations. The vicissitudes of Oedipus, from the unloved infant to the reigning parricide, seem to appoint the equally tragic alternatives for all posterity to explore. The most superficial inspection, from Oedipus to old Karamazov, must convince us that what makes the relationship so apt a symbol for the historical process is that one quality it shares in equal intensity with both literature and history— unceasing conflict with atonement at its end. As for the atonement between the father and the son in whom he is well pleased, it is in actuality a pious wish, in literature a posthumous reconciliation more formative of a religious belief than a real human relationship.

Within any given epoch conditions arise which determine the outcomes of these conflicts, and certain historical periods seem to be entirely exempt from viewing the conflict as tragic. In these periods arise situations such as are dealt with in the theatre of Plautus in which *juvenis* outwits and conquers *senex*, or in the Restoration theatre in which spindleshanks is hoodwinked by his young stud of a son. Such a struggle is, as Northrop Frye suggests in his essay, "The Argument of Comedy," essentially comic.

It is, I suppose, in those situations where life turns back upon itself and breaks where it should begin, that the tragic, historical significance of the father-son relationship occurs. One thing seems fairly certain—that literature abounds more in those situations in which David destroys Absalom, and Rustum, Sohrab, than those in which Theseus succeeds Aegeus and Prince Hal, King Henry—and more often than not denies the biological truism of youth succeeding age. It represents instead the efforts of an innately hostile father, who, by force of sheer vitality, or by the inertia of his established position, reverses the flow of progress and overshadows the son.

Recently new elements have been introduced into the literature of such conflicts. Their nature has been subtilized, introverted. The question has retreated from the palpable borders of physical survival or of moral superiority to the most elemental of all bases—the natural psychological ambivalence inherent in the relationships between fathers and sons, the recognition that with all the manifest good will in the world fathers and sons are more often than not mutually destructive entities. Not that the psychological ambivalence has not always existed, but now it has come forward to claim its right as the central subject, with the older, more public issues as mere corroborative appendages.

The old public battlefields—the promethean rebellion of the more spiritual son against the harsh fact of the brutal repressive father—the desertion of the family *business* in favor of the personal *vocation,* the preference for the kingdom of love over the safe-deposit vaults of mammon, the whole flight from gross reality—no longer offer a sound footing for waging the conflict. Fathers and sons are no longer warring socio-economic or cultural entities. When the artist follows the psychologist into the green room of family relations where the masks of character are laid aside, he finds not oppositions but strange complicities. Love and hate and all the acts of the conscious will are a part of the public pantomime. The moral content of the struggle becomes a rational fiction. The real pathos grows from the artist's ability to construct his characters from their non-volitional bases, and to be able to translate their mute appeals for help or understanding or their inchoate threatenings into an intuitively coherent language of significant character traits and forms of action. He must, in order to grasp the whole of his theme, make the ultimate commitment and postulate, as Dostoyevsky does, an unconscious—the things "which a man is afraid to tell even to himself." The impulse to make this commitment arises, of course, from our having accepted in the other, nonaesthetic quadrants of our lives, certain psychological data as our guide to the understanding of ourselves, data which Freudian psychoanalysis has systematized into a science. From having been mildly concerned with the psychologically accurate components of a literary work of art, the artist has come to insist that they be accurate, and that psychological inaccuracy put as heavy a tax on probability as the miraculous.

The psychoanalyst Otto Fenichel defines the new entente between the artist and the psychologist:

> It is in no way true that in discussing events of human life one has to choose between the vivid, intuitive description of an artist and the detached abstractedness of a scientist thinking only quantitatively. It is not necessary and not permissible to lose feeling when feeling is investigated scientifically. Freud once stated that it was not his fault that his case histories gave the impression of a novel.[2]

Freud himself appears to have been aware that a new subject for literature was emerging from the psychoanalytic recognition of neuroses and character traits as products of the conflict between inward strivings and environmental frustrations. We might object that "Sophocles long ago had heard it on the Aegean," but it is Freud's original contribution that he brought the recognition up to full consciousness. He has written, in effect, an addendum to Aristotle's *Poetics*, a rational guide to the composition of a work of art. In a posthumously published essay he deals directly with the drama:

> If religion, character, and social drama differ from one another, chiefly with respect to the arena in which the action takes

place, from which the suffering has its origin, we may now follow the drama to still another arena where it becomes the psychological drama. For it is within the soul of the hero himself that there takes place an anguished struggle between impulses, a struggle which must end, not with the downfall of the hero but with that of one of the contending impulses, in other words, with a renunciation. . . . The psychological drama becomes the psychopathological when the source of the suffering which we are to share and from which we are to derive pleasure is no longer a conflict between two almost equally conscious motivations, but one between conscious and repressed ones. Here the precondition for enjoyment is that the spectator shall also be neurotic. For it is only to him that the release, and, to a certain extent, the conscious recognition of the repressed motivation can afford pleasure instead [as in the non-neurotic whose repression is counterbalanced by the original force of the repression] of merely making for unacceptance. It is only in the neurotic that such a struggle exists as can become the subject for drama.[3]

I should like to consider, with what I trust is neurotic sensibility, Saul Bellow's *Seize the Day* as a novel in which the character and the action of the central figure, Tommy Wilhelm, are determined by and represent the neurotic conflict between instinctual cravings and outwardly determined frustrations. The conflict between father and son is central to the novel, but its repressed content is latent throughout until the last moment, when, as Freud describes it, "the repression is shattered." The novel is interesting, too, in that without deserting the psychoanalytic point of view one can apprehend in the action certain cultural implications. When I finished reading *Seize the Day* I was struck by what appeared to me to be the premeditated delineations of the character and psychopathology of Tommy Wilhelm. But I was equally struck by the unpremeditated affinities of both Tommy Wilhelm and his father with Kafka father and son as they appear in Kafka's "Letter to His Father." It is this affinity that suggests an extension of the neurotic problem— the outwardly determined frustration which is the product not of a single cultural milieu, but of an encounter between two conflicting milieus.

Kafka, writing in the cosmopolitan city of Prague, lives, in the "Letter to His Father," in a psychological ghetto, stoning

himself with marvelous, and I think semiconscious irony, for
the heresies of sensitivity, physical infirmity, and cultural
breadth in the presence of the father whose insensitivity, brutality, and intolerance Kafka praises as the virtues of a patriarch.
In the "Letter" we see in its most acute form what must
invariably take place within any cultural minority: the transi-
tional generation arrested, as Kafka says, "without forebears or
progeny," between the microcosm and the macrocosm. In
Kafka's case, because he was both a neurotic and an artist, we
see him draining his genius white to justify his father's ways to
himself, at the mercy of repressed infantile fantasies in which
the father must be conciliated at all costs. The family situation
which we can infer from Kafka's writings is typical of Jewish
culture in its struggle to survive. The patriarch dies a hard death,
adapting himself to the urban wilderness by shedding his
Yahwistic dignity in favor of a religious concern for business.
And the matriarch, whose only weapon against the hostile, un-
Jewish environment, against perhaps the now predatory father,
is tenderness and submission, teaches these questionable virtues
to her overprotected, breast-loving children. Kafka himself
describes it:

> Mother unconsciously played the part of a beater during a
> hunt. Even if your method of upbringing might in some un-
> likely case have set me on my own feet by means of producing
> defiance, dislike, or even hate in me, Mother cancelled that out
> again by kindness . . . and I was again driven back into your
> orbit . . . one could always get protection from her, but only in
> relation to you.[4]

In *Seize the Day* when his father forgets the date of his wife's
death, Tommy Wilhelm, who has asked the question disingenu-
ously, thinks, bitterly, "what year was it! As though he didn't
know the year, the month, the day, the very hour of his mother's
death."[5]

Kafka wrote to his father about his father's Judaism:

> Later, as a boy, I could not understand how with the insignifi-
> cant scrap of Judaism you yourself possessed, you could re-
> proach me for not (if for no more than the sake of piety, as
> you put it) making an effort to cling to a similar insignificant
> scrap. . . . And so there was the religious material that was
> handed on to me, to which may be added at most the out-

stretched hand pointing to "the sons of the millionaire Fuchs," who were in the synagogue with their father at the high holidays.[6]

Tommy Wilhelm

often prayed in his own manner. He did not go to the synagogue but he would occasionally perform certain devotions, according to his feelings. Now he reflected, In Dad's eyes I am the wrong kind of Jew. He doesn't like the way I act. Only he is the right kind of Jew.[7]

Kafka describes to his father the answer he gave him when the son asked his father for sexual advice:

It is not easy to judge the answer you gave me then; on the one hand, there was after all, something staggeringly frank, in a manner of speaking, primeval about it. . . . But its real meaning, which sank into my mind even then, but only much later came partly to the surface of my consciousness, was this: what you were advising me to do was, after all, in your opinion at that time, the filthiest thing possible. . . . The main thing was . . . that you remained outside your own advice, a married man, a pure man, exalted above these things.[8]

Similarly when Wilhelm asks his father for advice, the old man's impulse is to degrade the son in his own eyes. One of Wilhelm's numerous failures was in his job as a salesman. Dr. Adler asks him why he left the job:

"Since you have to talk and can't let it alone, tell the truth. Was there a scandal—a woman?"
Wilhelm fiercely defended himself. "No, Dad, there wasn't any woman. I told you how it was."
"Maybe it was a man, then," the old man said wickedly.[9]

Kafka's father reproached his children, Kafka wrote,

for living in peace and quiet, warmth and abundance, lacking for nothing, thanks to your hard work. I think here of remarks that must positively have worn grooves in my brain, like: "When I was only seven I had to push the barrow from village to village."[10]

Wilhelm's father angrily tells his son why he is a success:

"Yes. Because of hard work. I was not self-indulgent, not lazy. My old man sold dry goods in Williamsburg. We were nothing, do you understand? I knew I couldn't waste my chances."[11]

These are parallels only between Kafka's autobiographical letter and *Seize the Day*, and they exhibit a cultural frame of reference, dramatically abnormalized, within which one can consider the work of either writer. But when we turn to comparisons between *Seize the Day* and Kafka's fiction we are aware of only a pivotal connection—the mutilated relationship between sons and fathers. Kafka's gray Petrouchka-like protagonist and his two-dimensional, expressionistic backgrounds expand into the extremely dimensionalized Tommy Wilhelm and his crowded hour on upper Broadway. But the psychic conflict is identical, and the outcome, while it would not be one Kafka would have chosen, is at least Kafkan.

The desolation of Tommy Wilhelm is a very carefully determined event whose determinants are only explainable in psychoanalytic terms, and whose aesthetic achievement is valid only if we accept the somewhat invidious precondition for enjoyment Freud proposes. In Kafka the neurotic is in the artist, not in the work. The work itself is delivered over, in a manner of speaking, to the controlled insanity of Kafka's world; the interpretive potential is manifold. In *Seize the Day* the neurotic is in the work—and the interpretive potential is singular, a matter of reconciling the events in the novel to the character of Tommy Wilhelm, of explaining the manifest in terms of the repressed.

The day Saul Bellow seizes on which to describe Tommy Wilhelm is the day of one of Wilhelm's many undoings, distinguished from the rest only by the lyric and poetically desirable revelation purchased at the price of everything he owns.

On the day in question Wilhelm has been refused money and love by his father; his wife badgers him for more money; the bogus psychologist Dr. Tamkin has power of attorney over Wilhelm's remaining funds, which have presumably been invested in lard and rye futures. The lard and rye fall; Wilhelm is wiped out, and Tamkin disappears. Wilhelm's reaction to these misadventures is best described as despair; tempered at the very outset by resignation, neurotic fatalism:

> But at the same time, since there were depths in Wilhelm not unsuspected by himself, he received a suggestion from some remote element in his thoughts that the business of life, the real

business—to carry his peculiar burden, to feel shame and impotence, to taste these quelled tears—the only important business,
the highest business, was being done. Maybe the making of
mistakes expressed the very purpose of his life and the essence
of his being here. Maybe he was supposed to make them and
suffer from them and suffer from them on this earth. . . .

How had this happened, but how had his Hollywood career begun? It was not because of Maurice Venice, who turned
out to be a pimp. It was because Wilhelm himself was ripe for
the mistake. His marriage too had been like that. Through such
decisions somehow his life had taken form. And so, for the
moment when he tasted the peculiar flavor of fatality in Dr.
Tamkin, he could no longer keep back the money.[12]

The broadest psychoanalytic category within which Tommy
Wilhelm operates is that of the moral masochist, the victim,
for whom suffering is a *modus vivendi,* a means of self-justification. This aspect of Tommy Wilhelm is the most explicitly
realized level of his character. But it deserves closer study as
the basis for other, more subtle elements in the novel. The
person to whom Wilhelm is masochistically attached is, of
course, his father, Dr. Adler, before whom he exhibits his helplessness. And it is equally apparent, even to Wilhelm, that, with
individual differences, the other figures on whose mercy he
throws himself, are in a declining series, fathers—Maurice
Venice, the Rojax Corporation, Tamkin, Mr. Perls, and Mr.
Rappaport. He even appreciates the masochistic commitment,
when, in considering old Rappaport's devotion to Theodore
Roosevelt, he thinks: "Ah, what people are! He is almost not
with us, and his life is nearly gone, but T. R. once yelled at him,
so he loves him. I guess it is love, too."[13]

What determined Wilhelm's fixation on this all-powerful
father in the past is supplied in the novel to the extent that we
can reconstruct his childhood—the love and protection of his
mother and the stern, sadistic disciplinarianism of his father—
followed by his mother's death at the moment of his first failure
in Hollywood. The death of one parent, in fact, any intimate
bereavement, induces a retreat from adult effectiveness toward
dependence, and a heightened dependence on the surviving
parent. Dr. Adler was pressed, willy nilly, into service as the
mother in addition to his role as the father. But Dr. Adler's

tyrannical, uncompromising character has anticipated what might in Wilhelm's life have been a momentary lapse from effectiveness into fixed regressive patterns, has rendered his son incapable of independence. In this sense, a psychoanalytic irony enters into the description of the relationship between father and son, in that the doctor's forthright disgust with his son's weaknesses is a disgust with a situation of which he himself is the author. There is more truth than Dr. Adler is aware of in his "What a Wilky he had given to the world!" But, we can reasonably argue, Wilhelm is not always unsuccessful. He has assumed adult responsibilities over twenty years of his life, and until the ultimate day of his latest failure, he has not invoked his father's help. However, we must consider that as a neurotic personality, Wilhelm is not completely *hors de combat*; he is crippled, not dead, and his ego, besieged from without and betrayed from within, is still in command. He knows a hawk from a handsaw.

What the day of the novel exhibits is the phenomenon known as traumatophilia. The neurotic calendar is crowded with grotesque anniversaries, the observance of which offer a certain relief to the mechanism of repression, worn out in the service of the ego. The consciousness must be allowed from time to time to participate in the unconscious strivings of the individual, as Ferenczi suggests, to "equalize" the effects of the original painful experience throughout the psyche. It is the return of the repressed. In Wilhelm it is the masochistic necessity to fail, to be destroyed at the hands of the punishing father, in order, under the terms of the moral masochistic commitment, to retain his love, and, in less obvious ways, to memorialize certain events in the past.

What might save Wilhelm from a complete debacle on this particular day would be his insistence that Tamkin withdraw from the market before the lard and rye drop. Tamkin agrees reluctantly to pull out, but Wilhelm then allows his money to ride. Certain fatalities intervene and paralyze his will. The first and most apparent is his father's cold, overt hostility, and the passionate review of the past that has taken place in Wilhelm's mind in the morning. A second recollection involves Wilhelm's distress that his mother's grave has been vandalized, and that his father cannot remember the date of her death. With this renewed grief over his mother's death Wilhelm's old dependence returns, displaced now to his dependence on Tamkin. "Poor Mother! How I disappointed her," he thinks, as he comes down for breakfast. And his next act unconsciously reveals the renewal of his own bereavement. He returns, as Otto Fenichel suggests that bereaved people return, to an oral phase of his development.[14] Wilhelm must suckle. "He turned to the Coca-Cola machine. He swallowed hard at the Coke bottle and coughed over it, but he ignored his coughing, for he was still thinking, his eyes upcast and his lips closed behind his hand."[15] It is a caricatured representation of the nursing child.

An external contribution to the significance of the day appears in the form of an actual anniversary. The month is late September, and it is, as old Rappaport reminds Wilhelm, the eve of *Yom Kippur*, the Jewish holiday immediately following the Jewish New Year. *Yom Kippur* is the Day of Atonement for the Jews, when one makes formal acknowledgment of one's sins. *Yiskor*, which falls on *Yom Kippur*, is the service at which one remembers and prays for the dead. "Well, you better hurry up if you expect to say *Yiskor* for your parents," old Rappaport tells Wilhelm.[16] And Wilhelm remembers his mother's burial, and his father's indifference, and his having paid for having prayers sung for her. A moment later he allows Tamkin to let their combined investment ride to its loss.

I propose now to deal with Wilhelm's moral masochism, its causes and symptoms and contributions to his traits of character. Freud's first concept of the masochistic personality—the moral masochist specifically, to differentiate him from the sexual masochist, for whom sexual perversion is the outward enacting of his drive—was based on an intrapersonal conflict. The original sadistic impulse directed at the parent, recoiled to become parentally derived superego which commanded certain self-sacrifices as the penalty for aggressive fantasies. Thus Freud conceived of Dostoyevsky's psychic epilepsy and gambling mania as a self-determined punishment for having willed the father's death. From this concept arises the accepted notion that self-degradation is simply the mirror image of hate. But though this concept falls short of explaining the dramatic conflict in Wilhelm's character, it requires co-ordination rather than replacement. Part of Wilhelm's character (his gambling almost immediately suggests itself) is explained, but the concept does not completely explain his relationship with his father, although, as we shall see, it makes finally a major contribution to the end of the novel.

Bernhard Berliner in his essay, "On Some Psychodynamics of Masochism,"[17] while accepting Freud's motivational basis for masochism (guilt, need for punishment) describes moral masochism, not as a pathological way of hating, but as a "pathological way of loving." It is not, as Freud described it, an intrapersonal problem, but one involving an interpersonal relationship. "In all cases the disturbance of the interpersonal relationship leads to and is maintained by a peculiar character formation. Masochism is a character neurosis."[18] The subject

> relives and re-enacts in interpersonal relations a submissive devotion to and need for love of a hating or rejecting love-object, . . . originally a parent or a preferred sibling or some other unfriendly person of his childhood, and who lives in his superego. It is the superego that keeps the original situation alive through transference to any suitable person or set of circumstances in later age.[19]

The history of masochists reveals accompanying the unhappiness of childhood an abnormal need for oral satisfaction. In contrast to the more normal adjustment to dislike (the giving up of the hating object), the person represses the hatred, and in adulthood submissively accepts the cruelty as love. "Simultaneously he represses any hostile reaction against the loved object because that also would cause its loss. . . . Masochism is the hate or sadism of the object reflected in the libido of the subject."[20] It is not, Berliner insists, an instinct, like love or sadism, but it is a "neurotic solution" to a "conflict between manifestations of those two instincts."

The moral masochist exhibits "the servility of the beaten dog," with the human awareness that suffering enhances one's own value. "Suffering has come to mean being worthy of love. This narcissistic position fails in reality in that one must continually work out the old trauma."[21]

The deeper underlying motivation of this unhappiness is the wish to please a hating parent, or to placate or ingratiate himself with the parent by being unhappy, by failing, or, in other cases, by being helpless or stupid. It is the wish to be loved by the parent who hates or depreciates.[22]

Guilt, in the moral masochist, is not a reaction to sadistic impulses on the child's part, but stems from the oral need for love from the punishing parent who has engendered the guilt; the masochist adopts the parent's view of himself as wrong and the parent as right. He "makes himself the whipping boy for the benefit of a sadistic parent. In adult proportion, any external reality or fate may take the form of this parent."[23]

If the moral masochist is aggressive, it is

an intensified bid for affection, in which the suffering gives him a claim for being loved, and, also for prestige and domination. . . . He welcomes being hurt, not because it makes him right above others. . . . Making someone sorry, by self-sabotage, is intended both to hurt the love-object and make it concerned for the subject.[24]

Unconsciously the masochist tries—unsuccessfully, because the love object is beyond "magic" control—to deny and libidinize the hatred and sadism of the love object by making aggressive demands on it, as if love and punishment were casually connected.[25]

The ultimate sacrifice of the moral masochist to the love object accounts for his greatest paradox, his perverse refusal to "please" the parent in any rational sense of the word. The masochist identifies himself with the hating love object. He turns against himself, not his own sadism but the sadism of the parent. His guilt becomes the guilt the hating parent should feel if his cruelties are unjust. Since the parent cannot be wrong, the child must then feel guilty for him. He must be the bad child who deserves such chastisement. Turned against the world, these perversely "good" actions can be criminal, a psychopathic flouting of the law:

To accommodate a hating person he may make himself as unlovable as he feels that parent wants him to be. He may deny his good qualities, or his intelligence, often to pseudoimbecility. . . . He is stigmatized with unwantedness and displays his stigma as his bid for affection.[26]

As a person the moral masochist has a weak ego, is dependent and love seeking, and forms, because of his oral fixation, strong transferences. Unlike the anal-sadistic, compulsive neurotic, who punishes himself for hating, the masochist wants only to gain love. As Berliner differentiates between them, "The compulsive neurotic is paying imaginary debts, not knowing what the real debt was: the masochist is presenting an old unpaid bill for affection."[27]

Using this as our point of departure let us re-enter the world of Tommy Wilhelm. On this day of days his whole personality has been given over to an exhibition of his neurotic symptoms. And the external world obliges by offering him a realistic basis for such an exhibition. Systematically and seriatim, the more-or-less loved objects from his present punish him—his father, his estranged wife, and Tamkin. Their betrayals evoke the memories of earlier betrayals and humiliations, finding their ultimate source in the original mistreatment by his father. To illustrate in a single example the relation between his masochistic submission to the father and the oral nature of the masochism I will take up one of the *leitmotifs* of Wilhelm's thoughts.

Thinking indignantly about his father's self-love, Wilhelm recalls from his college literature course the line from Shakespeare's sonnet 73—"love that well which thou must leave ere long":[28]

> At first he thought it referred to his father, but then he understood that it was for himself, rather. *He* should love that well. "This thou perceivest, which makes thy love more strong."

The memory of this line reminds him of the anthology (Lieder and Lovett's *British Poetry and Prose*) and with it another poem he loved—"Lycidas," the line he remembers being "Sunk though he be beneath the wat'ry floor."

Later in the course of the morning, when, arising from his argument with his father, he has decided that it is his "peculiar burden to feel shame and impotence," the lines from "Lycidas" again return, this time coupled with a line from Shelley's "Ode to the West Wind," "that dirge of the dying year." The line is "I fall upon the thorns of life! I bleed!"

And though he had raised himself above Mr. Perls and his father because they adored money, still they were called to act energetically and this was better than to yell and cry, pray and beg, poke and blunder and go by fits and starts and fall upon the thorns of life. And finally sink beneath that watery floor— would that be tough luck, or would it be good riddance?[29]

The fourth poem comes to Wilhelm when Tamkin reminds him that he was an actor. Wilhelm remembers a job he had as a film extra. He had to blow a bagpipe. He "blew and blew and not a sound came out. . . . He fell sick with the flu after that and still suffered sometimes from chest weakness."

Margaret nursed him.

> They had had two rooms of furniture which was later seized. She sat on the bed and read to him. . . .
>> Come then, Sorrow!
>> Sweetest Sorrow!
>> Like an own babe I nurse thee on my breast![30]
>
> Why did he remember that? Why?

Of the four fragments the line from the sonnet is the one Wilhelm most immediately apprehends. Throughout the day Wilhelm's thoughts about his father's age and imminent death undergo revealing vicissitudes. He excuses his father's self-love as the fear of death. He reproaches his father, at the same time, for ignoring the fact that he himself must also die. But his most moving thought is what his father's death will mean for him.

"When he dies, I'll be robbed, like. I'll have no more father."

> "Of course, of course, I love him. My father. My mother—" As he said this there was a great pull at the very center of his soul. When a fish strikes the line you feel the live force in your hand.[31]

His feelings about his father are in apposition to the sonnet in which the older man calls attention to his approaching death, not to arouse compassion, but to impress the younger man (presumably the sonnet is addressed to a young man) that he faces a great loss.

Even if we disallow the homoerotic nature of Shakespeare's sonnet and its bearing on Wilhelm's feeling about his father, we find, in the line from "Lycidas," an overdetermination of the homoerotic element, and in its combination with the line from Shelley's poem (the cruelty with which Shelley's father treated him, Shelley's doctrine of nonviolence, and his actual drowning reinforce the line of poetry) a willingness to be the sacrificial victim. Wilhelm has "fallen on the thorns of life," and the prospect of sinking beneath the ocean's watery floor is not such a distressing one. It is consistent with Wilhelm's masochistic character that the line has come to mean for him to return to the womb, the death instinct that is a component of masochism. Implicit, too, in the context of the novel, the lines suggest that achievement of superiority which is the bitter consolation of the victim, although Wilhelm makes an ironic distinction between his superiority to Mr. Perls and his father, and his abjection.

The fourth poem, the lullaby, and its autobiographical context, stands in relation to the first three as symptom stands to repressed aim. The sonnet names the object of Wilhelm's masochistic strivings; "Lycidas" and the "Ode to the West Wind" describe the wished for torment and oblivion, falling on the thorns and sinking. The lullaby and its context indicate the mental and physical character-components of the masochist.

The suckling dependence of the moral masochist is symbolically described here as well as the frustrations that accompany deprivation. Wilhelm's orality has expressed itself in character-formation in that he has been attracted to acting, speech being an acceptable oral survival. But his career as an actor was a failure, and the memory of Hollywood that returns to him returns him also to the roots of the failure. He is blowing a false bagpipe, "blew and blew, and not a sound came out." Bagpipe as breast and sound as milk are perfect correlatives. Wilhelm is "sucking a dry teat." He has lost his mother, who, because of his peculiar needs, epitomized the only generosity he can ever know. From his father, to whom he has attached himself, he can only draw the sour milk of sorrow, the masochistic substitute for real nourishment. His wife, Margaret, also figures here, nursing him as Wilhelm's immediate substitution for his mother, but along with his father equally unsatisfactory. Sorrow —"Like an own babe I nurse thee on my breast!"—is Wilhelm's baby. The thought of his mother drives him to the Coke machine; the ill-treatment of his father compels him to eat not only his own breakfast, but a large part of his father's. Denied any overt love on his father's part, Wilhelm works out a primitive solution; he eats from his father's plate:

> Wilhelm understood he was being put on notice and did not express his opinion. He ate and ate. He did not hurry but kept putting food on his plate until he had gone through the muffins and his father's strawberries and then some pieces of bacon that were left.[32]

Another element remains to be explained in connection with the last poem Wilhelm remembers. It is his "chest weakness" which has never left him, the sense of suffocation he feels at critical moments during the day, especially at those moments when either his father or his wife is either rejecting him or making demands on him. Both are situations which cause anxiety connected with oral fixation. The one, the father's refusal, involves a denial of nourishment, a traumatic weaning; the other, Margaret's own sadistic demands for money, is a projection of Wilhelm's own insistent need on to the woman. The flow is reversed; the woman drains the man. For the orally fixated man, orgastic discharge perverts the unconsciously infantile relationship between himself and the woman:

> Well, Dad, she hates me. I feel she's strangling me. I can't catch my breath. She just has fixed herself on me to kill me. She can do it at long distance. One of these days I'll be struck down by suffocation or apoplexy because of her. I just can't catch my breath.[33]

Throughout the day Wilhelm suffocates in the presence of his tormentors. But this is not so much a "chest weakness" as it is a conversion hysteria, Wilhelm's repressed ideas expressing themselves in physical symptoms. Respiratory disorders are frequently associated with acute anxieties, centering mainly, according to Otto Fenichel, around "the repressed idea of castration," and the "reaction to separation from the mother."[34] Wilhelm has reason to fear both; his sense of suffocation is induced by both. A further insight into the hysterical nature of his behavior is afforded by the correlation of his dramatic acting out of the strangulation; and the fantasy he has woven about Margaret:

"Strange, Father? I'll show you what she's like." Wilhelm took hold of his broad throat with brown-stained fingers and bitten nails and began to choke himself.[35]

(Note even in the "brown-stained fingers" and the "bitten nails," the additional stigmata of Wilhelm's oral frustrations.) Fenichel identifies "irrational emotional reactions" at anologues to hysterical attacks. They serve to "reactivate infantile types of object relationships" when some associatively connected experience occurs. They involve a hysterical introversion, a turning from reality to fantasy:

However, hysterical "acting" is not only "introversion" but is directed toward an audience. It is an attempt to induce others to participate in the daydreaming, probably to obtain some re-assurance against anxiety and guilt feelings (or to evoke punish-ment for the same reason). . . . It is an attempt to return from introversion to reality, a kind of travesty of the process under-lying artistic productivity.[36]

When Wilhelm turns from his father to find a kinder father, his choice of object is determined for him by the same orality that governs his relations with his father. But with this difference, that as a singular individual his biological father must frustrate any preconceived fantasy on Wilhelm's part as to what his father should be to him. Wilhelm's masochistic submission to Dr. Adler represents the extent of his compromise. This is not so when he is free to exercise his fantasy and find in the real world the father who suits him. Dr. Tamkin (and Bellow in-vests him with a comic-grotesque unreality) is the answer to Wilhelm's dreams, and I will limit my discussion of him at this point to his appearance in Wilhelm's fantasy life.

In his retreat to orality, Wilhelm returns to the infantile belief in the omnipotent parent, who grants in return for dog-like trust and acceptance, full protection and endless beneficence. Wilhelm describes himself when he describes his beloved dog Scissors to his father:

He's an Australian sheep dog. They usually have one blank or whitish eye which gives a misleading look, but they're the gen-tlest dogs and have unusual delicacy about eating or talking.[37]

Tamkin is magic; he reads Wilhelm's mind. He is what Fenichel calls a "magic helper," whose relationship with Wilhelm, Karl Abraham describes in these terms:

> Some people [oral sucking types] are dominated by the belief that there will always be some kind person—a representative of the mother, of course—to care for them and to give them everything they need. This optimistic belief condemns them to inactivity.[38]

As Wilhelm thinks about him, "That the doctor cared about him pleased him. This was what he craved, that someone should care about him, wish him well."[39]

I have considered so far those qualities in Tommy Wilhelm which represent him as a willing sacrifice to fate, and indeed this would seem to be the only side of Tommy Wilhelm to consider. His last appearance, all alone, beweeping his outcast state at the bier of a stranger, would seem to be his last and most satisfying submission to the austere, intractable father image which dominates his being.

But in allowing this as the basis for *Seize the Day* we are ignoring an important portion of the statement I had considered axiomatic to the enjoyment of psychological literature: that the struggle within the soul of the hero "must end, not with the downfall of the hero, but with that of one of the contending impulses, in other words, with a renunciation."

Tommy Wilhelm's downfall, at the end of the novel, is not a downfall in the acute singular sense of the word as in classical tragedy. In the timeless world of Wilhelm's psyche the downfall has been a *fait accompli* almost from the beginning. The failure in the stock market is its latest and most vivid instance. Likewise the act of renunciation, the outcome of an inner conflict between opposing impulses, has taken place before, and now finds its perfect expression and, on an emotive level, recognizes itself beside the old man's coffin:

> Oh, Father, what do I ask of you? What'll I do about the kids —Tommy, Paul? My children. And Olive? My dear! Why, why, why—you must protect me against that devil, who wants my life. If you want it, then kill me. Take, take it, take it from me. . . .
> The flowers and lights fused ecstatically in Wilhelm's blind, wet eyes; the heavy, sea-like music came up to his ears. It

poured into him where he had hidden himself in the center of the crowd by the great and happy oblivion of tears. He heard it, and sank deeper than sorrow, through torn sobs and cries toward the consummation of his heart's ultimate need.[40]

The symphonic orchestration of such an ending must presuppose something besides an unchecked drift toward submission. There must be a crisis, a conflict, symphonic in its nature. At one point, before this resolution has been achieved, the brasses must have risen up against the violins and been, not without a struggle, silenced.

I have dealt thus far with the character of Tommy Wilhelm at its furthest remove from effective, mature activity. In doing so I have isolated the level of regression descriptive of such abject helplessness, the position of the infant at its mother's breast. But there are no "pure" strains of orality past actual infancy, while Wilhelm is denied, perhaps permanently, any successful adult accomplishment—the masculine self-sufficiency and self-esteem, the ability to have good relationships and pursue realistic rather than fantastic schemes for survival—his helplessness is more the helplessness of a strong man caged than a weak man at liberty. To see him otherwise is to deny him his quality as a protagonist and to dismiss him as Freud dismisses the "full-blown and strange neurosis. . . . We call the physician and deem the person in question unsuitable as a stage figure."[41]

What I must deal with now are those traits of character and neurotic symptoms which belong, in psychoanalysis, to the oral and anal-sadistic types of regression. To this aspect of Wilhelm's personality such concepts as Freud's original theory of masochism are more germane. We will deal with tendencies in which, although it is repressed, aggressive hostility takes the place of submissive exhibitions of suffering. Every phase of a child's development has its erotic and aggressive subdivisions. At the mother's breast the mouth is the pleasurable organ and suckling the means to that pleasure. With its first teeth, and the experience of weaning, come the first feelings of deprivation and frustration. The so-called biting stage sets in, in which the infant displays ambivalent feelings toward objects, compounded of aggressions against them and a wish to eat them. The withheld breast becomes an enemy to be taken by force. The old complicities of mother and child become a battle between the hungry infant and the alien world. At the same time another source of pleasure and aggression supervene in the form of the anal period. The feces, the first objective products of the body, become a source of pleasure in their retention or elimination and, for the same reason, a source of power and aggression.

Because of the inauguration at a very early age of the discipline of bowel training and the overt disapproval of the infantile pleasure in fecal play, anal erotism is regularly repressed. In its place appear the aggressive qualities connected with bowel discipline—the "stool pedantry" Ferenczi describes. To these pregenital sources of pleasure and power, psychoanalysis attributes a whole system of orifice psychology. Good suckling and good weaning, good evacuation and good discipline are thought to constitute the basis for good work habits and good character traits in the mature human being. If, for a multiplicity of reasons, one or any of these stages is accompanied by a frustration or trauma, or if it offered a great deal of satisfaction, or if the stage following brought with it pain instead of pleasure, a fixation takes place. Anal-oral fixations survive in adult life as character traits and neurotic symptoms. But because the mouth can still retain its primacy as a pleasurable orifice—as in eating and speaking and kissing, these functions need not undergo repression to the same extent as the anal component of infantile sexuality.

Psychoanalysis has long observed the connection between the emphasis on the discipline of anal drives and the character of Western culture. William Menninger observes that "our own emphasis on production, value of time, material possessions, wealth and power, is evidence of what might be called an 'anal phase' of civilization."[42] From this observed connection psychoanalysis has been able to describe the variations in character and the neurotic behavior of the adult in terms of fixations and anxieties related to various stages of sexual development. Otto Fenichel describes the relationship: "The prevalence of anal character formation in modern times and the 'drive to become wealthy' present a particularly good field for the investigation of the relation between social influence and instinctual structure."[43]

Tommy Wilhelm's aggressions are more inhibited, necessarily, than his masochistic bids for love. As distorted as they are, his gestures of submission achieve a certain level of completion. His aggressions are literally choked off, turned aside, or rendered as opposites of themselves.

Dr. Adler lives in his tight, tidy, old man's world of money saved. He has gone into his old age retaining everything, "a fine old scientist, clean and immaculate."[44] His entire philosophy of life is costive, parsimonious. Love means expenditure, and he cannot give it. His anal-sadism reveals itself in his cruelty to Wilhelm; his coarse suggestion that perhaps it was not a woman who caused Wilhelm's failure in his job, but a man, and his repeated injunction to his son, "I want nobody on my back. Get off!" are graphic revelations of the doctor's own anal preoccupations. "Concentrate on real troubles—fatal sicknesses, accidents."[45]

Poor Wilhelm can only lumber after his father in an apelike distortion of the thrifty anal character. He has accepted the economic objectives of society but he recognizes them as a form of cruelty, intimately connected in his case with his father. He is incapable of accomplishing the socially acceptable anal traits, the thrift and industry and self-discipline that distinguish his father. He cannot "retain" money; his retentions, like so many of his other traits, are at an infantile level. His principal character trait is his messiness, his dirt, the barely acceptable substitute for feces:

> A faint grime was left by his fingers on the white of the egg after he had picked away the shell. Dr. Adler saw it with silent repugnance. . . . The doctor couldn't bear Wilky's dirty habits. Only once,—and never again, he swore—had he visited his room. Wilhelm, in pajamas and stockings had sat on his bed, drinking gin from a coffee mug and rooting for the Dodgers on television. . . . The smell of dirty clothes was outrageous.[46]

His playing the stock market is, like his gin rummy, a form of gambling, in which he contrives to lose. Freud, in his "Dostoievsky and Parricide," describes the act of gambling as a compulsive, repetitive act, in which the anal-sadistic hostilities toward a parent are displaced to the gaming table. To make a "killing" at the table (or in the market) is to kill a hated object.

But Wilhelm's aggressions are characterized by their abortive quality. He commits, instead, financial suicide:[47]

> For the last few weeks Wilhelm had played gin almost nightly, but yesterday he had felt that he couldn't afford to lose any more. He had never won. Not once.[48]

His pockets are full of "little packets of pills, and crushed cigarette butts and strings of cellophane," and pennies. His hatred of "the world's business" represents merely a diversion from aggressions directed against his father, for whom a large income is the mark of success. "Holy money! Beautiful money! It was getting so that people were feeble-minded about everything except money. While if you didn't have it you were a dummy, a dummy!"[49] Wilhelm's speech patterns are interesting as they reveal his oral-anal sadism. He is given to violent, explosive, scatological utterances, in which anal function has been displaced upward. "In certain neurotics," writes Karl Abraham, "speaking is used to express the entire range of instinctual trends . . . every kind of bodily evacuation, including fertilization."[50]

> Too much of the world's business done. Too much falsity. He had various words to express the effect this had on him. Chicken! Unclean! Congestion! he exclaimed in his heart. Rat race! Phony! Murder! Play the game! Buggers![51]

But Wilhelm exhibits even more pronounced symptoms of repressed hostility, which translate themselves into tics, involuntary physical gestures, which reveal in an abstract movement of the body a repressed impulse. Rage or sexual excitement or grief are represented by a gesture. They are, says Fenichel, "an archaic means of communication."[52]

> But Dr. Adler was thinking, why the devil can't he stand still when we're talking? He's either hoisting his pants up and down by the pockets or jittering with his feet. A regular mountain of tics he's getting to be. . . . Unaware of anything odd in his doing it, for he did it all the time, Wilhelm had pinched out the coal of his cigarette and dropped the butt in his pocket, where there were many more. And as he gazed at his father the little finger of his right hand began to twitch and tremble.[53]

Wilhelm also stammers, a "slight thickness in his speech," especially when he speaks to his father. In this too he reveals his concealed hostilities, the death wish. Stuttering is

exacerbated in the presence of prominent or authoritative persons, that is, of paternal figures against whom the hostility is
most intense. . . . Speaking means the uttering of obscene,
especially anal words, and, second, an aggressive act directed
against the listener.[54]

The most direct form of aggression on Wilhelm's part ap
pears as its opposite, as a reaction formation to Wilhelm's death
wish. It appears as Wilhelm's fear of giving pain and his preoccupation with his father's death. He remembers explaining to
his mother why he does not want to study medicine. "I can't
bear hospitals," he tells her. "Besides, I might make a mistake
and hurt someone or even kill a patient. I couldn't stand that."[55]
He is obsessed with the thought that all his father thinks about
is his own death:

> And not only is death on his mind but through money he forces
> me to think about it, too. It gives him power over me. He
> forces me that way, he himself, and then he's sore. If he was
> poor, I could care for him and show it. The way I *could* care,
> too, if I only had a chance. He'd see how much love and re-
> spect I had in me. It would make him a different man too.
> He'd put his hands on me and give me his blessing.[56]

"When he dies," Wilhelm tells Tamkin, "I'll be robbed, like.
I'll have no more father."

It is out of these elements, which we have considered as
being to the highest degree ambivalent expressions of love and
hate—a wish to preserve, a wish for an omnipotent father and
a paranoid fear of an omnipotent father—that we can construct
the unconscious process by which Wilhelm comes to his act of
renunciation.

When Wilhelm looks at the dead man he sees what his soul
has wanted to see all during the terrible day; he sees his father
dead. He sees, too, his own death, mirrored in the face of the
gray-haired, "proper" looking, but not aged man before him. It
is here that the renunciation proper to the psychological drama
takes place. Wilhelm gives up his death wish against the father
and accepts, but without the masochistic insistence that characterized his earlier courtship of paternal cruelty, his own role
as victim.

A few minutes before this he has been standing over the

body of his father stretched out on a table in the massage room of the hotel, "the thighs weak, the muscles of the arms had fallen, his throat creased." He makes a last plea to his father for help, which will include not only money, but understanding. The father, as impatient with his suffering as he is with his dependence, sends him away with an old man's curse:

> "Go away from me now. It's torture for me to look at you, you slob!" cried Dr. Adler. Wilhelm's blood rose up madly, in anger equal to his father's, but then it sank down and left him helplessly captive to misery.[57]

The dead man in his coffin is the symbolic fulfillment of two alternatives—the wish to destroy the hated father and the wish to be destroyed. In giving up his death wish Wilhelm passes through what amounts to a phylogenetic process by which he is reconciled to his living father. The theme of *Totem and Taboo* is recapitulated here and extended beyond the suggestion that the only good fathers are dead fathers. Karl Abraham writes:

> The results of psychoanalysis justify us in coming to the conclusion that it is only when he thinks of him as a dead person, or wishes him to be so, that the son elevates his father to the level of a sun-god. These death phantasies give expression to impulses of hate, hostility and jealousy on the part of the son. They rob the father of his power so that he is in reality helpless and harmless. An omniscient power is then subsequently granted him as a compensation.[58]

But Wilhelm goes beyond this cycle of death and apotheosis. He has accepted Tamkin's existentialism; he no longer wishes for his father's death, can give up his helpless hatred, and with it, his equally hopeless love for this degraded, fragmented man of money.

The broadest cultural implications of *Seize the Day* involve the father's representing symbolically the sadistic, profit-seeking culture, and the son's willingness to be destroyed by it rather than share its heartless infamy, or fight against it.

That this cathartic experience will mark a new beginning for Wilhelm in a fatherless world would be a vain, Dickensian assumption. When we return *Seize the Day* to its coherences as art, its momentary solution is what must satisfy us. That moment of rest, like that moment in Joyce's *Ulysses* when Bloom and Stephen almost recognize their relationship, in which Tommy Wilhelm sees the futilities of his love-hate relationship with his father, is perhaps to be followed by the imperative *da capo* of his neurotic servitude.

Dr. Tamkin, the psychologist, is a problem.

He is a palpable fraud; the realistic hyperbole that envelops him is hazardous to the realism of the novel. He abuses Wilhelm's confidence and loses his money for him, and yet he is wise, accurate psychologically, and responsible for Wilhelm's final enlightenment. He discusses the "guilt-aggression cycle,"[59] as if he had been reading Menninger's essay on character derivatives from the anal phase. He is aware of the relationship between counting as a sadistic activity and killing. He explains the market to Wilhelm in these terms.[60] "You have an obsessed look on your face,"[61] he tells Wilhelm, who could easily have an obsessed look on his face, having immediately before been thinking about his father's death. "You have lots of guilt in you."

A transference appears to have been effected. Tamkin has been "treating" Wilhelm "secretly," and Wilhelm has responded to this paternal benevolence by finding himself able to remember his past with more clarity than ever before, "the poems he used to read."[62] More significantly the sadistic homosexual phrase his father had used has shifted to Wilhelm's dependence on Tamkin:

> And Wilhelm realized that he was on Tamkin's back. It made him feel that he had virtually left the ground [a dream symbol for erection] and was riding upon the other man. He was in the air. It was for Tamkin to take the steps.[63]

And Tamkin's advice is irreproachable; it enters the fabric of Wilhelm's mind as his vision of the authentic life. About his marriage Tamkin says:

> "Why do you let her make you suffer so? It defeats the original object in leaving her. Don't play her game. Now, Wilhelm, I'm trying to do you some good. I want to tell you, don't marry suffering. Some people do. They get married to it, and sleep and eat together, just as husband and wife. If they go with joy, they think it's adultery."[64]

"This time," thinks Wilhelm, "the faker knows what he's talking about."

> "The real universe. That's the present moment. The past is no good to us. The future is full of anxiety. Only the present is real —the here and now. Seize the day."[65]

I can only speculate on Tamkin's formal function in the novel, and my speculation leads me invariably beyond the bounds of the novel itself. I conceive of literary psychoanalysis as a truncated form of psychoanalysis. One does not willingly knock on the door of the artist's life. But I can see in the character of Tamkin—beyond of course his simpler level of function in *Seize the Day*—only an ironic portrait of a psychoanalyst and his patient, even to the fact that the patient gives all that he has in order to discover the unprofitable truth about himself. There is much to be said, if we accept this supposition, for the representation of the psychoanalyst as a figure of fun, whom even the patient can think of as being part faker. He combines areas of experience which have hitherto been combined only in comedy —the excremental with the spiritual (Freud's *ecclesia super cloacam*), the facts of life with the fantasies of love—his solemn and costly considerations of the trivial have added to the repertory of *The New Yorker* and *Punch* cartoonist what law and medicine added to the art of Hogarth and Daumier. But whatever Tamkin's extraordinary functions in *Seize the Day* may be, I cannot object to his presence. He is an accessory to the understanding of the novel.

Notes

1. Saul Bellow, *Seize the Day* (New York, 1956), Viking.
2. Otto Fenichel, *The Psychoanalytic Theory of Neurosis* (New York, 1945), p. 9.
3. Sigmund Freud, "Psychopathic Characters on the Stage," *The Psychoanalytic Quarterly*, XI (2, 1942), p. 462.
4. Franz Kafka, "Letter to His Father," *Dearest Father*, tr. Ernst Kaiser (New York, 1954), p. 163.
5. *Seize the Day*, p. 27.
6. Kafka, p. 173.
7. *Seize the Day*, p. 87.
8. Kafka, p. 186.
9. *Seize the Day*, p. 51.

10. Kafka, p. 158.
11. *Seize the Day*, p. 50.
12. *Ibid.*, p. 58.
13. *Ibid.*, p. 103.
14. Fenichel, *op. cit.*, p. 94.
15. *Seize the Day*, p. 15.
16. *Ibid.*, p. 86.
17. Bernhard Berliner, "On Some Psychodynamics of Masochism," *Psychoanalytic Quarterly*, XVI (4, 1947), pp. 459-471 *passim*.
18. *Ibid.*, p. 460.
19. *Ibid.*, p. 461.
20. *Ibid.*, p. 462.
21. *Ibid.*, p. 463.
22. *Ibid.*, p. 461.
23. *Ibid.*, p. 464.
24. *Ibid.*, p. 466.
25. *Ibid.*, p. 467.
26. *Ibid.*, p. 468.
27. *Ibid.*, pp. 470, 471.
28. *Seize the Day*, p. 12.
29. *Ibid.*, p. 56.
30. *Ibid.*, p. 89.
31. *Ibid.*, p. 92.
32. *Ibid.*, p. 42.
33. *Ibid.*, p. 48.
34. Fenichel, *op. cit.*, p. 250.
35. *Seize the Day*, p. 48.
36. Fenichel, *op. cit.*, p. 528.
37. *Seize the Day*, p. 48.
38. Karl Abraham, "Oral Erotism and Character," *Selected Papers on Psychoanalysis*, tr. Douglas Bryan (New York, 1954), p. 400.
39. *Seize the Day*, p. 73.
40. *Ibid.*, p. 118.
41. Freud, *op. cit.*, p. 464.
42. William C. Menninger, "Characterological and Symptomatic Expressions Related to the Anal Phase of Psychosexual Development," *The Psychoanalytic Quarterly*, XII (2, 1943), pp. 161-192 *passim*.
43. Fenichel, *op. cit.*, p. 487.
44. *Seize the Day*, p. 12.
45. *Ibid.*, p. 55.
46. *Ibid.*, p. 36.
47. Sigmund Freud, "Dostoievsky and Parricide," *Collected Papers*, tr. Joan Riviere (London, 1950), V, 222-242 *passim*.
48. *Seize the Day*, p. 7.
49. *Ibid.*, p. 36.
50. Abraham, *op. cit.*, p. 400.
51. *Seize the Day*, p. 17.
52. Fenichel, *op. cit.*, p. 317.
53. *Seize the Day*, p. 28.
54. Fenichel, *op. cit.*, pp. 312, 313, 316.
55. *Seize the Day*, p. 16.
56. *Ibid.*, p. 57.

57. *Ibid.*, p. 110.
58. Abraham, "Transformations of Scoptophilia," *Selected Papers on Psychoanalysis*, p. 232.
59. *Seize the Day*, p. 64.
60. *Ibid.*, p. 69.
61. *Ibid.*, p. 57.
62. *Ibid.*, p. 12.
63. *Ibid.*, p. 96.
64. *Ibid.*, p. 98.
65. *Ibid.*, p. 66.

9·SEVEN IMAGES

BELLOW IS more interested in "metaphysical" questions than in mere craftsmanship, but he realizes that he can most effectively communicate his concerns through images. These images are not odd or forced. They are "natural"; they provide the "scene" in which his characters live. They make us experience the pains of existence. Although the following discussion is "schematic" or "abstract," I do not mean to suggest that the images are simply manipulated. Bellow *feels* them as do his characters.

I. WEIGHT

Bellow often uses images of weight to express those "pressures" of existence which disturb his heroes.[1] In *Dangling Man* Iva "supports" Joseph, hoping that she can make life more tolerable for him. But her attempt is futile. Life continues to be a "loathsome burden." This burden is often a kind of "weariness of life"—as Goethe says.

The physical environment is a burden for most of the novel. Winds "buffet" Joseph on his daily walks. He sees the battered chicken on his mother-in-law's sink, and the "raveled" entrails are a dark reminder of his own. He looks outside at the Christmas preparations: "immense wreaths were mounted on buildings in the green, menacing air. . . ." Bodies are burdens. Minna's body is "pinched" by Abt when he hypnotizes her; her eyes "flinch" under her lids. Joseph beats Etta after she annoys him —she yields with shrieks to his repeated slaps. The spanking resembles his own childhood haircut that he remembers—that

142

haircut "hurt" his curls. And his grandfather is part of the memory—his head "hangs over his grandson," threatening him, weighing him down. A later incident is also remembered: the drops of blood on a quarreling drunkard's face, drops "falling from his head like the first slow drops of a heavy rain in summer. . . ." The present burdens of nature then reassert themselves: fog "hovers" over Joseph; the street lamp "bent over the curb like a woman who cannot turn homeward until she has found the ring or the coin she dropped in the ice and gutter silt." Each person—each new day—is "dark, burdensome." Perhaps the most impressive, "sustained" imagery of weight is in this passage:

> To many in the fascinated crowd the figure of the man on the ground must have been what it was to me—a prevision. Without warning, *down*. A stone, a girder, a bullet flashes against the head, the bone gives *like glass* from a cheap kiln; or a subtler enemy escapes the *bonds of years*, the *blackness comes down; we lie, a great weight on our faces, straining toward the last breath which comes like the gritting of gravel under a heavy tread.* (my italics)

The Victim is also full of burdens, pressures, weights. Even the epigraph contains them: the Ifrits's son is slain by stones (from dates) thrown at him. Elena "pressures" Asa into coming to Staten Island. The muggy air presses continually down upon him.

These various pressures—of the body, mind, and atmosphere —are found throughout Asa's adventures, not merely in the first two chapters. Here are some more. Allbee appears and threatens him, "crowding" him on the park bench. After his initial appearance, the clouds are "heavily suspended and slow." Under them Asa remembers his burden as a Jew at a party, then in Rudiger's office—no place is free. Although Asa does "not look as burdened as he [feels]," he must carry his cross.[2] On the ferry he thinks of the laborers in the engine room working the huge thing: "each turn must be like a repeated strain on the hearts and ribs of the wipers there near the keel." In Elena's rooms he sees "hovering" flies, menacing dishes. Her mother, with "the severity of her head pressed back on her shoulders," threatens him. Asa philosophizes about these various pressures: "Oh, there was a smashup somewhere, certainly, a smashup and a tragic one. . . . Something crushing, a real smash." Later "his high, thick chest [feels] intolerably bound and compressed, and he [lifts] his shoulders in an effort to ease his breathing." But what's the use? He continues to be crushed—like Mary's letter in his hand.

The images are dense in the latter half of the novel. Asa goes to the park and finds there an "overwhelming human closeness and thickness"—millions seem to touch him. Allbee strengthens this feeling when he tells his victim that ". . . the world's a crowded place . . ." even the dead "get buried in layers . . ." His very presence is a "great tiring weight." Asa is "mauled" as children—like Philip or Mickey—are mauled. Perhaps the heaviest weight is found here: "He had the strange feeling that there was not a single part of him on which the whole world did not press with full weight, on his body, on his soul, pushing upward in his breast and downward in his bowels."

Of course, *The Adventures of Augie March* are "lighter" than those of Asa and Joseph because the hero is a *luftmensch* —a man of air. But still there are burdens. Despite the fact that Augie immediately informs us about his "free" style, he does come from Chicago, "that somber city" of crowds, pressure-winds. Can he be less heavy than the physical atmosphere?

Augie is perhaps more interested in the burdens of history —as are Joseph and Asa, who constantly think of the family weighing them down—than the physical environment. He must breathe while other eras—previous greatness—lie on him. Thus we have an image which recurs throughout his adventures: Augie carries Einhorn:

> [I] got him on my back. He used to talk about himself as the Old Man of the Sea riding Sinbad. But there was Aeneas too, who carried his old dad Anchises in the burning of Troy . . .

As Augie carries Einhorn, Grandma Lausch carries the March family, and Simon later carries his relatives.

Everywhere people bear things. Augie is so much a part of his "dark, burdensome" environment that his language itself is loaded with things—lists of people or heavy objects or feelings. His epic catalogues are really "labored" enumerations: "gift robes and wrappers, venetian mirrors and chateaux-in-the-moonlight tapestries . . ."³ The people are often in "absolute abasement" to his language as, he tells us, the children were to Elisha's bear or the "cracked-down" Jew was to "divine blows."

We could multiply these images of weight. The bargain department under the sidewalk where Augie thinks people trample him; the "thickened and caked machine-halted silence" felt by Einhorn; the "machine materials that withstand steam, gases, and all inhuman pressure"; the "heavy nourishing air" which doesn't last—all these burden Augie, who screams out: How can I remove the mass of "uniform things?" His question is never answered.

Tommy Wilhelm, the "man of sorrows," tries to lighten his burden by "casting off" his real name—heredity itself. But he cannot do this, as he cannot really get rid of his own "thickness of speech." The "peculiar burden of his existence [lies] upon him like an accretion, a load, a hump. In any moment of quiet, when sheer fatigue prevented him from struggling, he was apt to feel this mysterious weight . . ." This mysterious weight produces "suffocation or apoplexy." Even Dr. Adler refuses to carry anyone—including his own son—on his back. Life is enough of a burden already. As Tommy realizes more dramatically: "they ride on me with hoofs and claws." Because he does see his burden eventually, he becomes Christlike. (His father talks about crosses, and the burdens are crosses). But even when he lightens his load in ecstatic crying, the tears convulse him, "bending his stubborn head."

On the first page Henderson has a "pressure in the chest," thinking of the facts of his disorderly life. His entire body is a "great weight." He believes that he can lighten his existential burdens by shifting them, by doing manual labor, but the voice within pressures him. As if "there were strangulation in [his] heart," he clutches the violin, trying to reach his dead father. The weights continue to lie on him.

He sees life in America as *junk*—like the "bottles, lamps, old butter dishes," etc., that he finds in the old woman's cottage. But even in Africa there is junk. The frogs—great, powerful, spotted—lie in the cistern. By blasting them out, Henderson can lift some of the burdens of the Arnewi tribe and his own. However, he destroys the cistern as well as the frogs. The Wariri ruler, Dahfu, lives in a dense atmosphere—witness the "volupté" of the Amazons which "presses" him and Henderson. The rituals themselves are supposed to free humanity from divine weight. That is why Henderson strains to lift Mummah, even though his body has been "loaded" with "vices, like a raft, a barge." He speaks to the idol. " 'Up you go, dearest, no use trying to make yourself heavier; if you weighed twice as much I'd lift you anyway.' " And he does. But he also meets the lion, to see if "man is a creature who cannot stand still under blows." Dahfu doesn't flinch under the lion's weight. Henderson does. Finally he learns to let go—and his own lion qualities come out after being inhibited for such a long time. When Dahfu hunts his father-lion, he must lie above the animal's cage. Suddenly he falls and the animal *stamps* him to death. Henderson realizes then that the pressures, burdens, and weights of life are never lifted.

II. DEFORMITY

Bellow often uses images of deformity or disease to express the painful mortality we bear. His employment of such images is "traditional": Oedipus, Samson, and St. Paul are blind. Bellow joins many ancient writers in asserting that the body itself —"shapeless," clumsy, or crippled—is less beautiful than the will or spirit. It is the necessary "weight" we carry. (For the purpose of this essay I have separated these two images but they are often united, as are all the images I discuss.)

Dangling Man presents the "deterioration" of Joseph. Living in a "narcotic dullness," he is sick like "coughing" Vanaker next door or his "unmanly" father-in-law—but his sickness is of the soul. Still, he sees universal physical deformity: Minna's hypnotized body; the "crooking" vein on Iva's temple; his own "crammed feeling" at his heart; his grandfather's "withered fist"; the street of his childhood where a cripple who taunted his brother and beggars "with sores and deformities" lived; the "cuttings and waste from the body"; the "Parisian cripple" renting out his hump; and Walter Farson's baby with a gag in her mouth. Two illnesses are stressed. Joseph sees a man fall in front of him—a heart attack—and he cannot resist gazing at his "swollen lips," his "helpless tongue." Mrs. Kiefer, the landlady, has a stroke that paralyzes her legs. Her illness dominates his thoughts for a good part of the novel. She drags Joseph along—as does the old woman with a scarred forehead who offers him religious pamphlets. (The latter's face "burns and wastes" under his eyes.) The total effect of these deformities is great: Joseph realizes that the body is crippled, imperfect; only the will can —and should—be strong. But he cannot fully regain his health.

The Victim begins on a note of sickness: Asa finds out that his nephew is bedridden. This illness is repeated throughout the novel. Thus Mr. Beard, Asa's boss, has a "face enlarged by baldness." Elena's eyes are "anxious, altogether too bright and too liquid"; there is a "superfluous energy in her movements . . ." Asa has "unreliable nerves," an occasional tremor. Allbee's "lower jaw slipped to one side, his glum, contemplative eyes filled with a green and leaden color." Asa remembers everyone years ago speaking of "brain fever"—this in reference to his mother's illness. Elena's mother resembles an "ugly old witch."

Why is there so much disease? Asa is preoccupied with disease because it signifies the "freakish" process of living, that process which singles out one disease from one person: "One child in thousands. How did they account for it? Did everyone have it dormant? Could it be hereditary? Or, on the other hand, was it even more strange that people, so different, did not have more individual diseases?" Such questions plague him. He sees disease as "metaphysical"—as do *The Magic Mountain, The Rack, Lady Chatterly's Lover,* and *The Idiot.* Perhaps Thomas Mann's remarks help to explain Asa's preoccupation:

> The truth is that life has never been able to do without the morbid, and probably no adage is more inane than the one which says that "only disease can come from the diseased." Life is not prudish, and it is probably safe to say that life prefers creative, genius-bestowing disease a thousand times over to prosaic health; prefers disease, surmounting obstacles proudly on horseback, boldly leaping from peak to peak, to lounging, pedestrian healthfulness. Life is not finical and never thinks of making a moral distinction between health and infirmity. It seizes the bold product of disease, consumes and digests it, and as soon as it is assimilated, it is health.[4]

Surrounded by disease, Asa is forced to seek "healthy" answers to existence—if any exist. Although he never achieves "prosaic health," to use Mann's phrase, he does learn to cope with life as disease and, paradoxically enough, becomes less diseased as a result: "The consciousness of an unremitting daily fight, though still present, was fainter and less troubling. His health was better, and there were changes in his appearance."

In 1949 Bellow published "A Sermon by Doctor Pep," which pursues the subject of disease.[5] The "doctor" leans on a crutch and speaks not of yogurt but of the linkage of disease and health. He suggests that we cannot separate them: "in health we are in the debt of a suffering creation." Although he has only one foot, he values his deformity; it has taught him to walk with a new step, to see life as it really is. He is better than the healthy ones dying of satiety; they keep death too near by "secret care." Pep and the crutch are married!

And the cripples multiply in *The Adventures of Augie March*. Augie lovingly depicts the various deformities of people he knows—he delights in his occult knowledge of disease. Unlike Joseph and Asa, he is not terrified; he remains full of pep.

Remember that we first see the March family discussing new glasses for Mama. Mama has few teeth left, large feet; Grandma Lausch is as "wrinkled as an old paper bag"; Georgie is an idiot with "stiff" feet; even the dog Winnie is "loud-breathing." Augie is somehow healthy, but he suffers from mental turmoil. Their friends are also deformed or diseased. Friedl Coblin has the "impediment of Moses whose hand the watching angel guided to the coal . . ." Anna Coblin "butchered on herself with pains and fears . . ."; she is likened to a martyr with a "mangled head." Coblin's eyes blink "just about to the point of caricature." Mama March gets sick; she lies "dumbly" in bed. Einhorn is a cripple whose hands function weakly; he resembles the deformed Hephaestus, who made "ingenious machines"— a god of "cranks, chains, and metal parts." The world itself becomes for Augie a place of "special disfigurement." Later he repeats this comment when he looks at the West Side station:

> It was very dark. It was spoiled, diseased, sore and running. And as the mis-minted and wrong-struck figures and faces stooped, shambled, strode, gazed, dreaded, surrendered, didn't care . . . you wondered that all was stuff that was born human and shaped human, and over the indiscriminateness and lack of choice.

No wonder that love itself is a "peculiarity."

Tommy Wilhelm also lives in a world of "freaks." When he greets Rubin, he notices the man's "poor" eyes. The other man gazes at him, making him self-conscious. Then Tommy looks at himself in the mirror, thinking that he is sick: "A wide wrinkle like a comprehensive bracket sign was written upon his forehead, the point between his brows, and there were patches of brown on his dark blond skin." He calls himself a "fair-haired hippopotamus!" Dr. Adler, on the other hand, takes good care of his body, but this, in itself, is a kind of sickness; as Tommy realizes, such "health" is diseased. Mr. Perls walks with a heavy cane; he has "dyed hair and fish teeth." Dr. Tamkin is deformed: "His bones were peculiarly formed as though twisted twice where the ordinary human was turned only once, and his shoulders rose in two pagoda-like points." His eyes are full of "strange lines." He thinks the world is a hospital—businessmen "spread the plague." Mr. Rappaport is blind; he has to be led across the street by Tommy. Like Augie March, our hero has a vision of *sick humanity*. In the subway tunnel he sees the "haste, heat, and darkness which disfigure and make freaks and fragments of nose and eyes and teeth . . ." Right here he loves the "lurid-looking people." Though he gets "all choked-up" later, he heals himself—that is, he sees his disease, and realizes there is no *cure*.

In *Henderson the Rain King* the underlying image becomes "exaggerated," until it is the basis of philosophical discussion. Again Bellow suggests the symbolic nature of disease; *"description" is idea*.

Like all of Bellow's heroes, Eugene Henderson is deformed. Just look at him: "At birth I weighed fourteen pounds, and it was a tough delivery. Then I grew up. Six feet four inches tall. Two hundred and thirty pounds. An enormous head, rugged, with hair like Persian lambs' fur." And a "great nose." He is somewhat "loony," smashing bottles, wallowing in mud. Everyone he knows suffers from disease or deformity. Lily wears a bridge—like Henderson; she is nearly six feet tall; and she has ugly dyed hair. (But she is "beautiful" for her husband.) The dead neighbor, Miss Lenox, has a "small, toothless face." In Africa Henderson learns the significance of disease. His "physical discrepancies" are discussed by Willatale and then by Dahfu. Willatale herself—toothless, the "flesh of her arm overlapping her elbow"—is not particularly beautiful. She appreciates the peculiarities of Henderson, finding in his physical appearance a great longing for spiritual elevation. When she agrees that he should study medicine—note how the doctor-figure reappears —he is happy, so happy that his gums itch. She *and* he know that happiness is always tinged with illness. *Humanity is never "healthy":*

> Oh, it's miserable to be human. You get such queer diseases. Just because you're human and for no other reason. Before you know it, as the years go by, you're just like other people you have seen, with all those peculiar human ailments.

Humanity is a "regular bargain basement of deformities."

Dahfu, a "medicine man," can help cure Henderson. His conversation circles about notions of health: Man is an artist; his principal work of art is the body. "Disease is a speech of the psyche." Because no one is ever completely free—"divine"—he is always sick, developing bodily symptoms. It seems that Dahfu has read Thomas Mann, Nietzsche, and Dostoyevsky as well as Wilhelm Reich.

Does Henderson ever become healthy? No, if we mean that he is free of the "body-speech" of the psyche. He continues to endure his pain. Occasionally he feels well—cured for an instant—as in the end of the novel. The following passage sums up the significance of disease in all of Bellow's novels; it suggests that disease is the spirit talking poorly, health just the opposite.

> I told the kid, "Inhale. Your face is too white from your orphan's troubles. Breathe in this air, kid, and get a little color." I held him close to my chest. He didn't seem to be afraid that I would fall with him. While to me he was like medicine applied, and the air too; it also was a remedy.

Humanity should seek the *remedy* of love.

III. CANNIBALISM

One image which is less important than weight or deformity is cannibalism. Bellow associates cannibalism with our "diseased" condition; people *consume* each other as the germ consumes the body.

Dangling Man gives us the following examples: Joseph, in talking about his plight, says: "I am deteriorating, storing bitterness and spite which eat like acids at my endowment of generosity and good will." He is "fed up." When he goes to the Almstadts, he describes in details the consumed chicken, "its yellow claws rigid, its head bent as though to examine its entrails which raveled over the sopping drain board." He later describes his grandfather's head "devouring" him. History itself consumes us, joining our own cannibalistic feasts. So do our idealizations: they "consume us like parasites . . ."; yet we invite such parasites, "as if we were eager to be drained and eaten." Joseph, depleted by the parasites around and within him, remains "hungry," even after eating a large dinner, a whole package of caramels, and a bag of mints.

One way of regarding *The Victim* is seeing Allbee and Asa as parasite and host (or vice versa). Even before we recognize this hideous relationship, Bellow gives us references to food. Asa Leventhal is "hungry" after he visits Elena; his hunger is, in a way, an outward sign of psychological needs. He "satisfies" his hunger with a good meal; "his mood gradually improved." But something makes him feel empty again; he drinks the milk in the refrigerator. Asa is being consumed, but he doesn't know the cause. After Allbee begins to taunt him, we get vicious consumption: Asa thinks of "little burning worms that seemed to eat up rather than give light," he sees Allbee as a parasite; he begins to see that hideous things, "cannibalistic things," exist in the world. In a complete vision he sees humanity in terms of food—an egg: "We were . . . running as if in an egg race with the egg in a spoon. And sometimes we were fed up with the egg, sick of it . . ." He continues to be hungry—but unable to "swallow another bite."

The imagery of food—of starvation and parasitism—strongly asserts itself in Dr. Pep's sermon: Humanity "kills and devours"; death inhibits the bite, it poisons each mouthful . . ."; we "turn our appetite on ourselves." But Dr. Pep suggests that there is always hunger which must be satisfied. Even divine food is devoured: "Or turn your thoughts to eucharistic wine and wafers. 'You shall eat my body and drink my blood.'" Jesus and the hamburger are related; both are needed to satisfy our hunger

—we consume as we love. This "secret of health and eating," Dr. Pep tells us, is found in a Paschal lamb, a fish, the holy wafer. "Is there any real love short of eating?" Although the doctor realizes that our hunger—base, "other directed"—cannot be completely satisfied, he hopes that it forces us to eat more substantial food—divinity itself.

This mad sermon resembles an essay written by Bellow's close friend, Isaac Rosenfeld, on Jewish taboos. The essay, entitled "Adam and Eve on Delancey Street," stresses the symbolic nature of food. Here are some fascinating passages which throw some light on the doctor's concerns:

> The simple act of eating has become for us the Jews a complicated ceremonial, from the preparatory phases of ritual slaughter, through *milchigs* and *fleishigs*, kosher and *treif*, to benedictions and postprandial prayers. It is for such reasons, among others, that the Jewish religion enjoys the reputation of being one of the most worldly and immanent, one of the most closely connected with daily life. What Sacred Communion is to Catholics, the everyday mealtime is to Orthodox Jews.[6]

> There is great charm in a religion that can thus run coalesced along the two lines of sacred and secular without any apparent break; it avoids the usual dualism, the conflict in belief or realm against realm.[7]

Dr. Pep's advice also avoids the "usual dualism"; in fact, he is perhaps a healthier individual than the Jew who, according to Rosenfeld, represses his needs by submitting to food taboos.

Although Augie March doesn't preach any sermon about cannibalism, parasitism, or the true consumption of food, he is disgusted—and fascinated!—by the immense meals Anna Coblin prepares. Eating becomes a wholly monstrous activity, "self-centered," materialistic, and lacking any spiritual meaning. The Coblins—and most of Augie's friends and relatives—are cannibals; they devour people as they do their luxurious meals. They are "human barbecuers." In his discussion of the "axial lines of life," Augie mentions Osiris, the god torn apart by his followers. Osiris is an ideal because the "devoured" god is somehow regenerated. Is Augie?

Food is emphasized in *Seize the Day*. When Tommy decides to have Coca-Cola with his breakfast, Mr. Perls and Dr.

Adler are shocked. Eating is as unbalanced as his whole life. As
he devours himself with guilt, so he eats and eats: "He did not
hurry but kept putting food on his plate until he had gone
through the muffins and his father's strawberries." Tommy is
always hungry, more so than Asa. So is Dr. Tamkin, who even
manages to devour food after the stock fluctuations. Of course,
he is a parasite—he uses the word himself to describe the pretender soul: "Biologically, the pretender soul takes away the
energy of the true soul and makes it feeble, like a parasite." He
feeds upon Tommy; that is why our hero is always hungry. Later
Tommy refers to his environment as food, wanting to breathe,
once again, the "sugar of the pure morning." But he eats un-
satisfying Coca-Cola and pills.

Henderson, like Tommy, is "hungry" for some meaning;
his *I want! I want!* is an "infant's" cry for food. Wherever he
turns, he sees parasitism or cannibalism. He remembers the
octopus in the aquarium: "the creature seemed also to look at
me and press its soft head to the glass . . ." Does the creature
—a symbol of death?—want to eat him? In Africa the Arnewi
cows are "dying of thirst"; the frogs feed upon them by polluting
their water. Henderson is so conscious of food that he feels sorry
for the nursing infants who are taken away from their mothers'
breasts (the mothers, by showing them to him, disrupt their
meal). (Once, he remembers, he wanted to feed a baby seal, but
one of the beachcombers objected, saying that if he fed the seal
it would "encourage the creature to be a parasite on the beach.")
Is there any proper food in life?

Henderson learns that love can transform food. Dahfu
shows him that the lion will not devour him, although lions
hunger for flesh. But the lesson is forgotten after Dahfu is consumed by his false lion-father. Parasitism remains. So does Henderson's spiritual appetite.

IV. PRISON

The previous images suggest that life is dangerous, ugly, and
heavy. Thus Bellow's characters consider themselves imprisoned.

In *Dangling Man* Joseph is locked in his room, rarely leaving it. The boarding house, itself, is a prison for the inhabitants
—for him, Vanaker, and the landlady. The mental environment

is also a prison: Joseph tries to keep himself "intact," shut-up, so that his feelings will not overly upset him; Minna is rigid, entrapped by Morris' hypnosis. People in general, Joseph says, are no longer impenetrable—they are always "invaded." Even if they want to remain alone in their "mental rooms," they cannot: someone knocks. The "craters of the spirit" are visible. (Does the emphasis on craters link our hero to the biblical Joseph who finds himself in several pits?) People constitute an "empire of ice boxes."

Three extended descriptions reveal the underlying claustrophobia of the novel. At one point we learn this from Joseph:

> I, in this room, separate, alienated, distrustful, find in my purpose not an open world, but a closed, hopeless jail. My perspectives end in the walls. Nothing of the future comes to me. Only the past, in its shabbiness and innocence. Some men seem to know exactly where their opportunities lie; they break prisons and cross whole Siberias to pursue them. One room holds me.

When he visits his childhood room, he discovers that this "great good place"—to use Henry James' phrase—is also a kind of prison from which he never escapes. "Home" does not really exist—only an ambiguous prison.

> The room, delusively, dwindled and became a tiny square, swiftly drawn back, myself and all the objects in it growing smaller. This was not a mere visual trick. I understood it to be a revelation of the ephemeral agreements by which we live and pace ourselves.

The third passage occurs in one of his many nightmares: Joseph finds himself in a "low chamber" with rows of large cribs in which corpses are lying. The corpses look "remarkably infantile." He likens the long room to the rooms in the Industrial Museum —to the terrors of Gehenna his father once conjured for him. The nightmare not only presents the "tomb" of his present existence—it suggests that Joseph is in Hell. There is "no exit" for him.

Tombs, prisons, rigid confinement—all these reappear in *The Victim*.

We first see Asa trying to leave the subway car; he barely squeezes through the "black door of the ancient car," uttering curses as he does. But he will not gain freedom—his own mind is a "box" which holds ambivalent attitudes. He continually sees prison around him—he imagines the men locked in the engine room abroad the ferry, their naked, oily bodies; he feels the press of crowds in the park; and the closeness of his own apartment (he leaves "the doors in the flat standing open; it made him feel easier.") This claustrophobia becomes "metaphysical": "You couldn't find a place in your feelings for everyone or give at every touch like a swinging door the same for everyone with people going in and out as they pleased. On the other hand, if you shut yourself up, not wanting to be bothered, then you were like a bear in a winter hole . . ." Life offers a swinging door or a locked room, but both choices are deceptive. The images continue: the "cashier's dazzling cage" in the restaurant; Asa's clasped hands "which would require great effort" to open; Allbee's claim that Jews keep "their spirit under lock and key"; the locked gate of the railroad station in Asa's dream; Allbee's statement that the world's an "overcrowded place"; and the story of the man on the subway tracks, "pinned" against the wall. Responding to so many images, Asa resembles the "man in a mine who could smell smoke and feel heat but never see the flames."

Surprisingly enough, *The Adventures of Augie March* contains many prisons—we wonder if Augie can avoid them more successfully than Asa or Joseph. On the first page he tells us that he will knock at the door of life—"sometimes an innocent knock, sometimes a not so innocent." He shuns confinement—there are open doors! But Augie finds that there are many doors which remain closed, even after he knocks. Several "institutions" are significant in this respect: George's "dummy-room" at the "penal-looking school" which has the "great gloom inside of clinks the world over . . ."; the Home to which George is sent—that home with "wired windows, dog-proof cyclone fence, asphalt yard, great gloom"; the home for the blind where Mama is sent; Grandma Lausch's institution; and the university with the old-world-imitated walls. Perhaps the very existence of such prisons of the spirit compel Augie to picture life a bit differently toward the end of the novel when he says: "we left what company we were in and went privately to take a few falls with our select antagonist in his secret room, like inside a mountain or down in a huge root-cellar." Everyone has a secret room where his furies lie—including larky Augie. No matter what preparations for life he finally makes, a man is always within "the walls of his being. And all high conversation would take place within the walls of his being. And all achievement would stay within those walls."

Tommy Wilhelm's hotel is the perfect setting for confinement—the drapes in the lobby keep out the sun; after breakfast the old guests sit down in the lobby and stay there the whole day. But the lobby is not his only prison. Tommy remembers the line of poetry: "Sunk though he be beneath the wat'ry floor . . ." because he himself is in a pit. Later he sees the moth trapped on the window pane; he thinks of the lack of space for his car. If only he can find a way out! But the novel insists on more entrapment, showing him that there is really no exit. Tommy "recognizes" death, the "end of all distractions," and of wrong tied tight within his chest," knowing he cannot stay in the same room with his father. New York City is a great hell; the "waters of the earth" are going to roll over him.

Slowly Tommy adjusts to the walls of his being. The imagery shows us his transformation: in the dark subway tunnel he blazes with love for the others—the tunnel, as hellish as it appears, holds a possibility of expansive love. So does the funeral parlor, another dark room. Like the corpse in the coffin, Tommy "recognizes" death, the "end of all distractions," and cries. His crying sinks deeper than his imprisoned being—so deep that it shows him an opening at the bottom. There is an exit!

Some of the short stories contain the same kind of images. Rogin in "A Father-to-Be" is trapped in the "water-filled hollow" of the sink; he submits to his "mother's" shampooing. Bellow implies the sink is a kind of womb; the image captures Rogin's oedipal plight. In "Looking for Mr. Green," the messenger, Grebe, sees many houses from which he is barred; all of them are old and ugly. Chicago itself is a "giant raw place," a "layer of ruins." Mr. Green, if he exists, doesn't live in any great, good place. The Wrecker, of course, realizes that he must destroy the prison of conventional marriage—imagistically, he wrecks his apartment, informing the onlookers: "the old must go down

. . ." He wants to "tear out the laths and get behind all the swellings"—to see new spaces.

In "Leaving the Yellow House," which appeared in the January, 1958 issue of *Esquire*, we again find the prison. Old Hattie does not want to leave her yellow house—it is all she has. But she and her neighbors understand that with her broken limbs, she cannot really take care of it. The house is "two-sided": it is the great, good place and prison. Perhaps Bellow suggests that before we can refashion dark prisons, we must accept them. Only then can imprisonment be "cozy." This is why Hattie wills the yellow house to herself:

> She resumed her letter of instructions to lawyer Claiborne: "Upon the following terms," she wrote a second time. "Because I have suffered much. Because I only lately received what I have to give away, I can't bear it." The drunken blood was soaring to her head. But her hand was clear enough. She wrote, "It is too soon! Too soon! Because I do not find it in my heart to care for anyone as I would wish. Being cast off and lonely, and doing no harm where I am. Why should it be? This breaks my heart. In addition to everything else, why must I worry about this, which I must leave? I am tormented out of my mind. Even though by my own fault I have put myself into this position. And am not ready to give up on this. No, not yet. And so I'll tell you what, I leave this property, land, house, garden and water rights to Hattie Simmons Waggoner. Me!"

Henderson resembles Augie and the Wrecker in trying to destroy all prisons. His expensive house is unpleasant; even his books are sinister containers of money. The cage in the aquarium more completely signifies entrapment. There an octopus presses its soft head to the glass—the creature is death itself. Henderson does not want to be locked in by money or biological factors; he wants to be in open space. But whenever he turns in America—that giant cage!—he sees more prisons: his father shut up in a room; the dead woman in the rubbish-filled cottage. Africa is not really different: the frogs lie in the cistern, contaminating the water. When Henderson wrecks the cistern, he doesn't see any hope for "proper shelter." And he is confined in an actual prison by the Wariri—in the room is a corpse which reminds him of the dead old woman, the octopus, his father. What if he himself is thrown into a pit? Henderson wonders. The rooms "increase." Dahfu, the Wariri ruler, lives in a luxurious palace which is actually a prison guarded by amazons. He suggests to the American that he is trapped by his tribal commitments; the only way he can "travel" is by reflection. Later both of them enter the dark tunnel where the lion is imprisoned; this reminds Henderson of the octopus' tank, suggesting death. Still afraid that there isn't any exit, he learns to adjust to prisons. He even accepts the tunnel. Unfortunately, he is trapped once more. When Dahfu falls into the lion's cage, meeting his death, Henderson realizes that mere acceptance of confinement will not *end* it—life is always a cage: *"my life and deeds were a prison."* Although we last see him in the open—"leaping, leaping, pounding . . ."—we realize that this is an interlude before another entrapment. Africa has taught him that any continent is a prison: one never leaves it.

V. BEAST

Another crucial image in Bellow's fiction is the beast. Not only are his characters pressed, trapped, devoured, or deformed —they are turned into animals. The image asserts itself in the early fiction, but it is fully developed later.

In *Dangling Man* we find several beasts: the "werewolf," Vanaker, a "queer, annoying creature" paces in the hallways and his room; the "nasty, brutish, short" quotation from Hobbes; the idea that "as animals instinctively sought salt or lime, we, too, flew together . . ." at high occasions to destroy one another. Joseph is convinced that the line between bestiality and humanity is very thin at times; *existence is a jungle.* Although we easily accustom ourselves to slaughter, he thinks, we are silly enough to take better care of pets than our neighbors. Even the physical environment is bestial—fog and rain make the street "an imagined swamp where death waited in the thickened water, his lizard jaws open . . ." No wonder that the "heart, like a toad, exudes its fear with a repulsive puff." Perhaps, Joseph thinks, the Egyptians were right in making one of their gods a cat—"only a cat's eye could see into the interior darkness . . ." without fear and trembling.

"The notions of inherent baseness, of human nature sharing the bestiality of nature itself . . ." are in *The Victim*; Asa like "each of Bellow's heroes finds the beast within."[8] Early in the novel the image asserts itself. Asa calls Mr. Beard a "God-dammed fish" after the employer starts to reprimand him. At home he thinks of mice darting along the walls. But the mice and fish are not so "full-bodied" as the later beasts. Asa begins to see animals everywhere—aboard the ferry he sees the yellow light on the water, which he compares to

> "the slit of the eye of a wild animal, say a lion, something in-human that didn't care about anything human and yet was implanted in every human being too, one speck of it, and formed a part of him that responded to the heat and glare, ex-hausting as these were, or even to freezing, salty things, harsh things, all things difficult to stand."

Nature itself is wild; is it any wonder that humanity reflects it? Asa's vision is not very comforting. Neither is his description of the "fly hovering below the tarnish and heat" of Elena's ceiling, or the "immense moths" filled with holes.

After Allbee enters, the images increase: we have many different creatures. The intruder seems "no more human" to Asa than a "fish or crab or any fleshy thing in the water." While he thinks this, he imagines that a mouse scurries past. Later Asa wants to be "like a bear in a winter hole," hiding from All-bee and the whole freakish process of living. The most sustained beast-description is found in the zoo incident. When he and Philip visit the zoo on their outing, Asa loses his sense of the "usual," seeing only the bars and cages, the dust and manure, the "ferocity of animal life"—so conscious of the animals is he that he immediately thinks of Allbee as a beast. Afterwards he reveals his feelings to his tyrant: "Everyday I see new twists. . . . They say you go to the zoo to see yourself in the animals. There aren't enough animals in the world to see ourselves in. There would have to be a million new feathers and tails. There's no end to the twists." Allbee counters by saying: You look like Caliban! The vision of bestial humanity becomes a vision of the bestial universe—possibilities, conditions, potentialities—all represented by the word "if"—"swing us around by the ears like rabbits."

The beasts appear in "A Sermon by Doctor Pep." Again this sermon points the way to new directions; here our animal-likeness is "accepted," even loved. Unlike Joseph and Asa, Dr. Pep realizes that to be human is to be animalistic—there is no way out—but the animalistic qualities are often "good," keeping us in touch with nature, not the mechanized city. Once we accept the delightful chirping of birds, we must also accept ferocious lions. Birds, lions, human beings—all creatures are *alive*. Consequently, Dr. Pep embraces the butterflies in the air, his own "dog-white hair," the lamb of Christianity, the "indiscriminate feasting sow," the "blood of steers," his fur-lined coat, the Lincoln Park Zoo as a favorite home—all these things "are images of spirit, icons, symbols, versions and formations."

Augie March is also at home with the beasts. Like the monkeys who see no evil, speak no evil, hear no evil, he accepts the bestiality around him, loving the "fighting nature of birds and worms" which Grandma Lausch has. Zeus, who appears on earth as an animal, symbolizes for him the bond of gods and beasts. The wonder of human beings is that they can be animalistic *and* godlike—that is, "exactly human." Of course, the bestial part of us is sometimes unpleasant—greedy, fearful—but we must be beavers ("I suffered like a beaver") or wolves (pacing in "the pit of the zoo" as Einhorn does during his deals) before we can show "stubborn animal spirit." The "male piercingness, sharpness, knotted hard muscle" of Chanticleer is achieved after the disturbed beauty of nightingales. Caligula, Thea's eagle, is viewed in two different ways by Augie. The eagle is brutish, sharp, fierce—but it is also an object of love (Caligula is less bestial than his trainer, Thea Fenchel). The eagle—like all the beasts—is dangerous and pathetic. It is almost human in its mixture. Thus Augie can later say about his soul, it's like other souls, as "one lion is pretty nearly all the lions." The soul and the lion—the image suggests their marriage.

Bellow suggests that one needs courage to accept the bestial soul. Tommy Wilhelm, like the weak Asa or Joseph, perceives only the threat or absurdity of animal-likeness, not "stubborn animal spirit." He sees himself as a "fair-haired hippopotamus"; Maurice Venice as a sloppy ox (there is also something "fishy" about the agent); his own bearlike posture; Mr. Perls as a "damn frazzled-faced herring with his dyed hair and his fish teeth . . .": The beasts here are "silly" (like herrings), not courageous (like lions). Because Bellow uses the imagery in a different way, he creates a *different zoo* in *Seize the Day*. It is too easy to say that he simply repeats the same kind of image; his beasts are carefully selected. When Tommy describes his "sheep dog," for example, he sees himself as the animal—gentle, friendly, but easily misled. When he looks closely at Dr. Tamkin, he sees a bird of prey with "hypnotic power" in his eyes, and "claw-like" nails. He can easily accept the charlatan's story about the lonely person "howling from his window like a wolf." Tommy's most extended description of beasts is this one: "On the road, he frequently passed chicken farms. Those big, rambling wooden buildings out in the neglected fields; they were like prisons. The lights burned all night in them to cheat the poor hens into laying. Then the slaughter." He sees himself, finally, as a "poor hen," devoured by the "claw-like" world.

Many critics have discussed the beasts in *Henderson the Rain King*. Daniel Hughes writes:

> Daniel's remark to Nebuchadnezzar, referred to throughout the novel, gives us the clue: "They shall drive thee from among men and thy dwelling shall be with beasts of the fields." This reduction (or exaltation) to the animal defines Henderson's characteristic experience. He begins as a breeder of pigs and returns with a lion cub; in between he suffers degradation in faintly parodic imitation of Lear, who is also forced to the animal and undergoes an actual and symbolic stripping.[9]

Henderson has many confrontations with beasts, as Mr. Hughes indicates; these affirm the bond between animal and human being. Here the beasts are not so "silly" as the ones in *Seize the Day*: they are stubborn, fierce, and strong. At the end of the novel Henderson profits from his savage encounters (especially with the lions), understanding that he cannot escape from his "heart of darkness." Here are Mr. Hughes' words:

> As with any resonant poetic symbol, no linear meaning can be attributed to the lion and lion-king of this novel. Indeed, this is a symbol, wholly integrated with Henderson's quest, thus forming an interesting contrast with the eagle-ritual that Augie March undergoes in a partly real, partly symbolic Mexico. . . . The lion kept under the throne by Dahfu is precisely what Henderson is not, something external, powerful, real. For all his boasting about reality, Henderson must undergo a savage en-

counter with something entirely foreign, and from this discover reality in himself.[10]

By crouching on all fours, imitating the lion, Henderson fulfills Daniel's prophecy. But he has one more confrontation—this time with Dahfu's lion-father, Gmilo (it turns out to be another lion). This new lion—like the octopus in the cage—symbolizes death; it can never be completely mastered.

The animal images in *Henderson the Rain King* are "deep"; they are more thoroughly developed than the few in *Dangling Man*, showing us again Bellow's consistent advancement.

VI. MOVEMENT

Because Bellow's characters feel trapped, pressured, and even devoured by the environment (and themselves), they want, at least consciously, to move. They *search* for answers to their predicaments. But their movements are usually erratic, circular, violent, or nonpurposeful.

Look at *Dangling Man*. Although Joseph is "imprisoned," he also sees himself as "dangling"—he insists that he "shall have to be cut down," before he can estimate the damage his "swinging" has caused him. There are other "useless" movements: Vanaker's mad pacing; Joseph's fearful walks—these are contrasted to the purposeful "rocketing" of Tad to Africa or regular seasonal change, which Joseph, quoting Goethe, would like to emulate. In this opposition of useless and purposeful movement, the useless movement asserts itself more strongly: fierce winds or rain; the blood-sopping draining board on which the chicken lies; the "grinding" movement of Christmas shoppers; the violent gestures of Joseph as he confronts Burns; the "hacking" of humanity; the graceless flying together of the bestial party guests; Joseph's mean spanking of Etta; his traumatic, early hair-*cut*—all these movements show us that *existence moves without grace*. At several points Joseph philosophizes in similar imagery. He tells us "there is a storm and hate and wounding rain out of us." The "hemispheric blackness" chatters, perhaps answering the human storm. When he tries to seek new directions, go to different places, he sees a man fall violently or a boy thrust a toy gun at him. "Who can be the earnest huntsman of himself when he knows he is in turn a quarry?" All his questions

produce this vision: "my mind flapping like a rag on a clothes-
line in a cold wind."

The Victim uses an epigraph from De Quincey's *The Pains
of Opium:* "Now it was that upon the rocking waters of the
ocean the human face began to reveal itself . . ." Existence in a
surging ocean. Immediately we are ready for the novel itself.
New York "seems to have moved from its place"—this unbalanced, crazy movement is juxtaposed to the "spiritual elevation"
of the lights climbing "upward endlessly into the heat of the
sky." Which of the two movements will win? Of course, there is
no real contest, as we can tell from other images on the same
page. Asa jumps up, struggles with the sliding subway door and
squeezes through it. Other frenetic movements follow: Mr.
Beard's hand trembles; Asa pushes his arm violently through his
coat-sleeve; Elena has "superfluous energy" in her movements;
Mary runs without grace (in Asa's memory).

Because Asa senses unconsciously the wasted movement
(around and within him), he thinks in terms of cessation of
movement or "transfer." The latter is evident in the many train
references: not only does he struggle with the subway door at the
beginning of the novel—he returns to the image in a "philosophical" way. He dreams about missing "the right train," after
running desperately to catch it. When he talks to Allbee, the
tyrant claims that all people are traveling in the wrong train,
headed in an obscure direction—driven by what? After many
years the two victims, now successful, see each other and start
talking about trains. Allbee says: "I've made my peace with
things as they are. I've gotten off the pony—you remember, I
said that to you once? I'm on the train." To which Asa asks: "A
conductor?" Allbee responds: "I'm just a passenger." *There is
no transfer: we remain passengers, not even knowing who runs
things.*

And the universal movement is violent, as more images tell
us. "Now it's all blind movement, vast movement, and the individual is shuttled back and forth." Sometimes there's a "smashup." Or we "go in all directions without any limit." Asa, "like
everyone else, [is] carried on currents, this way and that. The
currents had taken a new twist, and he was being hurried,
hurried." There is great "dizziness" in being human.

Both *Dangling Man* and *The Victim* are "closed" novels—
the various images of movement are under the surface; they
burst forth at important times to describe "blind, erratic"
motives (human or divine). In *The Adventures of Augie March*
Bellow gives us what he himself has called "catch-as-catch-can
picaresque."[11] Here the novel itself is "open," in motion: Augie
continually travels from one place to another, seeking metaphysical—or real—answers to his questions. The question is: Are
Augie's movements purposeful? Or are they as erratic as Asa's?
Again there is no simple reply because Bellow constantly juxta-
poses useless and purposeful movement, suggesting that life
holds both. But he does indicate that Augie is a more "successful" traveler than his earlier heroes.

Within the big movements of this novel, there are smaller
ones. Let us look closely at these. In the first chapter Grandma
Lausch instructs Augie and the others how to go on their mission
to the Charities office—*how to travel*. Although he listens to her
instructions, we can see already that he is a solitary traveler,
seeing his own sights in his own way. His style of movement is
reflected—or captured—in his narration. When he tells us that
"sometimes we were chased, stoned, bitten and beat up for
Christ-killers . . ." we note that his breathless pace is "larky and
boisterous," even though he describes painful movement. He
tells us often depressing things "on the run." The vital phrases
violate—render impotent—useless or cruel movement. They
incarnate "progressive," never-ending voyages.

But if we stop long enough to observe the kind of movement Augie "skips over" we find the blind process of *Dangling
Man*: the "snipping, cooing hubbub of paper-chain making" in
Georgia's school; the sly, often criminal movements of young
Augie; the "dizzy watchfulness" of Mama; the "angry giddiness"
of Grandma Lausch, her "human enterprise sinking and dis-
charging blindly from a depth"; the crippled, lurching gestures
of Einhorn; and the destroying fire in this cripple's house. These
movements are "countless disks," circles—not straight lines.
These disturb Augie: can he continue on his larky way, aware
as he is of erratic movement and dark prisons? He puts the
problem this way:

It was not only for me that being moored wasn't permitted; there was general motion, as of people driven from angles and corners into the open, by places being valueless and inhospitable to them. In the example of the Son of Man having no place to lay His head; or belonging to the world in general . . . I, with my can of paint, no more than others. And once I was under-way, street cars weren't sufficient, nor Chicago large enough to hold me.

Yes, he does keep moving, but he gradually begins to recognize that in "the free spinning of the world," breaking out of the small circle is not always completely successful. Out of one circle, he sees others: "Around some people the space is their space, and when you want to approach them it has to be across their territory . . ." It is not that easy to bound "the exploding oceans of universal space." The best one can hope for, according to Augie, is that he become aware of the "axial lines of life, with respect to which you must be straight or else your existence is merely clownery, hiding tragedy." Augie tries, if not to be straight in his movements, to be aware of the circular experiences of the race—the cyclical return of greatness. So we leave him still a traveler, a Columbus: "Why, I'm a sort of Columbus of those near-at-hand and believe you can come to them in this immediate *terra incognita* that spreads out in every gaze." Will he discover America or be shipwrecked? The question is open—like his crisscrossing, happy voyages.

Seize the Day has many movements which are, for the most part, violent, erratic, or useless. Tommy Wilhelm "sinks" throughout his adventures, although he longs to climb upward —when we first see him in the elevator, he sinks and sinks, and after the door opens, he sees the dark, uneven carpet "billow" toward him. Sinking, drowning—these images are contrasted to the bird that he sees beating its wings. Although we have two different kinds of movement, the "bad" will predominate. Thus Tommy's spirits are low; he remembers "Sunk though he be beneath the watr'y floor . . ."; he thinks of Los Angeles containing "all the loose objects" in the country that slide down there; he swallows hard at the Coke bottle; and he fears the *drop* in lard on the stock exchange. These images are not all; Tommy has to contend with violent movement as well as sinking. He thinks of constantly running out to move his car, gesturing wildly while driving, "rolling his blood-shot eyes barbarously," the wrenching of the cemetery bench by vandals, and kicking his bed to pieces. No wonder he needs tranquilizers! But even these cannot *steady* him; he continues to sink or move wildly. His self-control was going out like "a ball in the surf, washed beyond reach." He wants to stop going by "fits and starts and [falling] upon the thorns of life." He doesn't want to be drowned by the money-flow, wanting only to "march in a straight line." Dr. Tamkin's poem contains the images: it suggests that "Everyman" should stop "skimming" the earth's surface and, instead, remain at the foot of Mt. Serenity; climbing is dangerous. Tommy is so confused by the poem that he almost foams at the mouth, believing in effect, that the "waters of the earth are going to roll over [him]." After the stock exchange fluctuates madly, he runs to Tamkin's apartment and discovers that the charlatan has fled. Then he joins the pushing crowds and is carried into the chapel. Here the slow, steady movement captures him so much that he sinks into "the final thought"—like the corpse. (Again sinking—with a difference: one must sink in order to rise!) The epiphany of Tommy reasserts the images I have been tracing. He writhes with tears, sinking "deeper than sorrow," toward his heart's ultimate needs.

The short stories also contain movement. In "A Father-to-Be" Rogin rides in the subway (the road of life?), enjoying the trip at first. However, the peaceful journey stimulates his mind in unpleasant ways, making him think of time as a destructive current: "The life force occupied each of us in turn in its progress towards its own fulfillment, trampling on our individual humanity . . ." (He resembles Asa and Allbee in this thought.) Is there any way to stop the inhuman flow? Is there any way to shape movement? Rogin finds one answer in the "green and foaming" fluid in the sink, but he has simply submitted to Joan's current. In "Looking for Mr. Green," the messenger, George Grebe, regards himself as a hunter (like Augie?), seeking the answer to reality in the form of Mr. Green. But he finds that his quest is painful, not very successful, because he is an outsider. Climbing, walking through doors, pacing, and running

—finally he sees Miss (or Mrs.) Green and he achieves his goal. Or so he thinks. Has he shaped his quest or has he been carried along? The same question applies to Clarence Feiler, who hunts for Gonzaga manuscripts. "Fanatically" searching out relatives and friends of the dead poet, he seems to know where he is going. The imagery tells a different—more correct—story. We have such images as the following: "Holes are torn in the ocean bottom. The cold water rushes in and cools the core of the earth." Clarence thinks of the "pouring rain-cloud" (produced by atomic explosions?). The various references to earth-*shaking* bombs underlies our hero's reckless search: he is drowned—comically, of course—by the system's mad currents. It is appropriate that after he learns this, "the heavens [seem] to split; a rain [begins] to fall, heavy and sudden, boiling on the wide plain."

Now we are ready for the movement in *Henderson the Rain King*. Like Augie, Clarence, and the other voyagers, our hero is searching for reality. The question is: Is his hunt successful? The imagery offers clues to the meaning of the novel. It suggests that reality is erratic *and* orderly, wild *and* peaceful, high *and* low. It is mixed movement—this is the answer Augie accepts as do Asa and Allbee at the end of *The Victim*.

The novel begins with a "disorderly rush" as Henderson thinks of his experiences—this rush turns into chaos. He is pictured as shaking out books (to find his father's money), falling off a tractor and then running over himself, crawling with his pigs, and erratically playing the violin. Henderson decides, imagistically, to correct the rush by taking a trip, *ordering his movement*. Africa, the dark continent, will be chaos or heaven to him. (He is unaware that it is both.) In his airplane he feels at home—"dreaming down at the clouds." But the graceful movement soon ends. In Africa Henderson again sees violent movement: he wrestles with Itelo, falling to the ground; he thinks then that his "spirit's sleep" *bursts*; he blasts the cistern. However, during these bursts of chaotic movement, he dreams again of pink light which makes him "fly" over the white points of the sea at ten thousand feet; he hears Willatale affirm his belief that "the earth is a huge ball which nothing holds up in space except its own motion and magnetism and we conscious things who occupy it believe we have to move too, in our own space."

So the two kinds of movement continue after Henderson meets Dahfu. The ruler seems to "float" gracefully, even when he throws the skulls—he soars while Henderson thinks that *he* sinks. During the ritual "gouts of water like hand grenades burst all about and on him," not destroying but creating Henderson. When Dahfu tells him about cosmic force, the imagery reasserts itself—*man must move; he cannot stand still under blows*. Then it does not matter that Dahfu falls into the cage and is killed. Reality continues to flow, drowning some. But there are spots where it stops for a moment—they are as calm as the pink light. As Henderson thinks: "*Light itself was all Einstein needed*." Perhaps he puts it better this way: "The opposite makes the opposite." Chaos implies order; wildness implies peacefulness. And the last time we see Henderson, he is running "over the pure white lining of the gray Arctic silence." He is a pinpoint of moving light, "a little world made cunningly" of changing order.

VII. MIRROR

Bellow's heroes are obsessed by vision. As "visionaries" they tend to *see* existence in oblique or unbalanced ways. The mirrors demonstrate that their quests are frequently distorted.

Joseph, the dangling man, is unnaturally self-centered: the "others" reflect his preoccupations; they are inversions of his true image. Thus he sees the athlete, the tough boy, as an alien, who doesn't conform to the right code—his own. Always subject to such hallucinations, he can "reverse" the summer, making himself "shiver in the heat." When he looks at the ugly houses, streets, tracks, he wonders if the "people who lived here were actually a *reflection* of the things they lived among" (my italics). Again self and environment reflect each other: How can Joseph get out of himself and see other things? The question is especially compelling after he regards *himself* as a split image: the Joseph of a year ago—a cold, rigid conformist—and the present Joseph. Which one is real? he asks, knowing that he cannot continue to see himself as fragments. Burns, his old friend, cannot recognize him as *he* cannot recognize himself! Joseph partially recognizes that he has faulty vision: "he made mistakes of the sort people make who see things as they wish to see them or, for the sake of their plans, *must* see them." But he cannot correct it.

Continuing to emphasize the mirrors of self, Bellow gives us Minna's party—everyone here is *indistinct*: the "others remained grouped together indistinctly," we are told, and were recalled as "that fellow with the glasses" or "that pasty-looking couple." Abt, in hypnotizing Minna, dims the lights and closes her eyes—indistinctness leads to blindness. Later we listen to Joseph describing his brother, Amos, and his family. Like the tough boy mentioned earlier, Amos is an inverted image of his younger brother, who regards him as a "stranger." Etta, Amos' daughter, bears a "great resemblance" to Joseph: this resemblance "goes beyond the obvious similarities pointed out by the family." Can we not say that Etta, "a vain, self-centered, childish" person perfectly mirrors her uncle, who also stares at himself? In spanking Etta he spanks his own narcissistic image. Brooding about his niece, Joseph discovers that "the face, all faces, had a significance for me duplicated in no other object. A similarity of faces must mean a similarity of nature and presumably of fate." He recalls his grandfather's photograph, seeing in it a dim reflection of his own—one that would "reclaim" him "bit by bit." The grandfather and he are one as Etta and he are one. Life is a series of mirrors: "Alternatives, and particularly desirable alternatives, grow only on imaginary trees." It takes proper vision to choose the right ones.

Now we can understand why Bellow includes the "double" (the first of many in his novels). When Joseph sees a stranger fall from some kind of attack, he sees himself in the man—the fall reminds him of his own illness, his mother's death, Aunt Dina's scratching. A "pre-vision," he calls it. It results from his "melodramatic," fragmented view of existence. Everything is double—his two Josephs, Amos and Joseph—because life is a broken self-image; true vision, epiphany, is rare. Seeking it, Joseph constantly runs into distortions, grotesque reflections, as in his dream-double: he feels a touch on his back and turns: "Then that swollen face that came rapidly toward mine until I felt its bristle and the cold pressure of its nose; the lips kissed

me on the temple with a laugh and groan." Our seer resembles
Brydon of "The Jolly Corner," in love with a grotesque double,
or Poe's William Wilson. The interior darkness is dangerous—
"only a cat's eye" can see it truly.

So we leave Joseph in his old room, still not seeing wholly.
The room is delusive; it seems to "dwindle" and become a small
square. This is not a visual trick, he informs us. The visual trick
—like the other ones in the novel—is a *revelation* of life's
"ephemeral agreements." No wonder that Joseph rises "un-
steadily" from his rocker—he sees clearly that life is a cosmic,
distorting, treacherous mirror!

The Victim presents the same kinds of mirrors, implying
that "environment serves as an index for the exploration of
characters' attitudes toward themselves and their world and at
the same time as an index for the definition of an external
life."[12] Asa and Allbee cannot master reality—if such a thing
exists—because they see only themselves.

The very first sentence suggests that true vision is rare in
New York City, especially on a night when its citizens become
"barbaric fellahin." Asa Leventhal is the "one-eyed king" in
this "country of the blind." He walks in a foreign land, Staten
Island, seeing a "shimmer of fumes" or a "sunny" white cor-
ridor. He sees the "too bright" eyes of anxious Elena. All these
images prepare us for Asa's "hallucinations"—for his faulty,
self-centered, fragmented vision. His own eyes are clouded—
"they seemed to disclose an intelligence not greatly interested
in its own powers . . ." He sees mice darting along the walls.
He gazes at other eyes that seem softer and larger at night,
hoping to find something of value.

After Allbee enters, we are again confronted by the
"double"—this stranger holds Asa's secret desires for punishment and guilt, reflecting them as the stranger reflects Joseph's
death-wish. Unbalanced vision is more intense now. Asa stares
at the double's eyes and sees universal insanity there; later he
stares at the water and sees inhuman lions. Elena mirrors his
mother's madness and his own; Philip, her son, mirrors his
weakness; Max, his brother, mirrors his abdication of maturity.
"Horrible images" intrude: "hideous cardboard cubicles"
painted to resemble wood; men sitting on mission benches. As

Joseph stares at himself (a "Spirit of Alternatives"), so Asa sees himself: "he was able to see himself as if through a strange pair of eyes . . ." "Changed in this way into his own observer," he splits himself. He even *becomes* Allbee when he has "a strange close consciousness" of the other; the "look of recognition Allbee [bends] on him [duplicates] the look in his own." Such epiphanies suggest that each man is his own victim; *master and slave fragment the human image*. Existence is captured fully in the following image: "The imperfections of the pane through which Leventhal gazed suggested the thickening of water at a great depth when one looks up toward the surface."

The mirrors persist in *The Adventures of Augie March*, but they are less destructive. The general pattern is clear: Augie constantly meets people who reflect each other—Einhorn resembles Mintouchian who resembles Thea, etc. His world is a kind of "funhouse." Because his range of experience is so great (and, curiously, so limited to authoritarians), he must avoid becoming another reflection.

Here are some of the images of faulty vision, fragmentation, and distortion. There are several "mirrors" in the first chapter: we see the March family preparing to help Mama get new glasses—Grandma Lausch teaches her children how to get correct vision? Augie mentions the photograph of Grandma's husband; the photograph "doubled back between the portico columns of the full-length mirror." This *doubling back* is evident in all the adventures; it underlies his many comparisons to gods and generals. When he notes, for example, that he can't see his father as a "marble-legged Olympian" or his big mother as a "fugitive of immense beauty," he is suggesting that his friends and relatives are distorted, incorrect reflections of the gods: perfect beauty (or vision) exists in Heaven; earthbound people never see themselves properly. The three monkeys—see no evil, speak no evil, hear no evil—are fragmented deities. Augie begins to travel and meets other mirrors. Anna Coblin insists on seeing him as her own Howard, refusing to perceive that he is not a simple double of her son but a different person. Her religion is described this way: she "had things *segmented, flattened down,* and *telescoped* like the stages and floors of the Leaning Tower . . ." (my italics). A poor visionary with her "own ideas of time and place"! No wonder we see her "bothering the morning mirrors with her looks." Simon resembles her in having an "oriental, bestowing temperament"; he becomes the missing father. Contrasted to him, an inverted image, is Georgie, who doesn't stare at the world; on the contrary, he has a "subtle look" set on who knows what—a "seraphic" appearance.

The "true vision of things is a gift, particularly in times of special disfigurement and world-wide Babylonishness." But faulty vision is everywhere. Augie is taken for Mrs. Renling's lover; he thinks of Mr. Renling as a nightbird that "knows all about daylight" but flies toward darkness; Mama March is blind; Augie cannot become a "sun of the world," "Phoebus's boy"— he remains in the dark; Simon (who undergoes a grotesque metamorphosis) runs through lights and almost kills pedestrians; Caligula wears a hood. The net result of these "intimidations" for Augie is simple: existence, he believes, is double, mysterious, fragmented—as Mintouchian claims: "Do you say a double life? It's secret over secret, mystery and then infinity sign stuck on to that. So who knows the ultimate and where is the hour of truth?"

These images reappear in *Seize the Day*. Tommy sees his distorted reflection in the "darkness and deformations of the glass"; he resembles the hotel across the street, which looks like the "image of itself reflected in deep water." He feels, nevertheless, that fragmentation is better than being an "exact duplicate" of his cousin, who brilliantly conforms to the system. But Tommy cannot see clearly; the environment mirrors his failures: Venice, the agent, resembles him; so do Mr. Rubin and Mr. Rappaport. How to achieve clear vision? he wonders. Perhaps Dr. Tamkin, a visionary with "hypnotic power in his eyes," can help him. But the charlatan sees everyone as the "faces on a playing card, upside down either way." Although Tamkin writes in his poem: "Look then right before thee. Open thine eyes and see . . ." Tommy cannot even make out the figures on the stock-exchange board (resembling Mr. Rappaport who shouts, "I can't see"). Epiphany is rare, but it does occur when Tommy sees his image in the coffin. Can he keep this new vision?

I don't want to pursue the many mirrors in *Henderson the Rain King*. Again the crucial problem is how to achieve *insight*

—not an easy task when the hero is surrounded by *duplication* (he is like Lily's father in his suicide threat; the orphan at the end parallels Ricey's child); *grotesque reflection* (the lions are stronger than Henderson; one lion is a killer, unlike the other); *faulty vision* (Willatale *sees* despite her cataract; Henderson sits in darkness); or peculiarity of light. But Henderson does have visions: when he sees pink light—all that Einstein needed—he is no longer aware of the upside-down universe of things. Then he sees Deity—reality itself—as two-sided and one at the same time. Light, fire—these move but are steady; they distort but are clear: "The opposite makes the opposite." Or as he pictures his epiphany: "*It is very early in life, and I am out in the grass. The sun flames and swells; the heat it emits is its love, too. I have this self-same vividness in my heart. There are dandelions. I try to gather up this green. I put my love-swollen cheek to the yellow of the dandelions. I try to enter into the green.*" Every one, he says later, is "given the components to see: the water, the sun, the air, the earth . . ."

This survey of Bellow's imagery reveals several things: the images are "natural," archetypal, and carefully chosen.

Most critics of Bellow's fiction refer to his article, "Deep Readers of the World, Beware!"[13] Here he attacks symbol-hunters, asserting that the "deep reader . . . is apt to lose his head. He falls wildly on any particle of philosophy or religion and blows it up bigger than the Graf Zeppelin."[14] He is also against phony images (which become symbolic). What are true symbols? "A true symbol is substantial, not accidental. You cannot avoid it, you cannot remove it."[15] Of course, Bellow is right in rebelling against the artificial, non-substantial symbol, but he seems to flee partially from complex issues. The few examples he offers of true symbols don't tell us enough about "substantiality"; surely if any object—such as a crippled limb—reappears in a work of art, we cannot call it accidental—it is there! He takes no account of *patterns* of meaning. Although he believes the crippled feet of Oedipus are symbolic, he doesn't see that the feet join the blindness of Oedipus and Tiresias as part of a thoroughly developed gestalt.

The argument is perhaps a personal one. When *The*

Adventures of Augie March appeared, several critics saw "deep" symbols in it. Anthony West, for example, claimed that Bellow had "chosen to saddle himself with . . . a lead weight of Melvillean symbol."[16] The battle between Simon and Augie was not real: "Augie has a brother, Simon, who is intent on money and sex as Augie is on culture and love, not because families are liable to produce that kind of clash of personality but because America is split between materialism and idealism."[17] Now, Mr. West is "over-reading," but he does realize that the novel contains symbols. The question is: What do the symbols mean? I have suggested that certain images seem to recur so many times that they form a pattern or cluster of meaning. It is dangerous to call Augie a symbol of America; it isn't dangerous—*it is necessary!*—to see movement as a symbolic force in the entire novel.

We should not go to the other extreme and say that instead of handicapping his fiction with symbolic images, Bellow doesn't use *any*. Bellow himself in "Facts that Put Fancy to Flight," is for concrete realities—for social facts—but he asks for a "poetry of fact."[18] In other words, the writer should be realistic, knowing how many floors the Hotel Ansonia has, but he should realize Truth is more than such realism: The writer "may be realistic but not about the things that matter, the arrangements that shape our destiny. In this smaller way to stick to the facts limits him to minor schemes of social history, to satire, to muckraking and leveling, or to the penny psychology of private worlds. To this sort of 'objectivity' writers give all they've got. Strong on experience, they are much, much less strong on the truth."[19]

In my essay I have suggested that Bellow uses "natural" images—movement, resemblance, diseased limbs—but he uses them to portray the truths of existence. These images are shaped to symbolize our destiny. When he uses such exotic ones as those Henderson meets, they are still *natural in that particular Africa.*

The fascinating thing about these seven images is that because they are so real, they recur in all periods—they are archetypal. The pressures felt by Tommy Wilhelm or Asa Leventhal are "crosses" like the one borne by Christ; the disease appears again and again as a symbol (and fact) of our human condition not only in *Oedipus Rex* (remember Bellow's choice of Oedipus' feet as a true symbol) but in *Moby Dick* or *The Magic Mountain*; the beast is in medieval romance or *Gulliver's Travels*; the voyage is in—you name it. If we read Bellow's fiction with care—even the early *Dangling Man*—we see that as modern as his heroes are, they enact mythic trials. The images make Bellow's novels traditional; at the same time they don't destroy freshness or contemporaneity.

I have broken these images asunder. All seven reinforce one another; they coalesce as we read. The beast *moves* wildly; the crippled limbs *mirror* spiritual disfigurement; the weight *entraps* heroes. This is the terrifying "absurdity" of criticism: it elucidates and fragments a felt pattern of meaning.

Notes

1. Marcus Klein in "A Discipline of Nobility" (Chapter 7 in this book) mentions imagery of weight in general terms.
2. As I indicate at the end of this essay, Bellow's images are archetypal —weight is naturally related to the cross Christ bears.
3. Cf. Klein's essay for valuable comments on "stylistic weight": "And if all history and culture are rejected in a style that borrows widely from the world's accumulation of literature, that fact is more than irony. Bellow's style which beginning with Augie March has become a racy vehicle bearing great freights of knowledge, is a thing that simultaneously admits and dismisses clutter."
4. Thomas Mann, "Dostoevsky—in Moderation," Preface to *The Short Novels of Dostoevsky* (New York: Dial Press, 1945), p. xiv.
5. This "sermon" is important for suggesting new directions in Bellow's images and themes. But it is a wonderful achievement in itself. Herbert Gold chooses it for inclusion in his anthology, *Fiction of the Fifties* (New York: Doubleday, 1959).
6. Rosenfeld, *The Age of Enormity*, pp. 183-184.
7. *Ibid.*, p. 184.
8. Klein, "A Discipline of Nobility."
9. Daniel Hughes, "Reality and the Hero: *Lolita* and *Henderson the Rain King*" (Chapter 6 in this book).
10. *Ibid.*
11. In *Twentieth Century Authors:* First Supplement, ed. Stanley J. Kunitz (New York, 1955) p. 73.
12. Ralph Freedman, "Saul Bellow: The Illusion of Environment" (Chapter 5 in this book).
13. Saul Bellow, "Deep Readers of the World, Beware!" *New York Times Book Review*, February 15, 1959, pp. 1, 34.
14. *Ibid.*, p. 1.

15. *Ibid.*

16. Anthony West, *The New Yorker*, 29 (September 26, 1953), p. 142.

17. *Ibid.*, p. 140.

18. Saul Bellow, "Facts That Put Fancy to Flight," *New York Times Book Review*, February 11, 1962, p. 28.

19. *Ibid.*

10·BELLOW IN OCCUPANCY

PERHAPS the most striking thing about Saul Bellow's *Herzog* is its most unfashionable seriousness. Without using any of the easy rhetorics of exhibitionism to advertise the seriousness of his achievement, Bellow successfully persuades his reader that reading *Herzog* is an act of moral consequence. The reader is gently drawn into what turns out to be a most ungentle and painful debate. Positions are incisively defined, deserted, shifted, exploded, and then bewilderingly realigned, and the reader is forced to scuttle crabwise in order to keep himself upright. Not since the politically oriented thirties, I should think, has an American novel been able to sustain itself as a medium of social discourse or, better, a forum for sane argumentation and inquiry. We are now, however, thirty years removed from the dour intellectuality of the thirties; metaphysics has replaced economics as the subject of meaningful discussion, and perhaps *Herzog* may provide a crystallization of our contemporary confusions as Dos Passos' *U.S.A.* did in its day. And it may even be a sign of cultural maturity or desperation (or both) that gives the traditional novel of ideas this belated and amazingly popular appearance on the American scene.

For this, it seems to me, is what is new and exciting about *Herzog*. It is the production of a marvelously rich and more marvelously sane intelligence acting upon and reacting to the imponderabilities of normal human existence in the vivid darknesses of the mid-twentieth century. And this, unsymbolically! We have become unaccustomed to ideas naked—ideas freed from their always ambiguous, always symbolic containers. *Herzog* presents us with the frenetic play of ideas in their most natural habitat—a conscious, responsible human mind. And this old-fashioned rendering of the debater's platform is unsettling to us. It is not the dark and bloody ground of great mythic plantations, not the fluke-thrashed Pacific waters that engulf the soul. Neither gin nor jazz, neither drugs nor the orgasmic piece that passeth all understanding provides the rhythms for the debate. Bellow chooses as novelistic frame the square angularity of vision that the gross majority of literate Americans project upon the world. He invokes the absolutely square, bourgeois, middle-class ethic in his efforts *"to justify"*—to justify un-God's merciless ways to man-unkind, and this without disavowing the true prophecies of doom that make that ethic meretricious and logically indefensible. What is radical about *Herzog* is that it is a novel of ideas in which the ideas are unashamedly and merely ideas in a human mind. The world goes on; characters act or fail to act; the incessant flow of ideas changes nothing, averts nothing, saves no one.

And of course, *Herzog* is a comic novel. I should suppose that any modern effort to justify God's ways to man must be inherently comic. Justice, after all, is man's creation and the destruction of mankind is God's, and any attempt to harmonize the two must lead to that glottal stop that is usually death, but can sometimes be laughter. In Bellow's novel, the man of ideas, Moses E. Herzog, acts, suffers, fails and partially succeeds as a human agent without displaying any evidence that there is a causal connection between his thinking and his acting. The world of his ideas is a separate one. He entertains himself with it. He uses it to celebrate his soul, to upbraid himself, to pity his ignominies. But it is always a world separate and discrete from him, and this is a fact that he and the reader learn to regard as comic because any other reaction would be intolerable. Sprawled out in his hammock in the Berkshires like a caricature of a Transcendentalist, Herzog takes stock of the broken shards and disappointed hopes of his life. He has been twice divorced, he has failed in his friendships, fallen far short of his scholarly ambitions. He has found no sureties in sex, love, religion, philosophy, history, or human relationships. His mind—rich, exotic and delightfully erratic—recapitulates, reorganizes, resuffers the burden of his memories. Writing fragmented mental letters to the quick and the dead, re-enacting the salient scenes of his past, haranguing Nietzsche, Heidegger, General Eisenhower, Herzog finally subsides into mental silence. His mind offers no more ideas. No more words. He tells himself that he has accepted the dull brutal fact of his existence, but neither he nor we are able to know whether it is affirmation or sheer exhaustion that puts an end to his cerebration. And this, I take it, is comedy: a 341-page remembrance of things past in which the memories fail to cohere or explain—in which the movement of the main character is an illusory introspective spiral that comes out nowhere.

But *Herzog* is comic in other ways as well. "If I am out of my mind, it's all right with me, thought Moses Herzog." These are the opening words of the novel—a novel that takes place, after all, *in the mind* of Moses Herzog. Sometimes Herzog *is* out of his mind, sometimes not. But he is always aware of himself on two levels of awareness. That is, he is aware of himself as a man in the Berkshires engaged in a self-indulgent scrutiny of those past selves that his memory serves up to him. And, second, those recollected selves are themselves self-conscious; they too were self-aware in their moments of vital being. The possibilities for the ironic and futile play of identities within such a narrative focus are well-nigh inexhaustible. For, whether Herzog is in or out of his mind, the reader is usually kept within it, and this allows Bellow to manipulate the distances between his reader and his main character on the principle of a very complicated, double-motioned elevator mechanism. Sometimes we are allowed to look directly at Herzog, but more frequently the barrier of his personality is dissolved and we have to become Herzog looking at himself (or looking at himself looking at himself). And thus, although there are usually two layers of irony separating Bellow from Herzog when the focuses are working well, the reader is not always so shielded. And this, it seems to me, is what makes the reading of the novel so intimately painful and intensely comic at times. The same device of multiple perspective that separates Bellow from Herzog forces the reader into an overintimate identification. To be sure, the distances are not always successfully controlled. But when they are, *Herzog* becomes an almost terrifyingly impersonal book and the reader is caught in the most personal of engagements with it. The frustrated congestion of ideas becomes the personal property and obligation of the reader alone, and Bellow disappears from his own artifice. And this, too, is comedy—surreptitious, sadistic, even pedagogical in its demands.

But the modern comedy of identity has other uses as well, and Bellow's composition is an enormously artful one. We have already remarked the comic lack of movement in the main character's long progression from nowhere to nowhere. There is, however, something else that needs to be said. The device of multiple perspective tends to cancel out the actual lack of movement, since awareness of self-awareness creates a dynamic psychic motion in itself, and it is this rhythm that dominates the structure of the novel. When all is working well, the multiple perspectives engender an incredible circumambience of ironic directions; when the distances collapse, Bellow runs the danger of maudlin self-pity and sentimentality. In general, however, he is much more successful than unsuccessful in sustaining his balances in *Herzog;* and in this he is greatly aided by his happy conception of protagonist, that hammock-sprawling oxymoron, Moses E. Herzog. For he is, ultimately, a comic compendium of paradoxes: rational student of irrationality, skeptical believer, calculating, middle-aged innocent, self-effacing egotist, erotic intellectual, Montreal-born, Russian-Jewish American. He learns nothing, does nothing, slays no dragons, burns no bridges; and yet he is still in a supremely comic way, not only the hero of his novel, but an heroic character—a perfectly possible and viable figure of modern heroism.

"The hero is he who is immovably centered," wrote Ralph Waldo Emerson, a poet-thinker whom both Herzog and Bellow seem to respect. In spite of (or because of) the fact that he is constantly shifting his senses of self-awareness, Moses Herzog is an immovably centered man. In a way that Emerson may just have been guileful enough to have been suggesting, the centrality of self has changed from a reliance on some irreducible atomic entity like soul or spirit or immutable consciousness to a creative network of protean self-relationships. In this sense Herzog is a dazzling acrobat of consciousness, a prestidigitator of his constantly burgeoning selves, vulnerable or discoverable in no single one of them, immovably centered in their dynamic totality. The Wandering Jew—uprooted, displaced, always as detached and alien as consciousness itself—receives a comic apotheosis. It is he, the homeless one, who is able to establish a fruitful liaison with the world. In Herzogian terms, the Mosaic law has been amended to read, "Be it ever so humiliating, there's no place like home." And, perversely, on this level, the discrete world of ideas *does* become causally connected with man's actions. *To think*—even though it is possible only to think about oneself—becomes synonymous with *to act*. And the greatest actor, the largest hero of our time, would be the man who thinks most about his many selves in the most fluidly creative way. Thus, when Moses Herzog asks himself at the end of the novel what it is that he wants, his answer is both comic and momentously brave. "Not a solitary thing. I am pretty well satisfied to be, to be just as it is willed, and for as long as I may remain in occupancy." And at this point the reader should be aware that Herzog's lease of occupancy will extend to the temporal and psychic limits of his capacity for self-consciousness.

It would be possible to denigrate Bellow's remarkable accomplishment in this novel by overstressing the importance of some of its undeniable weaknesses. To do so would be petty, but not to point to them at all would be a critical disservice. Some of these weaknesses are probably inevitable in light of the immense strain that the restricted mode of composition must have imposed. I have already suggested that the ironic perspectives do not always function in balance. The passages directly concerned with the plot-triggering adulterous betrayal—the recollections of Madeleine and Valentine—smack too rawly of emotion untempered by art. There is also a tendency toward a wearying sameness in the over-all texture of the novel. Episodes, ruminations and characterizations merge together in an even consistency which resists discrimination and makes for monotony. The reader misses the urgency of anticipation that the conventional suspense-rhythm of narration usually supplies. Given the comic needs of Bellow's plan and his decision to remain within the associational field of one man's mind, this was perhaps a necessary sacrifice, but it is still a weakness. The prose style, on the other hand, is almost completely admirable—sensuous, lucid, satirical, grotesque, erudite and racy of the urban soil. It is only when Bellow attempts a purely lyrical flight that I find him deficient. And except for the Sono episodes (which are deliciously funny), the erotic scenes (especially with Ramona) seem to me forced and unconvincing. The reminiscent encounters between Herzog and his familial circle, by contrast, possess the authenticity of art at its very highest. Bellow's muse is essentially comic and unfashionably rational and *Herzog* is a resounding success, a joy to read and a painful delight to reflect upon.

But I must briefly pursue one final—possibly irrelevant—reflection. I have tried to show that this is a highly comic novel of ideas, intransigently social, and desperately honest in trying to face up to the soul-crushing intellectual challenges of our times. I think that Bellow is the most important novelist we have and I think that *Herzog* is his richest and fullest achievement. And yet when one invokes the still palpable ghosts of Faulkner and Hemingway, not to mention the nineteenth-century American giants, we are immediately aware of his lesser stature in comparison to them. They too were passionately concerned with the ambivalences of self, identity, and the implacable hostility of the universe. They too were in their differing ways comic. But their stances in relation to their art and the world show some cardinal differences from Bellow's. They were each of them, in some sense, "provincials"; he is not. They were each of them capable of rejecting or ignoring the world in order to construct their own worlds; he cannot do this. Their majesty consists in their ability to have built counterworlds in despite of the actual worlds around them. And the actual world has come to embrace their mythic structures as actualities and it has moved on its axis to come into accord with the rhythms of their imaginations. Bellow may conceivably surrender too much of his private myth to the exigencies of the world. His intellectual and emotional cosmopolitanism, his commitment to a social good, may cause him to modify the structuring shapes of his own dreams to accord with the world-as-it-is. And if this speculation should possess some truth, it is the world's loss as well as

Bellow's, for the world will have no choice except to absorb his work, which changes it not. His accomplishment is a major one. Yet might it not be even greater if he could compel the world to move in the measures of his own vision?

11 · HERZOG: A Review

PERCHED ON a cement block outside his former house, peering through the screen he left up last fall, looking for his ex-wife Madeleine's lover (his own former friend, adviser, and beneficiary), Moses Herzog has two bullets in Father Herzog's old nickel-plated gun and vengeance in his heart. But while he watches red-and-gold maned, gimp-legged Valentine Gersbach, "the poet of mass communications," giving his little daughter June Herzog a bath, the evil drains out of Herzog's heart with the bath-water. "The human soul is an amphibian, and I have touched its sides," Herzog reflects as he steps down, reminding both himself and us that the soul may be a monster or a bird, or a computing machine with a taxicab's heart, or the buzz of a message on the telephone—or, maybe just darkness, or light, or silence. For the world has entered Herzog's soul, his heart, his nervous system, his cerebral cortex, and his digestive tracts, and he spends his exuberance trying either to check the flood of, or throw his arms around, or press his own shape on (the mixed metaphors are an essence of Herzogism), what Yeats called "magnanimity of his own desire." And he does it with the absurd heroism of an absurd intellectual who can surprise us and himself by saying "Much of my life has been spent in the effort to live by more coherent ideas. I even know which ones."

Herzogism (like quixotism) will probably become a catchword, but the book can bear even that, for *Herzog* is a great comic novel. Bellow has found a way of getting everything in —of including and making coherent the biggest chunk of reality

since Joyce got his into *Ulysses*. Consider who Herzog is. He is a
son, a father, an ex-husband (twice), a friend, a patient, a client,
a "Reality instructor"; he is a consoler, a wanderer, a nature-
lover, a Ph.D.; he interprets history, he knows he is responsible
for the future, he writes letters: to the newspapers and to presi-
dents, and to his own, the obscure, and the great dead, etc. etc.
He lives in, and absorbs into himself, Chicago, New York, the
Berkshires, subways, telephones, Western Union—in one of his
rare triumphs, though maybe it's only an in-joke, he outwits
Western Union by sneaking in a threat to Gersbach by crypto-
gram: *"Dirt Enters At The Heart"*—airplanes, trains, bedrooms,
taxis, law courts, the police desk, a jail cell, washstands, toilet-
bowls, bathtubs—the list could go on and on. The point is that
Herzog is (to adapt his own definition of Gersbach), "the poet of
personal considerations" who takes into himself the X-Ray par-
ticled reality which buzzes around and through us who live in
the city. We feel the city of the past covering us as dust drifts
down from buildings being demolished to move "metamorphic
New York" toward the future; it beats from the garment district
lofts, seeps up from the grotesque underground of bootlegging,
from decaying neighborhoods. The city of the present assaults
us in subways, in taxicabs, on streets, from skylines, and in Grand
Central and Penn Stations; it spills over onto Belt parkways and
into the Jersey Flats. Trains, planes, and buses are hustling the
present out into a too predictable future. Herzog's "wild internal
disorder" reflects it:

> And why? Because he let the entire world press upon him. For
> instance? Well, for instance, what it means to be a man. In a
> city. In a century. In transition. In a mass. Transformed by sci-
> ence. Under organized power. Subject to tremendous controls.
> In a condition caused by mechanization. After the late failure
> of radical hopes. In a society that was no community and de-
> valued the person. Owing to the multiplied power of numbers
> which made the self negligible. Which spent military billions
> against foreign enemies but would not pay for order at home.
> Which permitted savagery and barbarism in its own great cities.
> At the same time, the pressure of human millions who have dis-
> covered what concerted efforts and thoughts can do. As mega-
> tons of water shape organisms on the ocean floor. As tides pol-
> ish stones. As winds hollow cliffs. The beautiful supermachinery
> opening a new life for innumerable mankind. Would you deny

them the right to exist? Would you ask them to labor and go hungry while you enjoyed delicious old-fashioned Values? You —you yourself are a child of this mass and a brother to all the rest. Or else an ingrate, dilettante, idiot. There, Herzog, thought Herzog, since you ask for the instance, is the way it runs. On top of that, an injured heart, and raw gasoline poured on the nerves.

Herzog has the senses to respond, the emotions to care, and the mind to probe his surroundings, his people, and himself. He also has the conscience and the vision and the vitality to try to turn everything into a human reality—he is famished for the real, for everything, which is another way of saying that Bellow has been able to make a man and a novel which has room for and can pack in our statistical, fluctuating encyclopedia.

I use that notion with Flaubert and Joyce in mind, for Bellow has done for the 1964 "moving city" (New York-Chicago-Ludeyville) what Flaubert did for mid-nineteenth century Paris and what Joyce did for 1904 Dublin. Flaubert's Frederick Moreau receives the imprint of Paris in his heart, Bouvard and Pécuchet translate *idées reçues* into action with the enthusiasm of lovable but mindless automatons, Stephen Dedalus receives Dublin's material and moral atmosphere into his nerves and bloodstream before turning them off with his "patented refrigerating device," Bloom registers municipal Dublin in patience, meditation, dream, and regret. Herzog brings this history up to date. Herzog is not *l'homme moyen sensuel,* or the man in the street, or the artist, or the natural active man, though he includes these. He has, it seems to me, absorbed those ancestors (as Bellow has absorbed their authors) and found the best figure for the present American which we have had. Herzog's father was the perfect outsider (a European Jew who made his living in the Montreal slums as a bootlegger distilling fine scotch whisky for the U.S. market), two of whose sons have become wealthy American businessmen and the third (Moses) a professor. Thus Herzog comes from the provinces (Moreau), grows up in and out of a suffocating tradition (Dedalus), and becomes a pedlar of dreams (Bloom). But he does not sell ads; he is a Ph.D., and that is just right for the post-World War II "hero." Bellow does not use a professor because that is all he knows, but because he

wants the kind of man who has one foot in the world of specu-
lative intelligence and one in the active life.

Bellow has perfected "the academic novel" by *using* the
academic hero: that is, he does not put Herzog *in* the settings
and situations which are characteristic of such novels, but in
the center around which whirl centrifugally the campus, the
business world, the city of the mind, the sensual and emotional
life, the family, personal values, and politics and history. Or,
since he achieves a beautifully persuasive and moving proportion among these attractions, we can say with equal truth that
they are rushing in upon Herzog centripetally and so give him
his shape.

Herzog is heroically cosmopolite in women, ideas, and
places. He has had affairs with women from Japan to Poland;
he has a domestic ex-wife who is thought to be promiscuous but
isn't, and a bluestocking ex-wife who is thought to be a model
mother but wants to be promiscuous; as if that weren't enough
he is taking on a woman who, by having combined the old
Eve, the modern handbooks, and efficient business methods,
has made Eros the perfect servant and all-purpose problem
solver. Moreau and Bloom are brought up to date, for divorces
and dream-girls hang over every middle-class marriage, stirred
by romantic literature, by full-color ads, and by "the entertain-
ment industry." The intellectual counterpart of these scram-
blings to resolve emotional conflicts are the compulsive letters
Herzog writes to an expanding circle as his problems become
increasingly metaphysical: to friends, to those who are giving
him professional help, to fellow scholars who are interpreting
life and history, to Adlai Stevenson, General Eisenhower, and
Nietzsche, and finally to God.

An extraordinary wealth of what makes a man is brought
to bear. But this is not "a novel about Man"; it is a man's novel,
built up painstakingly and harmoniously from detail, character,
and situation. Herzog is *engagé*, or to use his own term, "a relating animal." He doesn't like being "with it," "falling into the
quotidian," but he can't exist otherwise, for he draws his exuberance from his reactions to people, places, things, and ideas,
and his reactions make him real. The book exists in a moving
present during which Herzog tries to come to terms with all of

his experience and to shape his future. He confirms that he has
a future, even if it is only to endure:

> *Survival!* he noted. *Till we figure out what's what. Till the
> chance comes to exert a positive influence.* (Personal respon-
> sibility for history, a trait of Western Culture, rooted in the
> Testaments, Old and New, the idea of the continual improve-
> ment of human life on this earth. What else explained Her-
> zog's ridiculous intensity?) *Lord, I ran to fight in Thy holy
> cause, but kept tripping, never reached the scene of the struggle.*

But he can't get out of touch; when he does he has his one moment of panic and of incoherency. His exuberance ("scope" and
"intensity," he calls it) is the true binding force of the novel and
of his reality. His sympathy draws him toward everyone, uniting
him with the human sufferer, and his intellect keeps him concerned with the secret cause, whatever it may be. The book thus
has the tragic dimension which Joyce defined, but it is bathed
in what Joyce called the perfect end of art, joy, which is most
fully realized in comedy. What Bellow has achieved is the
Shakespearean sense of variety which sees all around a situation
and a passion, and realizes it in character, scene, and meditation.
Herzog's obsessive "relating" makes all of his recollections and
gestures dramatic. His exuberance is almost compulsive (a true
condition of our time). In his passion to understand people and
himself he rehearses them in retrospective narration and drama.
These elicit his efforts to apprehend his experience in its con-
nectedness, his stabs at intellectual and ideological resolutions,
his letters to Anima Mundi. He makes us feel that we have experienced a contemporary anatomy of love, that (like Hamlet)
he includes all of the others whether he is raging or meditating.
His ecstatic amours, his imaginative flights, the theories spun
from his spidery entrails, his "most" story to his daughter Junie
in the police station, the cluttered pastoral at Ludeyville, are
part of the same man and the same world. He is not a picaresque
saint, for the network is too tightly woven; he exists *in* his world
so that both he and it are simultaneously alive, and he is too
much a man to be canonized.

What this means is that Bellow has written a novel with a
great form. Driving, prowling, under arrest in plethoric Chicago,
trying "out of its elements, by this peculiar art of his own or-

gans," to create his version of it, and so to reshape his past and his present, Herzog feels at home: "He was perhaps as midwestern and unfocused as these same streets. (Not so much determinism, he thought, as a lack of determining elements—the absence of a formative power." (cf. Dreiser, whose naturalism, whose Hurstwood and Clyde Griffiths light up in the background). Bellow has mustered such a formative power; he forces, into a reality which can be lived, the American east and west, the city and the frontier. In artistic terms, Bellow has achieved a beautiful balance of personality and impersonality by making the novelist's voice sound through the whole and unify the whole ambience; he is sometimes with his character ("I"), sometimes around him ("He"). His voice moves in and out, creating the comic aether; it reflects the fluctuating border between involvement and detachment, color and line, tragedy and comedy. It has both the narrative drive of outer events, and the meditative convolutions of the city-saturated modern soul. I am reminded that Pound called Henry James a "drinker of men, of things, of passions," whose voice could be overheard "weaving an endless sentence." *Herzog* is also what Pound called *Ulysses*, "a passionate meditation on life."

But Herzog is unmistakably modern: the vital interchange between the artist and his character is more nervous and compelling than that between Joyce and Bloom, and James's world of agreed-upon conventions and manners has properly given way to the fluid informality of a mass society. The artist is not paring his nails, nor can he have Olympian confidence in his milieu. Bellow's voice exploits his donnée fully, but it cannot be a calm voice, nor is Herzog drowned out by the garrulity of Molly Bloom. One might call it a combination of Cervantes' nostalgic voice and the agonized voice of Shakespeare's Hamlet, which is driving willy-nilly toward the future. I feel, as I read the book, that Bellow has opened up a new quixotism, a new hamletism, weighted with and weighted down by the very world which impinges upon us. Herzog is an American Josef K. with great powers of endurance, whose religious sense is freed from dogma, from the Freudian darkness, and from the terror of totalitarian inevitability. Bellow has included both the Idol of Refined Art and the Idol of Raw Life in a greater amalgam; he feels life, if not steadily (which surely it is not), at least whole. His voice is a great civilizing voice which picks up the challenge of D. H. Lawrence, for Bellow is willing to express "man alive" in his drive toward a transvaluation of values, a change of heart, a re-interpretation of the Holy Ghost (though none of these terms can define Bellow's voice or his tone precisely).

I have implied that Bellow's novel is something of a synthesis, one of those encyclopedic works which makes one feel that it has been built upon the work of the writer's predecessors, upon his own development as a writer and a man, and upon the work of his contemporaries. For instance, Bellow has reinvented the epistolary form to convey the sense of eighteenth-century urbanity and the sense of the present city-dweller who tries to get into events, and into *l'histoire morale contemporaine*, by writing letters to the editor. His use of the past, which today comes to us as fragments of racial consciousness, as theories, and as a fluid tradition, extends the Joycean use of literary and religious myth; it is more relevant to us, and it reflects the absence of any standard which would make the modern vision a satiric one (Pound's insistence that Joyce used Homer primarily as scaffolding, and that *Ulysses* strikes most forcibly our sense of the relation between life and art, as we live them, than upon art as an end—a view which is reasserted by Robert M. Adams in his *Surface and Symbol*—adumbrates the perspective in which Herzog should be seen. Allegorizing is a clear and present danger; even Malamud's *The Natural* has been reduced to allegory). Scenes recur: Herzog sitting on the toilet reading Pope measures exactly Bellow's sense of the difference between Herzog's reality and Bloom's: Flaubert's *encyclopédie d'idées reçues mise en farce*, and Bloom's archetypal meditations, have become creative ideas which measure and affect action. Frank Alpine braced in the dumbwaiter shaft to spy on Helen Bober while she takes a shower has been enriched by Herzog's balancing to watch Gersbach give Junie a bath. Herzog has rediscovered nature by extending and enriching S. Levin's adaptation from Thoreau. Again, his notes for a proposed "Insect Iliad" for Junie, inspired by tent caterpillars and containing ants, water-skaters, cicadas, a wasp, and a stag-beetle, which he gives up, nods at but eschews the metaphysical overtones of Thoreau watching the war of the ants and of Lt. Frederick Henry playing God over the ants on the burning log. From his own work, Bellow has combined the man dangling in himself, the victim imposed upon by his own conjured municipal nightmare, the urge to seize the day, Augie March on the move. He has pulled the lines formed by the sequence of his previous novels into a single grand circle and filled it; the synthesis reflects not only his growth, but a new grasp on reality. Instead of constructing an abstract metaphysical and symbolic system, as Yeats did, to enable him "to hold in a single thought reality and justice," he has taken "the tradition" as a series of achieved realities. His intensity has "used" it, transformed, to make intelligible a present world.

Herzog is, among other things, a history and synthesis of "The novel." It gathers in not only novels of the past and current novels, but part-novels and novels-manqué. It sweeps up the sociological scalpel-and-bludgeon novel, the bitch-goddess novel, the fairy-and-dyke novel, the sex-machine novel, the howl novel, the addict novel. One goes on and on as new connections light up on Bellow's switchboard. To change media, which suggests not only Bellow's method but also the extent to which *Herzog* is alive to visions of the contemporary reality, we are reminded of Fellini's camera and his impervious surfaces, of Antonioni's sense of the haunt of places, of the tone qualities which give *Dr. Strangelove* its civilizing atmosphere. As a final illustration I am reminded of Ermanno Olmi's sense of the world as an organization, especially of that ominous breathing on the soundtrack of *Il Posto*, which seems to be the respiration and heartbeat of the actors, and of one's companions (?) in the audience of the dark theater, but at the end is shockingly revealed to be the regular beat of the mimeograph machine. Bellow is aware of the realities of the past and of the present, and he conveys them.

What I am being led to say is that Bellow's style is able to present this comprehensive reality on a scale ranging from the directness of presentation and statement, to the obliqueness of the most subtle and revealing poetry. Take this description of Herzog coming up from the subway on his way to Ramona's perfect dinner-table, perfect bathroom, and perfect bed:

> This was his station, and he ran up the stairs. The revolving gates rattled their multiple bars and ratchets behind him. He hastened by a change booth where a man sat in a light the

color of strong tea, and up the two flights of stairs. In the
mouth of the exit he stopped to catch his breath. Above him
the flowering glass, wired and gray, and Broadway heavy and
blue in the dusk, almost tropical; at the foot of the downhill
eighties lay the Hudson, as dense as mercury. On the points of
radio towers in New Jersey red lights like small hearts beat or
tingled. In midstreet, on the benches, old people: on faces, on
heads, the strong marks of decay: the big legs of women and
blotted eyes of men, sunken mouths and inky nostrils. It was
the normal hour for bats swooping raggedly (Ludeyville), or
pieces of paper (New York) to remind Herzog of bats. An es-
caped balloon was fleeing like a sperm, black and quick into the
orange dust of the west. He crossed the street, making a detour
to avoid a fog of grilled chicken and sausage. The crowd was
traipsing over the broad sidewalk. Moses took a keen interest in
the uptown public, its theatrical spirits, its performers—the
transvestite homosexuals painted with great originality, the
wigged women, the lesbians looking so male you had to wait for
them to pass and see them from behind to determine their true
sex, hair dyes of every shade. Signs in almost every passing face
of a deeper comment or interpretation of destiny—eyes that
held metaphysical statements. And even pious old women who
trod the path of ancient duty, still, buying kosher meat.

The sense of his own bodily movements, the revolving and rat-
tling of bars and ratchets, the grotesque human figures, the tendency of the city to turn into a lush jungle, a human womb, a
sterile onanistic giant whose denizens have bettered nature by
"creating" of themselves inverted biological mechanisms: these
are indeed metaphysical statements in addition to being reflections of Herzog's own Ramona-dominated destination. But then,
the beautiful ironic "And" of the concluding sentence!

The whole atmosphere has been ominously prepared by
Ramona's siren-call over that emotional dentist's drill, the telephone, "drilling away at him," itself a primary instrument of
metaphysical incitement and penetration. While he is talking to
the lawyer Simkin about what justice he should invoke against
Madeleine and Gersbach—the call which leads him to the law
courts, to the vision of evil which drives him toward murder—
the telephone appears to be communicating the decision of The
Castle. But it is the ironic metropolitan version of the sea-shell,
which gives us back the sound of our own bloodstream: "The
telephone seemed to pick up the sound of his blood, rhythmic,

thin, and quick, washing within his skull. Perhaps it was only a nervous reflex of his eardrums. The membranes seemed to shiver." Without knowing it, Herzog is drifting into the perilous solipsism which almost makes him assume that his desire for personal justice is the world's; he is on the verge of the horror which has resulted in our time when mechanisms have broken down our civilized sense, then have become in turn handmaids of a primitive brutality which can end in a Hitler. Herzog's departure from Ramona before her flowershop (p. 206) evokes a similarly suffocating sense in which the mass and rhythms of body, sex, taxicab, city-become-hothouse-plants, plants-become-machines-and-exhaust gas, overwhelm Herzog and dull him into a thing.

This is the inescapable tendency in Bellow's book, and he handles it with beautiful modulation all the way from texture to situation to symbol. Everybody has become or is in danger of becoming a reflection of the machines of transportation, communication and computation. Madeleine willfully drives herself not only into slacks, but into Catholicism, the Ph.D. mill, and cosmetics (the fantastic scene in which, after she and Herzog have made love, she "labours to be beautiful" by encasquing herself in the cerements of an old woman to go to work, is an appalling, grotesque, but true image of one face of the American woman; to put on lipstick after dinner in a restaurant she looks at her reflection in a knife blade!). Gersbach makes his gimpy leg an asset: it rouses him to sexual Adonism and enables him to find the right combination of egotism, sentimentality, opportunism, and adaptability to become "the poet of mass communications" and a lay analyst. The Herzog lawyer, Sandor Himmelstein, is a hunchback who compensates with a savage lust for power, becoming a sickly combination of brutality and maudlinity. Herzog has a biologist friend whose idealized love object is Rocco the monkey. The culminating figure in the horror scenes in the law court is an epileptic, orthopedic-booted young woman, sexually abused since childhood, who has refused to give up her illegitimate child, has moved into a cheap hotel with a lunchroom porter, and finally has beaten her three-year-old child to death in a rage because he has not been toilet-trained and perpetually cries. Bellow uses this method to link encroaching mechanism and emotional deformity; psychiatrists, lawyers, law courts, and marriage, which purportedly adjust or cure deformations and violence, merely manifest creeping mechanism or try to "adjust" men and women to it. All of the "Reality instructors" have, as it were, been operated on by Charles Bovary and have become Charles Bovarys themselves. Even physical nature is drifting from organism to mechanism, from matter to energy, as human instinct and creative power lose their sympathy and resiliency. Bellow shows the Daughters of Memory (and Herzog's own Muses, his mistresses) turning from women into systems; Thomas Pynchon's V. is hovering on the horizon.

That is not to say, however, that *Herzog* is an apocalypse or a diatribe. Both Herzog and his creator display the saving sympathy of broad vision; neither shrinks into self-justification and repudiation. The book has the vitality, spirit, and gaiety of genial comedy; it is full of great meditations, great conversations, dazzling turns of wit, and great lines that explode in the mind and into laughter. Marvellous characters are everywhere. Madeleine is an awesome creation in the line of Molly Bloom, who makes other efforts to write about "the modern woman" look puny; she is admirable in distortion, an Amazon, a Titanic bitch-goddess. Gersbach, a lovely parody of Herzog and almost his alter ego, is a compelling supersalesman of "potato love" who, because he lives it, rises to an heroic mission as a secular prophet of the sawdust trail. Ramona is perfect. Asphalter, Edwig the psychiatrist, the literary academician Shapiro, Himmelstein, Madeleine's father ("the American Stanislavsky"), Herzog's first wife Daisy, Nachman, Sono, Father Herzog and Moses's mother, Simkin, Tante Taube, Phoebe Gersbach, Herzog's brothers Shura and Will, the Yankee Tuttles, and an astonishing cast of New York cabbies, judges, cops, deadbeats, perverts: all of these come to life because they are all vivid and relevant inhabitants of the world of Herzog's actions, emotions, and imaginings (he was in the U.N. when Khrushchev pounded the desk with his shoe). He is intelligibly *related* to all of them, and they are all related in Bellow's version of this world. They come alive in surface and depth in exact proportion as they bear in upon Herzog, and we are convinced that that is just about the proportion which we ourselves feel. The powerful scenes in the book occur one after another, but always given the proper rhythm by the modulations from scene to flashback, from intense drama to Herzogian epistolary meditation (how perfectly Bellow uses the letter to give just that sense of the blurred line between public and private, between memory and event, between history and contemporaneity, in which we live!).

I should end this review, but *Herzog* is an extraordinary book, and everyone will feel impelled to live with it, to come to terms with it, to discover its form. I'll make a stab at it. A critic or reviewer deserves his enthusiasms more than he does his antipathies (writers need such enthusiasms, I think). Having suggested how Herzog looks from without and how the book seems to grow from its historical context, I now want to look at Bellow's character from within, examine how his metaphysical odyssey unfolds, and try to define the impression it finally makes.* Above all, I want to suggest how *Herzog's* form shapes itself to the touch of the mind. So here goes . . .

Herzog is an historian of our still- or post-Romantic period who has gone to pieces and is testing fragments of reality to put himself back together. Immersed in the Berkshire summer at his sagging "estate," he tests in violent retrospect—observing, meditating, and writing—event after event, role after role, hy-

---

* While rereading *Ulysses* for another purpose, I discovered that Moses Herzog is a "hop of my thumb" tea-and-sugar merchant referred to by the garrulous Irish bill-collector at the beginning of "Cyclops"; the bill-collector has just been trying to get a plumber, Geraghty, to pay up on a transaction with Herzog. Herzog is also one of Bloom's pallbearers in "Circe," and joins the hue and cry after Bloom flees Bella's house. "Cyclops" is of course the great episode of aboriginal nationalism in which Joyce plays his Dubliners off against all the heroic ages (cf. Joyce's mythopoeic backgrounds and Bellow's letters; also Joyce's "hangmen's letters," by means of which he enters the dimension of metempsychosis, using Paddy Dignam's ghost as the medium). In "Cyclops" Bloom becomes "Herr Professor Luitpold Blumenduft," the "new Messiah for Ireland," and as "ben Bloom Elijah" ascends to heaven "like a shot off a shovel"; on everything, Bloom "had to have his say too about it," and his prescription for Ireland (which enrages the Citizen) is "Love." In *Herzog* we imagine a monolithic, municipal, monumental Paul Bunyan just out of perceptual range in the cosmic vestibule of symbol and myth. There are many other specific parallels to *Ulysses*; e.g. Bloom's potato and "potato love," "Vulcan" Gersbach, "bloody freemason" Herzog (cf. Don Giovanni, Papageno, and Sarastro). But much more striking is what Bellow has learned from Joyce's style; that will elicit the most extensive study by writers, critics, and scholars. It will be a long time before *Herzog* will be exhausted.

pothesis after hypothesis, to try to find out who and where he is. He may be a man who is keeping up a front, or a would-be do-gooder: "all the dead and the mad are in my custody, and I am the nemesis of the would-be forgotten. I bind others to my feelings, and oppress them." Maybe, like almost everyone else, he is one of the "Reality instructors" ("A very special sort of lunatic" who "expects to inculcate his principles"); or one of the listeners, psychiatrist, policeman, lawyer, judge. Ramona tells him he is "a man tempted by God, longing for grace, but escaping headlong from his salvation" (Ramona's version of salvation is for a world where "Now that it can't be political, it's sexual"). Thinking of his behavior while his mother was dying, he calls himself a "gesture-maker." He hits part of the truth when he considers himself a self-pitier who deliberately chose innocence and refused to know evil, so that "therefore others were appointed to do it to him, and then to be accused (by him) of wickedness." At any rate, he is lost in a welter of definitions of what he is to himself, of what others think of him, and of what he does to other people. Just out of jail, after his auto accident, and before his retreat to the Berkshires, he was

> A loving brute—a subtle, spoiled, loving man. Who can make use of him? He craves use. Where is he needed? Show him the way to make his sacrifice to truth, to order, peace. Oh, that mysterious cerature, that Herzog! awkwardly taped, helped into his wrinkled shirt by brother Will.

That is Bellow speaking, questioning with his beautifully modulated point of view and tone, pushing Herzog toward us with an appeal so that for a moment he trembles on the edge of motion, delicately tipping toward symbol; then, unobtrusively, he is drawn back to where he belongs.

Whatever he is, the climax of his quest begins with his vision of evil in the great lawcourt scene, which makes him revert to primitive eye-for-an-eye justice, and ends when he reaps the consequences despite the change of heart he has outside the bathroom window. The law-court scene occupies the place of Ivan's stories, Dmitri's dream, The Grand Inquisitor fable; of Hans Castorp's snowstorm vision of the savagery underlying pagan beauty, of the Circe episode in *Ulysses*, and of Kafka's

world of endless guilt. Herzog's wandering from sordid case to
sordid case brings up against the horrifying disparity between
naked, degenerate brutality, and the forms and veils with which
society must protect itself. Herzog's vision is neither Christian,
nor pagan, nor psychological, nor is it a parable, or a dream, or
an inner hell; but it subsumes all of those conditions and forces
their Manhattan counterpart on the modern man who has an
obscure sense of cosmic wrong and feels impelled to do something about it. The scene is overwhelmingly presented, and it
elicits from Herzog the powerful ambiguities of anguish. His
surprise and admiration at one judge's humane consideration
makes all the more annihilating his sudden sense that the im-
peccably mannered witnesses, the tolerant, matter-of-fact lawyers,
the clichés in which events are recounted, are hopelessly inade-
quate to the implications of the stolid, opaque mother and the
screams of a child savagely beaten to death. The sense of gratuitous suffering overpowers Herzog, flooding the personal wrongs
he feels and raising them in his heart beyond social to metaphysical crimes. Sickness or the terror of the child grips him; fighting to suppress his rising vomit, he leaves the courtroom. In the
hall

> . . . he concentrated. With all his might—mind and heart—he
> tried to obtain something for the murdered child. But what?
> How? He pressed himself with intensity, but "all his might"
> could get nothing for the buried boy. Herzog experienced noth-
> ing but his own *human feelings*, in which he found nothing of
> use. What if he felt moved to cry? Or pray? He pressed hand to
> hand. And what did he feel? Why he felt himself—his own
> trembling hands, and eyes that stung. And what was there in
> modern, post . . . post-Christian America to pray for? Justice—
> justice and mercy? And pray away the monstrousness of life,
> the wicked dream it was? He opened his mouth to relieve the
> pressure he felt. He was wrung, and wrung again, and wrung
> again, again.
> The child screamed, clung, but with both arms the girl
> hurled it against the wall. On her legs was ruddy hair. And her
> lover, too, with long jaws and zooty sideburns, watching on the
> bed. Lying down to copulate, and standing up to kill. Some kill,
> then cry. Others, not even that.

His ecstatic love has turned to evil; he absorbs fully the lesson his mother taught him: that Adam is dust, which she had

illustrated by rubbing her palm with a finger until the sweat and dirt produced a black particle (it does). But he has lost the spirit of wit which comes from resignation; the inner beating breaks down the boundaries of his life, "the force of balked longings coming back as stinging poison." Helpless against fact, reduced to wordlessness, his feelings swollen to meet the inrush of evil, he reverts to Chicago a man possessed. His journey by superjet and expressway, through sidestreets, in a rented Falcon, to his father's tomb-like house, to get his father's gun, represents terrifyingly a retrogression into the primitive by modern methods: not under the psychiatrist's control, which leads to acceptance, but by instruments which drive to action.

Bellow has evolved this backfall in a brilliant series of bathroom scenes, evoking the spectre of American and romantic infantilism in the comfort hall for which America is famous. Things had begun to go to pieces around Herzog while he was reading Pope in a cellar lavatory which had thick walls like a bunker. His psychological reversion began when he recalled how at the synagogue his only refuge from elders who kept telling him he would be a rabbi was the W.C. The most alluring of possible reliefs came as a bathroom meditation while he was cleaning up for Ramona's gourmet dinner and trimmings; he anticipated the luxury of self-justification, and recalled how Sono, his Japanese mistress, had soothed him by getting into the bathtub with him and washing him. In Ramona's bathroom he recalls adolescent sexual fantasies, luxuriates in her smooth tiles and medicine chest, and begins to write to the dead. After dinner and their upsetting discussion of his life, all is assuaged by Ramona's appearance, framed in the bathroom door, naked but for black lace panties and high heels: as whore-mother she fulfills his wishes. But at once, just before he went to the law court and after the upsetting conversation with Simkin, Herzog had seen his brute self. Casually becoming aware that seeking comfort in the bathroom has become one of his habits, he remembers requiring Madeleine to make love on the cold tiles; that awakens sudden awareness of a moment, previously unperceived, when Madeleine's love for Gersbach had showed itself; the urge to punish them by holding a blowtorch to their feet rushes in on him. Though he ridicules such justice, his fathered face in the mirror shows him a creature "Not human of itself," only "longing to be human." It is this glimpse which thrusts Herzog toward prehistory.

But reimmersion is a way. Bellow evokes the double sense of childhood: savage in its first flood, but able to enlarge the overcivilized consciousness. When Herzog views Gersbach and Junie through the bathroom window, gun in hand, he sees childhood in its shape of innocence, recognizing what it means to be a father. He understands that he himself has been one of the "bungling child-men, pure hearts in the burlap of innocence" (Bellow seems to be playing throughout on Huxley's Burlap and Beatrice, proponents of togetherness in the bathtub): "willingly accepting the necessary quota of consequent lies, he had set himself up with his emotional goodies—truth, friendship, devotion to children (the regular American worship of kids), and potato love." He realizes in the telegraph office, wiring Ramona, that "The necessary premise is that a man is more than . . . all the emotions, strivings, tastes and constructions which it pleases him to call 'My Life'." He has been driven by an "infantile terror of death"; but something incomprehensible, whatever it may be, includes both death and the self.

But Bellow does not stop with a change of heart. Herzog is still in Chicago, not Eden, and after his idyllic visit with Junie to the Museum of Science and the Aquarium he suffers the consequences of his homicidal intention: edging too cautiously onto the boulevard, his Falcon is struck from behind by a speeding truck, and the police find in his pocket the fatal pistol, for which he has no permit. Yet though he is humiliated, the ride to the police station through his old neighborhood makes him face for the first time the one incomprehensible evil of his childhood, an attack by a sex-pervert. This recognition accelerates his retreat from self-obsession, so that at the police station he can face Madeleine without losing his composure in either maudlinity or resentment.

What lies behind Herzog's ability to accommodate to himself both himself and his tormentors is his saving sense of drama, for adepts at self-dramatization have the knack of seeing life as scene and as *dramatis personae*. Leaving the bathroom window, he had become aware that Madeleine and Gersbach (like himself?) are "grotesque love-actors": "his intended violence turned into theater, into something ludicrous." The upshot of his insight, and of Phoebe Gersbach's refusal to help him expose her husband and Madeleine, is an impersonal, historical definition of his "emotional type":

> Herzog could not say what the significance of such generalities might be. He was only vastly excited—in a streaming state—and intended mostly to restore order by turning to his habit of thoughtfulness. Blood had burst into his psyche, and for the time being he was either free or crazy. But then he realized that he did not need to perform elaborate abstract intellectual work—work he had always thrown himself into as if it were the struggle for survival. But not thinking is not necessarily fatal. Did I really believe that I would die when thinking stopped? Now to fear such a thing—that's really crazy.

Moving thought replaces the bathroom as Herzog's psychological comfort station; he gets motions and words meshed again, and is once more in the state of mind to keep the creation of human reality going. As he says to his fellow-estranged Asphalter, who is trying to face life without his monkey Rocco by pretending that he has already died:

> it isn't a question of dread, or any such words at all . . . Still, what can thoughtful people and humanists do but struggle toward suitable words? Take me, for instance. I've been writing letters helter-skelter in all directions. More words. I go after reality with language. Perhaps I'd like to change it all into language, to force Madeleine and Gersbach to have a *Conscience*. There's a word for you. I must be trying to keep tight the tensions without which human beings can no longer be called human. If they don't suffer, they've gotten away from me. And I've filled the world with letters to prevent their escape. I want them in human form, and so I conjure up a whole environment and catch them in the middle. I put my whole heart into these constructions. But they are constructions.

The constructions at least give him "something great, something into which his being, and all beings, can go. He does not need meaning as long as such intensity has scope. Because then it is self-evident; it *is* meaning." And of course, for Bellow, and for us too, it is this novel.

But again, this is no final solution. The resolution, if the novel has one, is less a finality than a quality. One of the arguments about the book will be whether the conclusion brings us back to the beginning, so that Herzog pauses after full circle before another bout; or whether he gets himself and others sufficiently out from under his skin so that he can open himself to whatever will come and not be stampeded. He seems on the verge of some kind of new insight when he rejects the parlor Romanticism of "safe, comfortable people playing at crisis, alienation, apocalypse and desperation. We must get it out of our heads that this is a doomed time, that we are waiting for the end, and the rest of it, mere junk from fashionable magazines. Things are grim enough without these shivery games." Rejecting any "doctrine or theology of suffering," he sees his own suffering as merely "a more extended form of life, a striving for true wakefulness and an antidote to illusion" ("as people pinch themselves to feel awake"), and he takes no moral credit for it. He eschews metaphors (perhaps with Camus' Sisyphus in mind), and asks Nietzsche a friendly "question from the Floor" about the Dionysian spirit, especially its twentieth century perversion, concluding with greetings "from this mere border of grassy temporal light." In his letters he now seems to slough off erotic, mystical, and psychiatric interpretations of life. His last letter, written from where he feels "easily contained by everything about him *Within the hollowness of God,* as he noted, *and deaf to the final multiplicity of facts,* as well as, *blind to ultimate distances. Two billion light-years out. Supernovae,"* is to God:

> *How my mind has struggled to make coherent sense. I have not been too good at it. But have desired to do your unknowable will, taking it, and you, without symbols. Everything of intensest significance. Especially if divested of me.*

This telegram modulates us imperceptibly out of the flashback; we, Herzog, discover that we are at a point just after the beginning of his metaphysical odyssey. Something has happened in the present. For a moment Herzog feels peace, "Confident, even happy in his excitement, stable. The bitter cup would come round again, by and by. This rest and well-being were only a momentary difference in the strange lining or variable silk between life and the void." But for a moment he reaches *"out where it is incomprehensible. So . . . Peace!"*

If the book is circular, it is a spiral, for in the last pages

Herzog is either upon a new level, or down in the quotidian, or
both: for him they have at last become one and the same. Herzog
never stops living, and Bellow keeps it open; Clyde Griffiths'
romantic, self-deceiving "And yet . . ." has become a simple,
even gay, "Well, of course there is more to come." The book
began with Herzog swamped in cluttered pastoral: Thoreau's
nature, the scent of wild, and the wreckage of his "home." It
is the detritus of a life, of a civilization, after the break. We have
been through the retrospective journey, and we return to the
clutter once more. But people are coming back, Herzog remembers, when peace has at last turned him inside out. He cleans
himself up to greet his brother Will.

The conclusion is presented as a beautiful collection of
images, gestures, and exchanges. Will almost persuades him to
go to the Pittsfield hospital for a rest, but the spectre of psychiatric treatment saves him. For a moment Herzog has misgivings.
He thinks of the bird skeletons in his water closet, owls in the fix-
tures, a half-painted piano he has quixotically been refurbishing
for Junie, the remains of meals, the wife-deserted atmosphere;
but he fields these "bathroom" images carefully, realizing "My
balance comes from instability." He fights off Will's remedy by
feeling a "no" without words, merely gesturing, and finally re-
solving the crisis in gaiety when he compares his fantastic collection of wives, children, and a Berkshire estate to the picture
of Father Herzog and his sons deciding whether White Horse,
Johnnie Walker, or Haig & Haig should be the label of the day.
In a funny way, the Yankee Tuttle ("the master spirit of Ludeyville"), who is summoned to turn on the electricity, and his
frowzy wife, who comes to clean house, become for Herzog an
image of placid, practical, easy domesticity, replacing for him
psychiatrists or mother-and-father figures. Ramona's serious
metaphysical eros gets reduced in marvellous comedy: as he
invites her to dinner Herzog admires the courage and poise with
which she overcomes the quiver caused by her efforts to be "a
woman who took matters into her own hands," and her per-
fume stirs "the deep, the cosmic, the idiotic masculine response
—*quack*. The progenitive, the lustful quacking in the depths.
Quack. Quack."

Finally, Will leaves. Herzog is left alone while Mrs. Tuttle finishes her cleaning, waiting for Ramona to come for dinner (and to help with the dishes—that's *all!*). The last, two-and-one-half page scene, dense and beautiful, leaves us with the sense that perhaps Herzog was right, that perhaps intensity, if it can find scope, is, in the end, meaning. The human "word-models" for life give way for a moment to a fleeting sense that "the model of natural creation seems to be the ocean." This model and the amphibian human soul seem to sustain the human dwelling: "What keeps these red brick houses from collapse on these billows is their inner staleness. I smell it yawning through the screens. The odor of souls is a brace to the walls. Otherwise the wrinkling of the hills would make them crumble." Herzog turns on the water pump, the hermit thrushes sing the water-dripping song, and he thinks of the blackbirds gathering in waves to fly to their waterside nests (the skeletons in the water closet have their counterparts in life; water is not only a cause of death but also the source of life; the bathroom is fitted into a whole house, and the house into the world). In a last meditation he sings inwardly along with the birds, ending one last aspiring meditation with delightfully cautious acquiescence and unpretentiousness: "I am pretty well satisfied to be, to be just as it is willed, and for as long as I remain in occupancy." In the end, gestures only. Fetching the cold wine-bottles from the spring, he takes pleasure in the vivid cold of the water. For the table he picks flowers, then wonders if he has—a corkscrew—or a nail—or he *could* break them. He fills his hat with roses from the rainpipe and lilies from the cistern. The lilies wilt instantly. Shall he look for peonies? He checks his impulse: "How would it be interpreted?" Yet he decides not to throw his flowers away. But how can he give further evidence of his sanity? He'll stop writing letters. With that thought he goes to his Recamier couch (this is Herzog's final place of reclining, replacing the bed, the psychiatrist's couch, even the grass):

As he stretched out, he took a long breath, and then he lay, looking at the mesh of the screen, pulled loose by vines, and listening to the steady scratching of Mrs. Tuttle's broom. He wanted to tell her to sprinkle the floor. She was raising too much dust. In a few minutes he would call down to her, "Damp it down, Mrs. Tuttle. There's water in the sink." But not just yet. At this time he had no messages for anyone. Nothing. Not a single word.

The last dust-and-water image is a full, easy nod toward his mother's illustration that Adam is dust and sweat. Herzog is no longer in motion, he is not bathed in words; he chooses silence, "At this time." It is a great silence in a real place at a single moment. "Like a long-legged fly upon the stream His mind moves upon silence." We now wait for what Herzog and we will come up with.

But the question remains: is the ending an oversimplification? Is it really adequate to the weight and density and violence of the world Herzog has come from? Is that world itself a genuine and inclusive representation of the incredible world around us? Does it aim too much at the past, giving insufficient weight to those awarenesses of the present which are pushing us toward the future? The novel may be beautiful; is it true? I myself, at this time, would answer those questions in favor of the novel. But do I know the reality? It might properly be asked, though, does anyone except Bellow know that reality? Or, can anyone better it? Until they can, it is Bellow's and Bellow's is it. Another thought occurs: is the ending excessively pastoral? That is a harder question, one that has to be asked about the pastoral or near-pastoral endings of such city or "civilization" works as those of Lawrence (*The Rainbow, Women In Love, St. Mawr*), Joyce (*A Porftrait, Ulysses*), Pound (*The Pisan Cantos*), and Hemingway. The question does not come up in the same way with such archetype novelists as Faulkner, but those who move their resolutions away from the city whose pressures form their central milieu have to face it. It probably resolves itself into the extent to which a work safeguards itself against making too great claims for life. *Herzog* seems to make great claims, but perhaps its comic tone musters sufficient ironies to enable us to feel that exuberance and catharsis can be real.

At any rate, I think that *Herzog* is a great American novel, whose vision will provide perpetual delight and whose techniques will repay other writers for the study. As I said, I think that it makes a near-epical synthesis. Hemingway said "Every novel which is truly written contributes to the total knowledge which is there at the disposal of the next writer who comes"; Bellow's does that because he has been "able to understand and assimilate what is available as his birthright and what he must, in turn, take his departure from." *Herzog* has "the dignity of movement of an iceberg" whose bottom is in the tradition. We might ask, though, whether any book can really be a classic when it is centered too much in character, so that "action in character" replaces "character in action." Is there too little narrative? Is *Herzog* a *Sartor Resartus?* Again, Hemingway posed the problem aptly: "Prose is architecture, not interior decoration, and the Baroque is over. For a writer to put his own intellectual musings, which he might sell for a low price as essays, into the mouth of artificially constructed characters which are more remunerative when issued as people in a novel is good economics, perhaps, but does not make literature." Yet Bellow has made the ideas fiction, because he has made what Hemingway called "People": "People in a novel, not skillfully constructed *characters,* must be projected from the writer's experience, from his knowledge, from his head, from his heart and from all there is of him. . . . a good writer should know as near everything as possible." Bellow has tried to know all that, and has taken the great risk of trying to give it fictional form.

What kind of novel is it? We can find there the elements of the historical, ideological, metaphysical, romantic, anti-romantic, erotic, and picaresque novels; of the novel of manners, the anti-novel, the romance, etc. But above all, it is a great comic novel. As an anthology of ideas and speculations it even has the quality of being an education. Even if you know all the antagonists, colleagues, and ideas that set Herzog off (I didn't), his angle gives you a fresh view of things you know. Further, Bellow relates ideas immediately to life (that is another sense in which *Herzog* is *really* an academic novel—or an intellectual novel—though we never get onto a campus). No novel I have read makes me keep saying "that is just what life is like." Yet, it is also magnificent art; Bellow continually gives one confidence that he is creating a great form, one which includes multiplicity with the shape and rhythm of beauty. It is astonishingly modulated in that space between life and art which it tries to express, so that I feel I am experiencing the novel with all of my faculties.

I have not read a contemporary novel which comes as close to turning Hemingway's ingredients—the tradition, interior decoration, and experience—into a fictional form which can contain them and integrate them. But critics should keep in mind that *Herzog* is a great open form which is new (My interpretation is only provisional!—F.R.); that it calls for perspectives which can elucidate a form based upon our special "field" reality: the one which lies between—both separating and relating them, for it is their "stuff"—life and art, a man and the *res publica*, the infinite pulverizations of which we are made. Above all, there is Joyce's mild complaint about the critics of *Ulysses*, reported by Pound: "If only someone had said among all those critics, that the book is really damn *funny!*"

12 · THE COMPLACENCY OF *HERZOG*

FOR SOME YEARS now our immediate age has been under the most fantastic pressure to produce a novel we could all accept in good conscience as major. Not only have we felt we deserved such a novel. We have *needed* it to vindicate our belief that this age, with its enormous awareness of literary values, should be as creatively vital as it is sophisticated about creativity, that our intense dedication to the life of the mind ought naturally to find its corollary in the production of major works of the imagination.

Bellow's *Herzog* has lately been acclaimed by the intellectual community as such a work, and one of the chief reasons it has been is that it takes intellectual sophistication as its very subject and demonstrates that the life of the mind can in fact be as important and exciting a source of creative vitality as the life of the groin. It deals expertly with materials which most of our novelists have found immensely difficult to dramatize, the materials of consciousness itself, and it deals with them in such a way that we recognize them to be central to our experience, uniquely expressive of ourselves and our condition as intellectuals. Bellow of course sees the condition of intellectuality in *Herzog* as a mixed blessing, and it is proper that he should, since that is exactly what it is. It has given us our high cultural expertise, but it has also severely impeded us in the efficient pursuit of the practical and the amorous life. It has rendered large areas of experience unreal to us, and it has made almost impossible satisfactory relations with people who do not share our commitment to ideas. The character of Herzog embodies these contradictions and is even shown to be torn in two by them— until, that is, he achieves peace through positive thinking. Yet even as we perceive this and admire the honesty which prompted Bellow to lay before us both sides of the case, we also perceive that intellectuality, as he portrays it in *Herzog*, finally emerges as far more of a blessing than a blight. And it does so, interestingly enough, just because the blight has been *turned into* a blessing, just because Bellow makes it so clear that Herzog's suffering is right and admirable, and that suffering is not only the intellectual's occupational disease but his badge of honor, the very measure of his significance both as a person and as a dramatic figure. For it is ultimately his suffering that causes Herzog to seem worthy of major literary treatment and capable of achieving something of the largeness of reference of a major social and literary symbol.

Thus, Bellow has managed to make a virtue of what we had always supposed was our chief source of discomfort, and he has done this not only through his flattering treatment of Herzog's miseries but through his highly *un*flattering treatment of the people with whom Herzog is associated, and who are hell bent on causing him misery.

Bellow has always had the habit, which in his later work has tended to become a rather facile trick, of treating his secondary characters as if they were inmates of either a zoo or a madhouse. Augie March and Herzog in particular are depicted as quiet, deferential men set down among trolls in bedlam. Augie has to contend with the often antagonistic and at times downright berserk vitalism of Einhorn, Dingbat, the Magnuses, Mintouchian, Thea Fenchel, and Basteshaw, while Herzog is chronically badgered and exploited by Simkin, Gersbach, Shapiro, Himmelstein, Nachman, and the various other freaks and egomaniacs whom Herzog rather plaintively calls his "Reality instructors." Bellow's handling of these people constantly verges on caricature. In fact, there are moments when they seem to exist solely as verbal abstractions, creations of merely adjectival intensity. Yet their function is clearly not to suggest living people drawn from close observation of the real world. Rather, it is to provide a milieu of grotesque idiosyncrasy and self-preoccupation against which Herzog can be seen as saintly. To be sure, in comparison with them he is ineffectual, bumbling, and a fool—the very type of the silly intellectual helplessly adrift in the cutthroat world of practical affairs. But however ridiculous he may be, he is also so much more of a human being, so much more sensitive and responsible than they, that his ridiculousness becomes, like his suffering, a badge of honor, the mark of his moral superiority. For Herzog is selfless where they are selfish, loving where they are hateful, wryly comic where they are gruesomely grotesque, a wonderful, absurd, adorable Jewish Uncle Tom whose predicament is that he is finally too pure for this world. The intellectual is also too pure for this world, or so he has always secretly considered himself. But he has been obliged to assume that his purity was at best a negative virtue, one he had to settle for in place of the truly human virtues shared by those who are not intellectuals. Now, however, through the drama of Herzog, he is given abundant evidence that nonintellectuals are monsters, that if they are human, he is positively angelic, that, in fact, to be an intellectual among such people is perhaps to be the very best thing there is. For in Herzog human warmth and ideas, heart and high culture, are joined together to produce the most flattering image of the intellectual to be found in modern literature.

It would seem that Bellow could not possibly go beyond this in his effort to aggrandize Herzog and to persuade us to see him as a figure of transcendent meaning and saintliness. Yet this is actually only a modest rehearsal for the emergence of Herzog into the full glory of his ultimate incarnation in the role of the Jewish intellectual as symbol of contemporary Everyman. It would undoubtedly be even harder than it is to accept Herzog in this preposterous role if Bellow did not take care to create an atmosphere of such high fastidiousness about slick generalizations of just this kind that we almost became convinced that he hates them as much as we do and is standing guard for us against them. For example, he speaks with proper contempt of "the commonplaces of the Waste Land outlook, the cheap mental stimulants of Alienation," and that, along with his over-all wariness of tone, his apparent abhorrence of obvious and easy answers, would seem to serve as effective insurance against any lapse into other commonplaces and cheap mental stimulants. But it turns out that our trust is grievously misplaced, for Bellow slyly slips Herzog into the breach left by the banished Waste Land cliché. Herzog emerges, in fact, as the Waste Land cliché irrigated and transformed into the Promised Land, while the platitude of Alienation is converted into the even hoarier platitude of Accommodation and Togetherness. For what he finally holds up for our inspection is a new hopeful doctrine of potato love not uncolored by righteous disdain. The trolls may be killing us, he seems to say. We may be exploited, cuckolded, hounded out of house and home, reviled, and spat upon. But we can afford to be compassionate and gracious in our torment, remembering, as Nick Carraway's father once said, that "all the people in this world haven't had the advantages" that we have had.

At the end the novel heaves a fatty sigh of middle-class intellectual contentment. "I am pretty well satisfied," muses Herzog in his lawn chair, "to be, to be just as it is willed, and for as long as I may remain in occupancy." And we sense that Herzog will be a long time in occupancy. For if it has been demonstrated that intellectuals have a corner on the world's love and compassion, it is probable that they also have a corner on the world's powers of survival. And of course Herzog is finally as arrogantly complacent in his new-found affirmative position, about being stuck with his loving and erudite self, as Bellow dares to allow him to be. In fact, it would appear that in Herzog the many intellectuals who have long felt guilty and defensive about their role in life have found their bromide, their hero, and the justification they have long been seeking for their secret sense of superiority. The novel, in short, is as wholesome and nutritious as a dish of cornflakes, a clearly "major" Establishment work in the sense that it dramatizes a theme of considerable size with complete honesty and without once expressing an idea that could possibly give offense to anyone. On the contrary, it has brought much good cheer and glad tidings to the intellectual community, and as is so often the case, such service has not gone unrewarded.

13 · WHERE DO WE GO FROM HERE:
The Future of Fiction

WE KNOW that science has a future, we hope that government will have one. But it is not altogether agreed that the novel has anything but a past. There are some who say that the great novelists of the twentieth century—Proust, Joyce, Mann, and Kafka—have created sterile masterpieces, and that with them we have come to the end of the line. No further progress is possible.

It does sometimes seem that the narrative art itself has dissolved. The person, the character as we know him in the plays of Sophocles or Shakespeare, in Cervantes, Fielding, and Balzac, has gone from us. Instead of a unitary character with his unitary personality, his ambitions, his passions, his soul, his fate, we find in modern literature an oddly dispersed, ragged, mingled, broken, amorphous creature whose outlines are everywhere, whose being is bathed in mind as the tissues are bathed in blood, and who is impossible to circumscribe in any scheme of time. A cubistic, Bergsonian, uncertain, eternal, mortal someone who shuts and opens like a concertina and makes a strange music. And what has struck artists in this century as the most amusing part of all is that the descriptions of self that still have hold of us are made up of the old unitary foursquare traits noted according to the ancient conventions. What we insist on seeing is not a quaintly organized chaos of instinct and spirit, but what we choose to call "the personality"—a presentably combed and dressed someone who is decent, courageous, handsome, or not so handsome, but strong, or not so strong, but certainly generous, or not so generous, but anyway reliable. So it goes.

Of all modern writers, it is D. H. Lawrence who is most implacably hostile toward this convention of unitary character. For him this character of a civilized man does not really exist. What the modern civilized person calls his personality is to Lawrence figmentary: a product of civilized education, dress, manners, style, and "culture." The head of this modern personality is, he says, a wastepaper basket filled with ready-made notions. Sometimes he compares the civilized conception of character to a millstone—a painted millstone about our necks is the metaphor he makes of it. The real self, unknown, is hidden, a sunken power in us; the true identity lies deep—very deep. But we do not deal much in true identity, goes his argument. The modern character on the street, or in a conventional story or film, is what a sociologist has recently described as the "presentation" self. The attack on this presentation self or persona by modern art is a part of the war that literature, in its concern with the individual, has fought with civilization. The civilized individual is proud of his painted millstone, the burden which he believes gives him distinction. In an artist's eyes his persona is only a rude, impoverished, mass-produced figure brought into being by a civilization in need of a working force, a reservoir of personnel, a docile public that will accept suggestion and control.

The old unitary personality which still appears in popular magazine stories, in conventional best-sellers, in newspaper cartoons, and in the movies, is a figure descended from well-worn patterns, and popular art forms (like the mystery novel or the western) continue to exploit endlessly the badly faded ideas of motives and drama or love and hate. The old figures move ritualistically through the paces, finding, now and then, variations in setting and costume, but they are increasingly remote from real reality. The functions performed by these venerable literary types should be fascinating to the clinical psychologist who may be able to recognize in these stories an obsessional neurosis here, a paranoid fantasy there, or to the sociologist who sees resemblances to the organization of government bureaus or hears echoes of the modern industrial corporations. But the writer brought up in a great literary tradition not only sees these conventional stories as narcotic or brain-washing entertainments, at worst breeding strange vices, at best performing a therapeutic function. He also fears that the narrative art, which we call the novel, may have come to an end, its conception of the self exhausted and with this conception our interest in the fate of that self so conceived.

It is because of this that Gertrude Stein tells us in one of her lectures that we cannot read the great novels of the twentieth century, among which she includes her own *The Making of Americans*, for what happens next. And in fact, *Ulysses, Remembrance of Things Past, The Magic Mountain*, and *The Making of Americans* do not absorb us in what happens next. They interest us in a scene, in a dialogue, a mood, an insight, in language, in character, in the revelation of a design, but they are not narratives. *Ulysses* avoids anything resembling the customary story. It is in some sense a book about literature, and offers us a history of English prose style and of the novel. It is a museum containing all the quaint armour halberds, crossbows, and artillery pieces of literature. It exhibits them with a kind of amused irony and parodies and transcends them all. These are the things that once entranced us. Old sublimities, old dodges, old weapons, all useless now; pieces of iron once heroic, lovers' embraces once romantic, all debased by cheap exploitation, all unfit.

Language too is unfit. Erich Heller in a recent book quotes a typical observation by Hofmannsthal on the inadequacy of old forms of expression. Hofmannsthal writes,

> Elements once bound together to make a world now present themselves to the poet in monstrous separateness. To speak of them coherently at all would be to speak untruthfully. The commonplace phrases of the daily round of observations seem all of a sudden insoluble riddles. The sheriff is a wicked man, the vicar is a good fellow, our neighbor must be pitied, his sons are wastrels. The baker is to be envied, his daughters are virtuous.

In Hofmannsthal's *A Letter* these formulas are presented as "utterly lacking in the quality of truth." He is unable, he explains, "to see what people say and do with the simplifying eye of habit and custom. Everything falls to pieces, the pieces to pieces again, and nothing can be comprehended any more with the help of customary notions."

Character, action, and language then have been put in doubt and the Spanish philosopher Ortega y Gasset, summing up views widely held, says the novel requires a local setting with limited horizons and familiar features, traditions, occupations, classes. But as everyone knows, these old-fashioned local worlds no longer exist. Or perhaps that is inaccurate. They do exist but fail to interest the novelist. They are no longer local societies as we see them in Jane Austen or George Eliot. Our contemporary local societies have been overtaken by the world. The great cities have devoured them and now the universe itself imposes itself upon us, space with its stars comes upon us in our cities. So now we have the universe itself to face, without the comforts of community, without metaphysical certainty, without the power to distinguish the virtuous from the wicked man, surrounded by dubious realities and discovering dubious selves.

Things have collapsed about us, says D. H. Lawrence on the first page of *Lady Chatterley's Lover,* and we must each of us try to put together some sort of life. He offers us a sort of nature mysticism, love but without false romanticism, an acceptance of true desire as the first principle of recovery. Other writers have come forward with aesthetic or political or religious first principles. All the modern novelists worth mentioning aim at a point beyond customary notions, customary dramas, and customary conceptions of character. The old notion of a customary self, of the fate of an all-important Me displeases the best of them. We have lived now through innumerable successes and failures of these old selves. In American literature we have watched their progress and decline in scores of books since the Civil War, from buoyancy to depression. The Lambert Strethers, the Hurstwoods and Cowperwoods, the Gatsbys may still impress or please us as readers, but as writers, no. Their mental range is no longer adequate to these new circumstances. Those characters suit us better who stand outside society and, unlike Gatsby, have no wish to be sentimentally reconciled to it, unlike Dreiser's millionaires have no more desire for its wealth, unlike Strether are not attracted by the power of an old and knowing civilization.

This is why so many of us prefer the American novels of the nineteenth century, whose characters are very nearly removed from the civil state—*Moby Dick* and *Huckleberry Finn*. We feel in our own time that what is called the civilized condition often swings close to what Hobbes calls the state of nature, a condition of warfare, in which the life of the individual is nasty, brutish, dull and short. But we must be careful not to be swept away by the analogy. We have seen to our grief in recent European and especially German history the results of trying to bolt from all civilized and legal tradition. It is in our minds that the natural and the civil, that autarchy and discipline are most explosively mixed.

But for us here in America discipline is represented largely by the enforced repressions. We do not know much of the delights of discipline. Almost nothing of a spiritual, ennobling character is brought into the internal life of a modern American by his social institutions. He must discover it in his own experience, by his own luck as an explorer, or not at all. Society feeds him, clothes him, to an extent protects him, and he is its infant. If he accepts the state of infancy, contentment can be his. But if the idea of higher functions comes to him, he is profoundly unsettled. The hungry world is rushing on all continents toward such a contentment, and with passions and desires, frustrated since primitive times, and with the demand for justice never so loudly expressed. The danger is great that it will be satisfied with the bottles and toys of infancy. But the artist, the philosopher, the priest, the statesman are concerned with the full development of humanity—its manhood, occasionally glimpsed in our history, occasionally felt by individuals.

With all this in mind, people here and there still continue to write the sort of book we call a novel. When I am feeling blue, I can almost persuade myself that the novel, like Indian basketry, or harness-making, is a vestigial art and has no future. But we must be careful about prophecy. Even prophecy based on good historical study is a risky business, and pessimism, no less than optimism, can be made into a racket. All industrial societies have a thing about obsolescence. Classes, nations, races and cultures have in our time been declared obsolete, with results that have made ours one of the most horrible of all centuries. We must, therefore, be careful about deciding that any art is dead.

This is not a decision for a coroner's jury of critics and historians. The fact is that a great many novelists, even those who have concentrated on hate, like Céline, or on despair, like Kafka, have continued to perform a most important function. Their books have attempted, in not a few cases successfully, to create scale, to order experience, to give value, to make perspective and to carry us toward sources of life, toward life-giving things. The true believer in disorder does not like novels. He follows another calling. He is an accident lawyer, or a promoter, not a novelist. It always makes me sit up, therefore, to read yet another scolding of the modern novelist written by highly paid executives of multimillion-dollar magazines. They call upon American writers to represent the country fairly, to affirm its values, to increase its prestige in this dangerous period. Perhaps, though, novelists have a different view of what to affirm. Perhaps they are running their own sort of survey of affirmable things. They may come out against nationalism, or against the dollar, for they are an odd and unreliable lot. I have already indicated that it is the instinct of the novelist, however, to pull toward order. Now this is a pious thing to say, but I do not intend it merely to sound good. It should be understood only as the beginning of another difficulty.

What ideas of order does the novelist have and where does he get them and what good are they in art? I have spoken of Lawrence's belief that we must put together a life for ourselves, singly, in pairs, in groups, out of the wreckage. Shipwreck and solitude are not, in his opinion, unmixed evils. They are also liberating, and if we have the strength to use our freedom we may yet stand in a true relation to nature and to other men. But how are we to reach this end? Lawrence proposes a sort of answer in *Lady Chatterley's Lover*, showing us two people alone together in the midst of a waste. I sometimes feel that *Lady Chatterley's Lover* is a sort of *Robinson Crusoe* for two, exploring man's sexual resources rather than his technical ingenuity. It is every bit as moral a novel as *Crusoe*. Connie and Mellors work at it as hard and as conscientiously as Robinson, and there are as many sermons in the one as in the other. The difference is that Lawrence aimed with all his powers at the writing of this one sort of book. To this end he shaped his life, the testing ground of his ideas. For what is the point of recommending a course of life that one has not tried oneself?

This is one way to assess the careers and achievements of many modern artists. Men like Rimbaud, Strindberg, Lawrence, Malraux, even Tolstoy, can be approached from this direction. They experiment with themselves and in some cases an artistic conclusion can come only out of the experimental results. Lawrence had no material other than what his life, that savage pilgrimage, as he called it, gave him. The ideas he tested, and tested not always by an acceptable standard, were ideas of the vital, the erotic, the instinctive. They involved us in a species of nature-mysticism which gave as a basis for morality, sexual gratification. But I am not concerned here with all the particulars of Lawrence's thesis. I am interested mainly in the connection between the understanding and the imagination, and the future place of the intelligence in imaginative literature.

At this point in a lecture this is a rather large subject to announce, but what I have in mind is relatively simple. It is necessary to admit, first, that ideas in the novel can be very dull. There is much in modern literature, and the other arts as well, to justify our prejudice against the didactic. Opinion, said Schopenhauer, is not as valid as imagination in a work of art. One can quarrel with an opinion or judgment in a novel, but actions are beyond argument and the imagination simply accepts them. I think that many modern novels, perhaps the majority, are the result of some didactic purpose. The attempt of writers to make perspective, to make scale and to carry us toward the sources of life is, of course, the didactic intention. It involves the novelist in programs, in slogans, in political theories, religious theories, and so on. Many modern novelists seem to say to themselves, "what if," or "suppose that such and such were the case," and the results often show that the book was conceived in thought, in didactic purpose, rather than in the imagination. That is rather normal, given the state of things, the prevalence of the calculating principle in modern life, the need for conscious rules of procedure, and the generally felt need for answers. Not only books, paintings, and musical compositions, but love affairs, marriages, and even religious convictions often originate in an idea. So that the *idea* of love is more common than love, and the *idea* of belief is more often met with than faith. Some of our most respected novels have a purely mental inspiration. The results are sometimes very pleasing because they can so easily be discussed, but the ideas in them generally have more substance than the characters who hold them.

American literature in the nineteenth century was highly didactic. Emerson, Thoreau, Whitman, and even Melville were didactic writers. They wished to instruct a young and raw nation. American literature in the twentieth century has remained didactic, but it has also been unintellectual. This is not to say that thought is lacking in the twentieth-century American novel, but it exists under strange handicaps and is much disguised. In *A Farewell to Arms* Hemingway makes a list of subjects we must no longer speak about—a catalogue of polluted words, words which have been ruined by the rhetoric of criminal politicians and misleaders. Then Hemingway, and we must respect him for it, attempts to represent these betrayed qualities without using the words themselves. Thus we have courage without the word, honor without the word, and in *The Old Man and the Sea* we are offered a sort of Christian endurance, also without specific terms. Carried to this length, the attempt to represent ideas while sternly forbidding thought begins to look like a curious and highly sophisticated game. It shows a great skepticism of the strength of art. It makes it appear as though ideas openly expressed would be too much for art to bear.

We have developed in American fiction a strange combination of extreme naïveté in the characters and of profundity implicit in the writing, in the techniques themselves and in the language, but the language of thought itself is banned, it is considered dangerous and destructive. American writers appear to have a strong loyalty to the people, to the common man; perhaps in some cases the word for this is not loyalty, perhaps it might better be described as *fear*. But a writer should aim to reach all levels of society and as many levels of thought as possible, avoiding democratic prejudice as much as intellectual snobbery. Why should he be ashamed of thinking? I do not claim that all writers can think, or should think. Some are peculiarly inept at ideas and we would harm them by insisting that they philosophize. But the records show that most artists are intellectually active, and it is only now in a world increasingly intellectualized, more and more dominated by the productions of scientific thought, that they seem strangely reluctant to use their brains or to give any sign that they have brains to use.

All through the nineteenth century the conviction increases in novelists as different as Goncharov in Russia and Thomas Hardy in England that thought is linked with passivity and is devitalizing. And in the masterpieces of the twentieth century the thinker usually has a weak grip on life. But by now an alternative, passionate activity without ideas has also been well explored in novels of adventure, hunting, combat, and eroticism. Meanwhile, miracles, born of thought, have been largely ignored by modern literature. If narration is neglected by novelists like Proust and Joyce, the reasons are that for a time the drama has passed from external action to internal movement. In Proust and Joyce we are enclosed by and held within a single consciousness. In this inner realm the writer's art dominates everything. The drama has left external action because the old ways of describing interests, of describing the fate of the individual, have lost their power. Is the sheriff a good fellow? Is our neighbor to be pitied? Are the baker's daughters virtuous? We see such questions now as belonging to a dead system, mere formulas. It is possible that our hearts would open again to the baker's daughters if we understood them differently.

A clue may be offered by Pascal, who said there are no dull people, only dull points of view. Maybe that is going a little far. (A religious philosophy is bound to maintain that every soul is infinitely precious and, therefore, infinitely interesting.) But it begins perhaps to be evident what my position is. Imagination, binding itself to dull viewpoints, puts an end to stories. The imagination is looking for new ways to express virtue. American society just now is in the grip of certain common falsehoods about virtue—not that anyone really believes them. And these cheerful falsehoods beget their opposites in fiction, a dark literature, a literature of victimization, of old people sitting in ash cans waiting for the breath of life to depart. This is the way things stand; only this remains to be added, that we have barely begun to comprehend what a human being is, and that the baker's daughters may have revelations and miracles to offer to keep fascinated novelists busy until the end of time.

I would like to add this also, in conclusion, about good thought and bad thought in the novel. In a way it doesn't matter what sort of line the novelist is pushing, what he is affirming. If he has nothing to offer but his didactic purpose he is a bad writer. His ideas have ruined him. He could not afford the expense of maintaining them. It is not the didactic purpose itself which is a bad thing, and the modern novelist drawing back from the dangers of didacticism has often become strangely unreal, and the purity of his belief in art for art in some cases has been peculiarly unattractive. Among modern novelists the bravest have taken the risk of teaching and have not been afraid of using the terms of religion, science, philosophy, and politics. Only they have been prepared to admit the strongest possible arguments against their own positions.

Here we see the difference between a didactic novelist like D. H. Lawrence and one like Dostoyevsky. When he was writing *The Brothers Karamazov* and had just ended the famous conversation between Ivan and Alyosha, in which Ivan, despairing of justice, offers to return his ticket to God, Dostoyevsky wrote to one of his correspondents that he must now attempt, through Father Zossima, to answer Ivan's arguments. But he has in advance all but devastated his own position. This, I think, is the greatest achievement possible in a novel of ideas. It becomes art when the views most opposite to the author's own are allowed to exist in full strength. Without this a novel of ideas is mere self-indulgence, and didacticism is simply axe-grinding. The opposites must be free to range themselves against each other, and they must be passionately expressed on both sides. It is for this reason that I say it doesn't matter much what the writer's personal position is, what he wishes to affirm. He may affirm principles we all approve of and write very bad novels.

The novel, to recover and to flourish, requires new ideas about humankind. These ideas in turn cannot live in themselves. Merely asserted, they show nothing but the good will of the author. They must therefore be discovered and not invented. We must see them in flesh and blood. There would be no point in continuing at all if many writers did not feel the existence of these unrecognized qualities. They are present and they demand release and expression.

NOTES ON CONTRIBUTORS

LESLIE A. FIEDLER teaches at the State University of New York at Buffalo. He is the author of *Love and Death in the American Novel, No! in Thunder, Waiting for the End,* and other books.

MAXWELL GEISMAR is the author of *Writers in Crisis, The Last of the Provincials, Henry James and the Jacobites,* and other books.

RICHARD CHASE taught at Columbia University before his death. He is the author of *The American Novel and Its Tradition, Emily Dickinson, Walt Whitman Reconsidered,* and other books.

J. C. LEVENSON teaches at the University of Minnesota. He is the author of *The Mind and Art of Henry Adams.*

RALPH FREEDMAN teaches at Princeton University. Hs is the author of *The Lyrical Novel,* a study of Hesse, Virginia Woolf, and Gide.

DANIEL HUGHES teaches at Wayne State University. He is the author of *Waking in a Tree,* a volume of poetry.

MARCUS KLEIN teaches at the State University of New York at Buffalo. He is the author of *After Alienation: American Novels at Midcentury.*

DANIEL WEISS teaches at San Francisco State College. He is the author of *Oedipus in Nottingham: D. H. Lawrence.*

221

EARL ROVIT teaches at The City College of New York. He is the author of *Herald to Chaos: The Novels of Elizabeth Madox Roberts, Ernest Hemingway,* and *The Player King,* a novel.

FORREST READ teaches at the University of North Carolina. He is the author of several important essays on Ezra Pound; he is preparing an edition of Pound's letters to Joyce.

JOHN W. ALDRIDGE teaches at the University of Michigan. He is the author of *After the Lost Generation, In Search of Heresy, The Party at Cranton,* and other books.